The Archaeology of Ethnicity

The study of ethnicity is a highly controversial area in contemporary archaeology. The identification of 'cultures' from archaeological remains and their association with past ethnic groups is now seen by many as hopelessly inadequate. Yet such an approach continues to play a significant rôle in archaeological enquiry, and in the legitimation of modern ethnic and national claims.

Siân Jones responds to the need for a radical reassessment of the ways in which past cultural groups are reconstructed from archaeological evidence with a comprehensive and critical synthesis of recent theories of ethnicity in the human sciences. In doing so, she develops a new framework for the analysis of ethnicity in archaeology which takes into account the dynamic and situational nature of ethnic identification.

Opening up the important issues of ethnicity and identity, this book addresses important methodological, interpretive and political issues. It will provide invaluable reading for the student of archaeology and other disciplines in the human sciences.

Siân Jones is Parkes Fellow at the University of Southampton, where she is undertaking research on ethnicity in ancient Palestine. She is co-editor of *Cultural Identity and Archaeology: The Construction of European Communities* (Routledge, 1996).

The Archaeology of Ethnicity

Constructing identities in the past and present

Siân Jones

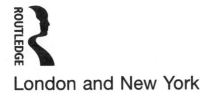

London and New York

First published 1997
by Routledge
11 New Fetter Lane, London EC4P 4EE

Simultaneously published in the USA and Canada
by Routledge
29 West 35th Street, New York, NY 10001

Quotation from *Oranges Are Not the Only Fruit*, Jeanette Winterson

Typeset in Garamond by J&L Composition Ltd, Filey, North Yorkshire
Printed and bound in Great Britain by Mackays of Chatham PLC, Chatham, Kent

British Library Cataloguing in Publication Data
A catalogue record for this book is available from the British Library

Library of Congress Cataloging in Publication Data
Jones, S. (Siân), 1968–
   The archaeology of ethnicity: constructing identities in the past and present / Siân Jones.
      p.   cm.
   Includes bibliographical references and index
   1. Ethnoarchaeology.   2. Ethnicity.   I. Title.
CC79.E85J66   1997
930.1'089–dc20   96–32658
                                                                     CIP

ISBN 0–415–14157–5 (hbk)
ISBN 0–415–14158–3 (pbk)

For P. J. U.

and for my mother and father

Contents

Figures

Preface

This book is largely based on my doctoral thesis, which was undertaken at the University of Southampton and completed in 1994. Drawing on recent theories of ethnicity in the human sciences, the aim of my doctoral research was to provide a theoretical framework for the analysis of ethnicity in archaeology. Despite a few important pieces of existing work, there was very little interest in this topic when I started the project in 1989. Many archaeologists dismissed the study of ethnicity either as the epitome of a seemingly outmoded paradigm, culture-history, or as an impossible task which had politically dangerous connotations. Consequently, on describing my research project I was often confronted with questions such as 'What has that got to do with archaeology today?' and 'Why are you doing that?' Fortunately, at the Department in Southampton I benefited from the foresight and perceptiveness of a number of individuals who made me realize the importance of the project at times when self-doubt and confusion might have made me abandon it altogether.

Half a decade later, ethnicity, along with nationalism, has become a very topical issue, both in archaeology and in society generally. Both ethnicity and nationalism are high on the agenda at archaeological conferences, and the literature focusing on the use of the past in the construction of contemporary identities is expanding exponentially. However, archaeologists have largely focused on the politics of identity in the present, frequently lapsing into more general discussions on the politics of archaeological enquiry, without taking the logical step of reconsidering the interpretation of identity groups in archaeology. In the absence of such a re-evaluation providing us with a stronger basis for the interpretation of past ethnic groups it is very difficult for us to engage successfully with the ways in which contemporary groups, national, ethnic, indigenous or otherwise, use archaeology in the construction and legitimation of their own identities. I hope that this book will contribute to the development of new approaches to the interpretation of past identities, and new perspectives on the use of the past in the construction of group identities today. With this in mind, I have written a new introductory chapter and expanded the conclusion of my Ph.D. thesis in order to highlight the need to consider simultaneously the construction of identities in the past and in the present.

This book has been a long time in the making and I am grateful to a considerable number of people for their advice and support during work on my thesis and subsequent revision for publication. I wish to acknowledge the Isle of Man Board of Education for providing funding for my Ph.D., and the Sir Robert Menzies Centre for Australian Studies for a scholarship which enabled me to go to Australia in 1990 to examine the construction of Aboriginal identity. During my time there Ian and Libby Keen, Gordon Briscoe, Iris Clayton, Jacquie Lambert and many others were a source of insight and advice. I am grateful for their help during a period which was formative in the development of the ideas presented here, and it is with much regret that a substantive discussion of the construction of Aboriginality eventually had to be left out of my Ph.D. thesis and this book.

Thanks to Tim Champion, Clive Gamble, Paul Graves-Brown, Claire Jowitt, Kris Lockyear, Brian Molyneux, Tim Sly, Dave Wheatley, Francis Wenban-Smith, and many other staff and postgraduates at the Department of Archaeology, University of Southampton and elsewhere, whom I consulted in the course of my doctoral research. They provided a stimulating and friendly environment in which to study, and the comparative and theoretically informed nature of archaeology at Southampton has influenced my work immeasurably. I would especially like to thank Stephen Shennan who has been particularly long-suffering over the years, providing invaluable commentary on endless drafts of my work.

In revising my thesis for publication Ben Alberti, Cressida Fforde, Antony Firth, Pedro Funari, Martin Hall, Richard Hingley, Quentin Mackie, Ingereth Macfarlene, Maggie Ronayne, Mike Rowlands and Jane Webster have also given their time to discuss problems and ideas. I am grateful for their input and their constructive criticisms. My ideas were also further developed whilst teaching a postgraduate course at the University of La Plata in Argentina and MA courses at the University of Southampton on the topics of ethnicity and nationalism. Thanks to all the students for their enthusiasm and, at times, challenging scepticism. I also wish to thank my colleagues at the Parkes Centre for the Study of Jewish/non-Jewish Relations, Tony Kushner and Sarah Pearce, for providing me with the space to work on this book despite the demands of other projects.

Thanks to Kathryn Knowles who produced figures 2.1, 2.2, 2.3 and 2.4. B. T. Batsford Ltd and Dr Anne Ross kindly gave permission for the reproduction of the map illustrating 'Culture provinces and expansions of the Celts' from *Everyday Life of the Pagan Celts*. Likewise, David Allen, the curator of Andover Museum, gave permission for the use of the 'Iron Age Warrior'. Both illustrations have been used for the cover of the paperback edition. Thanks to Jeanette Winterson and Vintage Books for permission to quote from *Oranges Are Not the Only Fruit*. Thanks also to Vicky Peters at Routledge for her enthusiasm and help along with the rest of the editorial team.

I owe a great deal to family and friends – who include many of the people referred to above, as well as Maj Bedey, Amanda Boulter, Sara Champion, Steve Dorney, Ruth Gilbert, Kat Hall, Jane Hubert, Ella Leibowitz, Gustavo Martínez, Michael Wells and others – for their love and support through difficult periods as well as good times over the last six years. Finally, my greatest debt is to Peter Ucko whose friendship and support has extended far beyond what is normally expected from a Ph.D. supervisor. Many thanks for providing indispensable advice and criticism, as well as being a source of inspiration, without which it is unlikely that I would have completed my thesis.

Definitions

The concept of ethnicity has a complex history and its meaning has been much debated. In Chapters 2 and 3 the history of the concept of ethnicity, among others, is critically examined, and following this, a working definition of ethnicity is proposed in Chapter 4. However, for the purposes of clarity it is necessary to define the way in which I use the terms 'ethnic identity', 'ethnic group' and 'ethnicity' throughout this book, except in instances where I am discussing other people's uses of these terms.

Ethnic identity: that aspect of a person's self-conceptualization which results from identification with a broader group in opposition to others on the basis of perceived cultural differentiation and/or common descent.

Ethnic group: any group of people who set themselves apart and/or are set apart by others with whom they interact or co-exist on the basis of their perceptions of cultural differentiation and/or common descent.

Ethnicity: all those social and psychological phenomena associated with a culturally constructed group identity as defined above. The concept of ethnicity focuses on the ways in which social and cultural processes intersect with one another in the identification of, and interaction between, ethnic groups.

She said that not much had happened between us anyway, historically speaking. But history is a string full of knots, the best thing you can do is admire it, and maybe knot it up a bit more. History is a hammock for swinging and a game for playing. A cat's cradle. She said these sorts of feelings were dead, the feelings she once had for me. There is a certain seductiveness about dead things. You can ill treat, alter and colour what's dead. It won't complain. Then she laughed and said we probably saw what happened differently anyway . . . She laughed again and said that the way I saw it would make a good story, her vision was just the history, the nothing-at-all facts. She said she hoped I hadn't kept any letters, silly to hang on to things that had no meaning. As though letters and photos made it more real, more dangerous. I told her I didn't need her letters to remember what happened.

(Jeanette Winterson, *Oranges Are Not the Only Fruit* 1985)

Chapter 1

Introduction

... the crucial theoretical question of archaeology today is that of national identity, or more specifically that of the relationship archaeology enjoys with the construction (or the fabrication) of collective identities.
(Olivier and Coudart 1995: 365)

... the expansion of archaeology's relation to nationalism and ethnicity in the construction of collective identity seems certain to continue. Partly the materiality of the archaeological record will assure this. Partly also the creation of alternative pasts is increasingly being used to legitimate land claims, ethnic territories and access to economic resources.
(Rowlands 1994: 141)

The role of archaeology in the construction and legitimation of collective cultural identities is coming to be perceived as one of the most important issues in archaeological theory and practice. Throughout the history of archaeology the material record has been attributed to particular past peoples, and the desire to trace the genealogy of present peoples back to their imagined primordial origins has played a significant role in the development of the discipline. This situation is not surprising given the emergence of archaeology as a discipline in the context of European nationalisms, and the very materiality of the evidence which seemingly gives body and substance to collective origin myths. Yet the relationship between archaeology and the construction of communities of shared memory has only become subject to self-conscious analysis and criticism at certain times, most recently during the 1980s and 1990s in the context of increasing concern with the socio-politics of archaeology, and in reaction to the perceived intensification of ethnic and national sentiments. What follows is in part a contribution to this re-evaluation of the way in which archaeological enquiry is intertwined with the construction of contemporary identities. Focusing on the nature of ethnicity, its relationship to material culture, and the validity of archaeological attempts to identify past ethnic groups, this book explores an area which has been both central to traditional archaeological interpretation, and at the heart of recent debates about the political implications of archaeological enquiry.

The classic example of nationalistic archaeology is the political manipulation of the past in Nazi Germany. The name of the German philologist and prehistorian, Gustaf Kossinna, is inextricably tied to the practice of ethnic interpretation in German archaeology, and the fascistic and nationalistic use of such interpretations by the Third Reich. Between 1895 and his death in 1931, Kossinna developed an ethnic paradigm which he called 'settlement archaeology' (see Härke 1991, 1995; Kossak 1992; Veit 1989; Wiwjorra 1996). The basic premise was that artefact types could be used to identify cultures and that clearly distinguishable cultural provinces reflect the settlement areas of past tribes or ethnic groups. But perhaps the most crucial aspect of his methodology with relation to its nationalistic tone, was the direct genealogical technique used in order to trace the presence of historically known peoples back to their supposed prehistoric origins. It was on the basis of this technique that Kossinna attempted to delineate the descent of the Nordic, Aryan, Germanic super-race to the Indo-Europeans (or 'Indo-Germans'); in the process a deep antiquity was attributed to the Aryan 'race', alongside a decisive, creative role in the course of history through its continuous expansion into new areas (see McCann 1990; Veit 1989: 38).

Kossinna was explicit about the nationalistic and racist overtones in his work, speaking of German racial and cultural superiority over others (Wijworra 1996: 174). He declared German archaeology 'a pre-eminently national discipline' in the title to one of his popular books, dedicating it, in the post-World War I edition, 'To the German people, as a building block in the reconstruction of the externally as well as internally disintegrated fatherland' (Kossinna 1921 [1914]: dedication, cited in Arnold 1990: 465). Moreover, Kossinna, along with other archaeologists, was actively involved in the production of propaganda during World War I and, following German defeat, he attempted to use the results of archaeological research to argue that areas of Poland had been part of the territory of the Germanic peoples since the Iron Age (see Arnold 1990: 467; Wijworra 1996: 176). However, it was after Kossinna's death, with the rise of National Socialism in Germany that his work was elevated to a position of dogma in support of the myth of the Aryan master race. Archaeology held an important position in the ideology of the Third Reich; it received considerable prestige and institutional support, and was appropriated by key Nazi figures such as Alfred Rosenberg and Heinrich Himmler, although Adolf Hitler himself was ambivalent towards their efforts (see Arnold 1990: 469). To obtain 'scientific' support for his ideas, Himmler founded the SS organization, *Deutches Ahnenerbe* (German Ancestral Inheritance), which organized archaeological investigations carried out by SS officers, and involved the obligatory use of Kossinna's 'settlement archaeology' method. Archaeological remains identified as 'Germanic' were prioritized over others, and the *Ahnenerbe*, along with other archaeologists, were particularly concerned to 'demonstrate' Germanic expansion in pre- and proto-history, for instance, eastwards into Poland, South Russia and the Caucasus (McCann 1990: 83–4; see Figure 1.1). A further example of the way in which archaeological research was implicated in the actions of the Nazi regime is provided by Himmler's attempts to link the physiology of the Venus figurines from the Dolní Vestonice excavations with that of Jewish women, and supposedly primitive 'races' such as the Hottentots (McCann 1990: 85–6). However, whilst a number of German archaeologists, such as Hans Reinerth and Herman Wirth, were actively involved in producing representations of the past in keeping with Nazi ideology, others did not lend explicit support to such representations. Indeed, many archaeologists, like other German citizens, remained passive bystanders (*Mitlaufer*) under the totalitarian regime, ultimately sanctioning the National Socialist Party by default, whilst a small minority expressed direct opposition, largely through critiques of Kossinna's work (see Arnold 1990: 472–3; Veit 1989: 40–1).

In his review of archaeological theory in Europe, Hodder (1991a: x) has argued that 'few archaeologists in Europe can work without the shadow of the misuse of the past for nationalistic purposes during the Third Reich'. The immediate reaction from German scholars in the postwar period was to distance themselves from the overtly racist character of Nazi archaeology, and in particular to vilify Kossinna, representing him as 'the evil mind behind all chauvinist and fascist exploitation of archaeology' (Härke 1995: 54). This was a convenient stance for those German archaeologists who had been passive bystanders in Nazi Germany, but condemnation of Kossinna as the main culprit in the nationalistic abuse of archaeology during the Third Reich was also the most prevalent response from other European archaeologists. Overt ethnic interpretations were rejected due to the traditional conflation of ethnic groups with races, and German archaeologists in particular retreated into a descriptive, empiricist approach with little reference to peoples such as the 'Germani' or the 'Indo-Europeans' (Härke 1995: 56; Veit 1989: 42). Furthermore, the direct genealogical method advocated by Kossinna for tracing historically known groups back into prehistory was largely abandoned. Nevertheless, despite these changes German archaeologists continued to use the basic ethnic paradigm, classifying material culture into groups known as archaeological cultures, which were implicitly regarded as the product of distinct groups of people. As Veit (1989: 42) points out, 'the "archaeological culture" . . . became a quasi-ideology-free substitute for the term "ethnic unit"', but one which still takes for granted the idea that peoples must be lurking behind such archaeological groupings.

Elsewhere in Europe, and in other parts of the world, German archaeological methodology continued to exert its influence up until the 1980s,

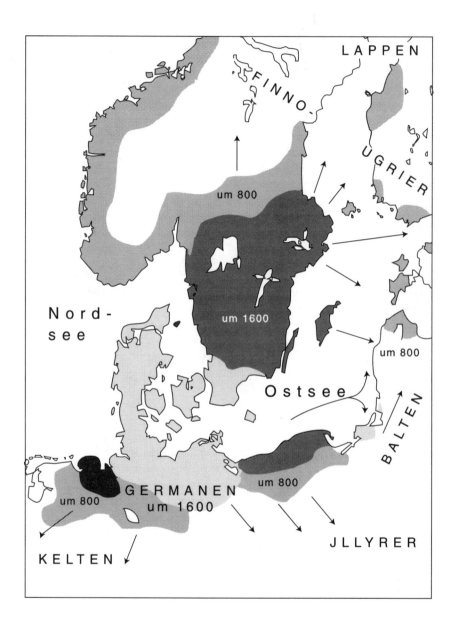

Figure 1.1 Map showing supposed 'Germanic' territorial expansion during the Bronze Age, which was produced in 1945 by the German archaeologist Hans Reinerth who worked for the Nazi organization, AMT Rosenberg (redrawn from Arnold 1990: 466).

either directly, for example in Namibia (see Kinahan 1995) and Argentina (see Politis 1995), or indirectly, through its initially influential role in the development of culture-historical archaeology in general. Culture-history can be characterized as the empiricist extraction, description and classification of material remains within a spatial and temporal framework made up of units which are usually referred to as 'cultures' and often regarded as the product of discrete social entities in the past. Despite variation between different regional and national traditions of culture-historical archaeology, it has been the main archaeological paradigm throughout much, if not all, of this century in Europe and elsewhere in the world (see Graves-Brown *et al.* 1996; Hodder 1991b; Ucko 1995b; see also Chapter 2). Thus, irrespective of whether or not explicit reference is made to past peoples or ethnic groups, the *same* basic paradigm which was used in Nazi Germany has also formed the rudimentary framework for archaeological enquiry worldwide.

The celebrated escape of archaeology from the confines of descriptive, empiricist culture-history is often associated with the 'new archaeology' of the 1960s and 1970s (see Willey and Sabloff 1974: 183–9; Renfrew and Bahn 1991: 34–5).[1] A predominantly Anglo-American development, new archaeology was influenced by social anthropology and entailed a reconceptualization of culture as a functioning system, rather than the homogeneous normative framework of a particular group of people (see Chapters 2 and 6). Analysis was, and in many cases still is, explicitly concerned with social processes and the production of generalizing explanatory models, drawing on anthropology, cultural ecology and neo-evolutionary theory. As a number of commentators have argued (e.g. Hodder 1991b: 6), the main contribution of the processual archaeology which emerged was in terms of the analysis of economic and subsistence strategies, exchange systems and social organization. Within this discourse there was very little concern with problems of nationalism, ethnicity and multiculturalism. Having dismissed the equation of archaeological cultures with ethnic groups, processual archaeologists in general did not regard ethnicity as an important focus of archaeological enquiry; it was merely seen as the product of an outmoded and unfashionable archaeological paradigm (Olsen and Kobylinski 1991: 10; see also Chapter 2). Furthermore, despite the critical intentions of some of its early exponents (Wobst 1989: 137–8), processual archaeology was, and to a large extent still is, firmly rooted in scientific notions of objectivity (e.g. Binford 1983). As a result, the use of archaeology by nationalists continued to be perceived as a discrete, external political influence on the discipline, leading to the distortion of scientific research.

The recent concern with socio-political issues, including a renewed interest in ethnicity and multi-culturalism, has been strongly linked to post-processual archaeology by both its advocates and its opponents. Yet post-processualism in itself represents a heterogeneous range of approaches, and a concern with the socio-politics of archaeology is by no means restricted to archaeologists whose work would be incorporated within this category. In fact, the World Archaeological Congress, one of the main forums for discussions about ethnicity, nationalism and competing perspectives on, and uses of, the past, has brought together a wide range of people representing diverse backgrounds, interests and theoretical perspectives (see Ucko 1987). Hence, it can be argued that post-processual archaeology, as a disciplinary movement, has in part set the context, and provided important critical perspectives, for exploring the nature of archaeology as a contemporary practice involved in the construction of cultural identity. However, broader social and ideological movements, and the various groups associated with them, have also contributed to the recognition of such concerns (see Moser 1995; Layton 1989b; Ucko 1983a, 1983b, 1987). Such influences exemplify the complex and recursive relationships that exist between archaeology as a particular practice concerned with the past and the rest of society.

In the context of critical reflection on the nature of the discipline, there has been a proliferation of research, evident in conferences, symposia and publications, focusing on the socio-politics of archaeology in general,[2] and also specifically on the ways in which archaeology intersects with the construction of cultural identity.[3] Trigger (1984: 358) has identified 'nationalist archaeology' as a specific type of archaeology, arguing that 'Most archaeological traditions are probably nationalistic in orientation.' Furthermore, many case studies have been undertaken which demonstrate that the use of archaeology in the construction and legitimation of national identities and territorial claims is far more extensive than has been generally assumed. In nineteenth-century Denmark prehistoric monuments, such as burial mounds and dolmens, figured strongly in the construction of a national, rural idyll, and archaeologists such as Worsaae were openly committed to rebuilding the national consciousness in the face of German aggression (Kristiansen 1992: 19–21; Trigger 1984: 358). In reaction to German expansionist claims based on archaeological distributions, the Polish archaeologist, Konrad Jażdżewski, published an archaeological atlas of Europe in 1949 illustrating the alleged expansion of the Slavonic peoples during the Bronze Age over much of central and eastern Europe (Kristiansen 1992: 18; and see Figure 1.2). In France, the Gallic resistance to the Roman Empire has played a central role in the construction of French national consciousness. The site of Bibracte, and the heroic figure of Vercingetorix, have been invested with particular importance in the modern nation-state, reflected in the considerable financial support and political patronage attached to the recent Mount-Beuvray excavation (see Dietler 1994: 584; Fleury-Ilett 1996: 196, 204). In the shadow of a history of English colonialism, the idea of an ethnically pure Celtic culture played a

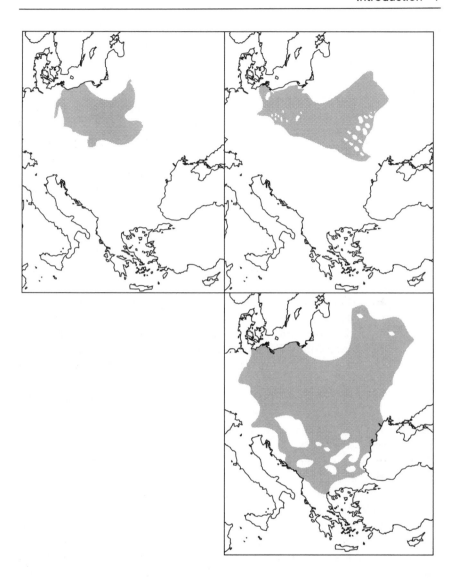

Figure 1.2 Three maps tracing the supposed expansion of the Slavonic people, produced by the Polish archaeologist, Konrad Jażdżewski, shortly after World War II (redrawn from Kristiansen 1992: 17). The first map relates to the Bronze Age, the second to the 'Migration Period' (AD 300--500), and the third to the Viking Age. There are obvious parallels in the mode of representation employed in these maps and that of the German archaeologist Hans Reinerth (see Figure 1.1), despite the fact that they present conflicting claims concerning the culture-history of the region that falls within modern Poland, and other areas in central Europe.

fundamental role in Irish national origin myths by the early twentieth century, resulting in an emphasis on the archaeology of the La Tène and early Christian periods, and a neglect of later 'Anglo-Norman' archaeology (see Woodman 1995: 285–6). Archaeology has also played an important role in younger nation-states, for example in the legitimation of the modern state of Israel a direct genealogical connection has been made with the ancient Israelite nation, resulting in considerable attention to the archaeological remains of the Iron Age in contrast to later periods (see Glock 1994). Furthermore, the site of Masada, which is said to be the scene of an heroic mass-suicide by a group of Jewish rebels in the face of Roman oppression, has become a particularly important symbol in Israeli national consciousness, forming the focus of military pilgrimage and ceremony (see Zerubavel 1994).

However, whilst it has been demonstrated that archaeology and nationalism are closely intertwined in many different contexts, it has also been shown that archaeology is involved in the construction of a much more complex range of collective identities.[4] Nationalism itself takes diverse forms (see Hutchinsen and Smith 1994; Kapferer 1989), and considerable change can occur in the historical and cultural representation of particular national traditions. Moreover, the nation-state is only one of the many possible foci for communal identity in the contemporary world, often leading to local rather than global conflicts; a point which was highlighted at the 1995 annual conference of the Association for the Study of Ethnicity and Nationalism in London (Targett 1995: 9). The so-called 'ethnic revival', the emergence of indigenous Fourth-World movements, the breakup of the Soviet Union and other former Eastern Block countries, and secessionist movements in other areas of the world, are some of the developments that have forced a recognition of the plural, multi-cultural realities of most contemporary states, whether or not diverse identities are acknowledged in state ideology. The situation is further complicated by supra-national entities which make a claim to the cultural identity of their members, such as the European Union, and fundamentalist religious movements such as The Nation of Islam. In the face of such diverse manifestations of communal cultural identity, many scholars of nationalism and ethnicity (e.g. Clifford 1988, 1992; Friedman 1989; Gilroy 1992; Hannerz 1989; Marcus 1989) have renounced the ideal of a world made up of distinct, relatively homogeneous nation-states as representing either a bygone era, or a modernist fantasy. Instead, they talk about a post-modern world characterized by opposing tendencies towards increasing globalization on the one hand, and the fracturing of identities resulting in hybridity, creolization and indigenization on the other (see Young 1995 for a critique of this trend). The image is one of diverse, unstable, competing configurations of cultural identity stretching from the local to the global, and engaging in multiple regimes of power (e.g. Clifford 1992: 101, 108).

Archaeological representations of the past are interwoven with such multiple and diverse forms of cultural identity which frequently do not coincide with the state. In addition to 'nationalist' archaeology, Trigger (1984) identified two further types: 'colonialist' which refers to the archaeology of countries where European powers have subjected native populations to various forms of institutionalized domination for considerable periods of time; and 'imperialist' or 'world-orientated', associated with a small number of states, such as the United Kingdom and the United States of America, which have exerted political domination over large areas of the world. There are many examples of such colonialist and imperialist archaeologies, for instance as in the various attempts by the Rhodesian colonial regime to attribute the construction of Great Zimbabwe to allochthonous peoples (Garlake 1982: 6; Hall 1995: 32–42), or archaeologists' denial of any ongoing relationship between living Australian Aborigines and their past which was defined as 'prehistoric' and 'dead' (see Ucko 1983a, 1983b: 14).

Yet, a decade further on, it is being argued that Trigger's categories are too superficial and generalized to address adequately the multiplicity of ways in which archaeology is used in the construction of identities in different regions of the world (e.g. Ucko 1995b: 9). Trigger (1984: 368) himself acknowledged that the types of archaeology he had defined were not comprehensive, indicating that there is some ambiguity as to whether Israeli archaeology should be classified as nationalist or colonialist, and whether German archaeology of the Kossinna school was nationalist or imperialist given the expansionist aims of National Socialism. However, what these ambiguities suggest is that such exclusive categories are perhaps not very useful for characterizing the archaeology of a particular region or country. For instance, the use of archaeology (e.g. the Bronze Age and the 'Celtic' Iron Age) in the construction of an exclusive representation of European cultural heritage and identity in the context of the European Union (see Jones and Graves-Brown 1996; Megaw and Megaw 1996) does not seem to fall readily into any of Trigger's categories. Moreover, colonial and neo- or post-colonial contexts illustrate the complex, ambivalent relationship between archaeology and the construction of particular cultural identities. In many post-colonial contexts western scientific archaeology, and in particular culture-history, has been co-opted for the purposes of cultural regeneration and nation-building following the subordination and dislocation brought about by colonialism (e.g. Mangi 1989). Yet, whilst such attempts to construct a unified national identity are often viewed in a positive light as the legitimate empowerment of formerly subjugated peoples, it is also evident that they sometimes involve the suppression of ethnic pluralism within the new state and in some instances the continuing denial of the existence of indigenous minorities (see Politis 1995; Ucko 1994). Furthermore, although a western form of archaeology may have played a role in the mobilization of liberation movements in North Africa (Mattingly

1996: 57–9) and India (Paddayya 1995: 141), it has also been party to ethnic and religious-based antagonisms which threaten the existence of contemporary states, as in the case of Muslim–Hindu conflict over the site of Ayodhya in northern India (see Rao 1994; Bernbeck and Pollock 1996). Finally, the ways in which indigenous Fourth-World communities conceptualize the past raise the possibility of alternative perspectives on the relationship between the past and identity which are not necessarily compatible with existing archaeological approaches (see Layton 1989b). Nevertheless, indigenous peoples are often forced into engaging with western conceptions of continuous, culture-historical development in order to legitimate their claims to land and heritage (see Clifford 1988: 336–43; Ucko 1983b: 16, 18). In such contexts the issue of whether archaeologists can identify ethnic groups and their continuity through time on the basis of distinctive material culture styles takes on immense political importance:

> For example, the archaeological 'evidence' of cultural continuity, as opposed to discontinuity, may make all the difference to an indigenous land claim, the right of access to a site/region, or the disposal of a human skeleton to a museum as against reburial.
>
> (Ucko 1989: xiii)

Thus, the intersection of archaeology with contemporary cultural identities is complex, extensive and often overtly political in nature; a point which is acknowledged by a growing number of archaeologists today. Yet the issue of what should be done about the potential problems arising from this situation continues to be a source of controversy within the discipline. Confronted by conflicting interpretations of the past, the crucial problem archaeologists face is when and how they should arbitrate between multiple, competing interpretations of the past. Can archaeologists distinguish between balanced, objective interpretations of the past and distorted ones? Or are different interpretations just a matter of competing subjectivities, and arbitration between one and another simply a matter of political expediency?

Such questions intersect with fundamental concerns about objectivity and the place of political and ethical judgements within the discipline of archaeology. The relationship between archaeology and the construction of contemporary identities, whether indigenous, ethnic or national, illustrates the socially and politically contingent nature of archaeological knowledge. In the light of this realization, the claim that archaeology provides the only legitimate and authoritative approach to the past has been questioned (e.g. Ucko 1989: xi), and respect for multiple, diverse interpretations of the past advocated (e.g. Shanks and Tilley 1992 [1987]: 245). Others, however, have been extremely critical of this stance, which they set up as a form of extreme relativism:

diversity becomes liability as any review of racist or chauvinist, nationalist readings of the past would demonstrate. The point is obvious and should not require belabouring, but apparently, many post-processualists in England and the United States operate under the illusion that such dangerous, undesirable tendencies are behind us and represent nothing more than an unfortunate episode in the history of the discipline. In the real world (e.g., Southeast Asia, China, the former Soviet Union, the Middle East, continental Europe) such 'readings' are still ubiquitous and still dangerous: the material culture record all too frequently is used to justify nationalist aspirations and land claims. In this light, post-processual archaeology seems absurdly academic.

(Kohl 1993a: 15)[5]

Yet amongst most archaeologists the only response to such qualms about the possibility of a relativistic slide into multiple, equal perspectives on the past, seems to be a demand for an orthodox set of disciplinary criteria for establishing the validity of competing interpretations of the past on an objective basis independent from the political realities of the present (e.g. Anthony 1995; Kohl and Fawcett 1995a; Yoffee and Sherratt 1993; Trigger 1995). In effect, they invoke the harsh realities of nationalist conflict as a mandate for archaeologists to act as arbitrators distinguishing on the basis of the evidence between 'objective', 'balanced' interpretations of the past, and 'distorted' or 'implausible' ones (e.g. Anthony 1995: 83–8; Kohl and Fawcett 1995a: 8; Kohl and Tsetskhladze 1995: 168–9).

Such a position is not new, and represents a similar one to that of German, and other, archaeologists in reaction to the use of the past for political purposes in Nazi Germany. The retreat to an empiricist position, buttressed by the notion of objectivity, allowed political interests to be situated as an external influence resulting in distorted interpretations of the past, distortion which could supposedly be revealed on the basis of the objective analysis of archaeological data. Archaeologists could stand aside or 'claim that "truth" was being manipulated by "others" for their own political ends' (Ucko 1995b: 16). However, as archaeological facts were considered to be neutral in themselves, archaeologists could only dispute competing interpretations on the basis of the precision with which the facts had been observed, including which material remains related to which particular past 'people' or ethnic group (see Veit 1989: 41). As Härke (1995: 56) points out, this retreat to a positivist and empiricist position was particularly ironic as it was precisely the kind of stance 'which had facilitated the Nazi exploitation of archaeology in the first place, and which may still have undesirable political consequences in spite of its claim to "objectivity"'. Indeed, it is on the basis of claims to scientific objectivity that particular subjective interpretations of the past (including nationalist and fascistic ones) have often gained legitimating power (see Shanks and

Tilley 1992 [1987]: 258), undermining the claim that such interpretations will gain greater validity in the context of recent critiques of objectivity (e.g. Anthony 1995: 85; O'Meara 1995: 427–8).

The idea of a dichotomy between political influence and value-free science continues to have considerable resonance with present day demands for the re-establishment of an orthodox scientific position to counteract the spectre of what is assumed to be extreme relativism. However, this dichotomy is in part founded on an ongoing archaeological naivety connected with the failure to examine the fundamental, but often implicit, assumptions that underlie archaeological interpretations of ethnicity, and consequently the use of archaeology in the construction of contemporary cultural identities. Until archaeologists explore the ways in which conventional archaeological epistemology itself may intersect with racist and nationalist ideologies, in particular through the identification of discrete, monolithic, cultural entities, a whole series of implicit values and presuppositions will go unrecognized (see Shanks and Tilley 1992 [1987]: 46). Furthermore, any effective engagement with the use of archaeology in the construction of contemporary identities must involve a reassessment of the relationship between material culture and ethnicity (see Ucko 1989: xiii). The need for such a project is amply illustrated by some of the contradictions evident in recent work on nationalism and the politics of archaeology (e.g. see contributions to Kohl and Fawcett 1995a). To give an example, Kohl and Tsetskhladze (1995: 151) begin their case study of nationalism and archaeology in the Caucasus by arguing that it is difficult to identify ethnic groups on the basis of their material culture. They then suggest that Georgian archaeologists have not been 'immune to the ubiquitous temptation to identify prehistoric ethnic groups on the basis of their material remains', leading to unascertainable attempts 'to identify the ethnicity and linguistic affinities of archaeologically documented cultures' (Kohl and Tsetskhladze 1995: 158–9). Yet two pages further on they assert that Georgians have a legitimate historical claim to their territory on the basis that Christianity has been an integral component of their culture and 'one simply cannot ignore those beautiful monastery complexes and churches with their Georgian inscriptions' (Kohl and Tsetskhladze 1995: 161). Ultimately then, it seems that the 'balanced', 'objective' and 'reliable' interpretations of past ethnic groups which they insist must be produced can only be made on precisely the same principles of interpretation that underlie the 'unbalanced' and 'distorted' representations of certain nationalist archaeologists!

Clearly there is considerable ambivalence about the basic interpretative methods and assumptions conventionally being used, but the desire to maintain the ideal of an objective and empiricist archaeology prevents a critical and theoretically informed re-evaluation of these methods and assumptions. Furthermore, diatribes against 'post-processual scholasticism' (e.g. Kohl 1993a: 16) ironically often dismiss the very kind of research concerning material culture and the formation of social and cultural identities (e.g. Hodder 1982a; Shanks and Tilley 1992 [1987]: 172–240) that may ultimately provide archaeologists with a stronger basis for engaging with nationalist reconstructions of the past.

There is a lacuna in the treatment of cultural identity in archaeology. On the one hand, the identification of *past* ethnic groups or cultures has been a major concern within the empiricist framework of traditional archaeology. On the other hand, recent critical studies have focused on the ways in which archaeological knowledge is used in the construction of identities in the *present*. However, neither has, for the most part, been concerned with formulating new theoretical frameworks for the interpretation of ethnicity in the past. There has been very little explicit analysis of the nature of ethnicity and the relationship between material culture and ethnic identity (exceptions include Dolukhanov 1994; Hodder 1982a; Olsen and Kobylinski 1991; Shennan 1989b). In contrast, there has been a rapid increase in research and theoretical debate about ethnicity in the human sciences since the late 1960s, resulting in a number of important changes in our understanding of socio-cultural differentiation. As yet these developments are largely ignored by archaeologists, many of whom continue directly to equate 'archaeological cultures', defined on the basis of repeated associations of distinctive material culture, with past ethnic groups.

The aim of this book is to provide a critical synthesis of a range of recent theories of ethnicity in the human sciences, and to develop a theoretical framework for the interpretation of ethnicity in archaeology. The approach adopted takes into account the ways in which the concepts and meanings that frame our present-day understandings of the past, and the objects of archaeological study, form part of one another and help to constitute one another (see Shanks and Tilley 1992 [1987]: 256–7; McGuire 1992: 217–18). Such a dialectic between past and present means that it is necessary to explore the ways in which the assumptions and concepts used in archaeological analysis have been, and continue to be, influenced by discourses of identity in the present (see Jones 1996). How, and in what ways, are the concepts and frameworks that are employed in the identification of past ethnic groups socially and historically constituted in themselves? Working from such a critical historicization of current discourses of identity, the processes involved in the construction of ethnicity and the relationship between ethnicity and culture can be examined in order to develop a comparative theoretical framework. The argument I develop counteracts the idea that ethnicity constitutes the basic, underlying essence or character of a group of people which persists through time and can be traced back to a unique origin. Instead, I argue that ethnic identity is based on shifting, situational, subjective identifications of self and others, which are rooted in ongoing daily practice and historical experience, but also subject to transformation and discontinuity. As discussed in the Conclusion, such a theoretically informed analysis of the dynamic and historically contingent nature of ethnic identity in the past *and* in the present has the potential to subject contemporary claims about the permanent and inalienable status of identity and territorial association to critical scrutiny.

Chapter 2

The archaeological identification of peoples and cultures

A desire to attach an identity to particular objects or monuments, most frequently expressed in terms of the ethnic group or 'people' who produced them, has figured at the heart of archaeological enquiry (see Hides 1996). From the Renaissance period onwards archaeological material has been attributed to historically attested peoples, such as the Britons, Romans, Saxons and Danes in England, and Germanic tribes of the Heruli and Cimbri in Central Europe. Moreover, the spread of nationalism during the nineteenth century provided fertile ground for an escalation of interest in archaeological remains, and in particular to tracing their national or ethnic pedigree (see Díaz-Andreu and Champion 1996a; Sklenár 1983; Trigger 1989). By the early decades of the twentieth century such interests had become explicitly formulated in the methodological principle that archaeological culture areas reflect past 'peoples' or ethnic groups, as in the work of archaeologists such as Kossinna (1911) and Vere Gordon Childe (1929).

CULTURE-HISTORY

Throughout the nineteenth century, chronological and spatial frameworks, such as the Three Age System and its regional variants, were being constructed on the basis of European archaeological material. A 'direct ethnohistorical' method was also being developed in the 1860s and 1870s by archaeologists such as Vocel and Montelius, who attempted to trace particular groups of people back into prehistory on the basis of find associations and horizons starting from a point where their presence could be documented by the synchronization of archaeological and historical sources (Sklenár 1983: 91). Other archaeologists, such as Rudolf Virchow, the founder of the German Society for Anthropology, Ethnology and Prehistory, were also concerned with chronology, and the definition of ethnic groups from archaeological material through the systematic compilation of typical object types and their geographical distribution (Kossack 1992: 80–2).

It was within this context that Kossinna defined and systematically applied the concept of an archaeological culture in conjunction with the 'direct ethno-historical' method in his book, *Die Herkunft der Germanen* (The Origin of the Germans), published in 1911. His 'settlement archaeology' was based on the axiom that 'in all periods, sharply delineated archaeological culture areas coincide with clearly recognizable peoples or tribes' (as cited in Childe 1956: 28). Cultures were defined on the basis of material culture traits associated with sites in a particular region, and at a particular time, and it was assumed that cultural continuity indicated ethnic continuity. On the basis of this methodology he claimed that it was possible to identify major ethnic groups, such as the Germans, the Slavs and the Celts, in prehistory on the basis of culture provinces, while individual cultures correspond with tribes, such as the Vandals and the Lombards (Trigger 1989: 165).

The work of Kossinna and others, such as Oswald Menghin, established the basis of German archaeological methodology until well into the twentieth century. Although there was often opposition to their particular interpretations, and also to the 'direct ethno-historical' method, research continued to focus on the identification of archaeological cultures, and, implicitly at least, ethnic groups or peoples (see Veit 1989). The work of Kossinna and Menghin also had an influence on British archaeology through the work of Childe, although he rejected Kossinna's Indo-Germanic interpretation of European prehistory and, to a large extent, his racist assumptions (e.g. see Childe 1933a, 1933b, 1935).

The early work of Childe (e.g. 1927 [1925], 1929) has come to be regarded as the defining moment in the establishment of culture-historical archaeology in Britain, and the development of the culture concept in the sense of the distinctive ways of life of discrete groups of people (e.g. Daniel 1978 [1950]: 247; Trigger 1980: 40, 43). However, although Childe was one of the first to produce a grand synthesis of European prehistory based on the systematic application of the culture concept, its use was fairly commonplace in the archaeological literature of the early 1920s. For instance, in an attempt to 'track down the historical Dorians' through archaeological research, Casson (1921: 212) associated the Dorians with 'the appearance and steady development of a culture, distinguished by objects of pottery and bronze, known as geometric'. Both Casson and those discussing his paper (e.g. Bosanquet 1921; Hall 1921) used the culture concept liberally, distinguishing between 'Dorian culture', 'Mycenian culture', 'Danubian culture' and so on. Likewise, in their discussion of the Llynfawr hoard, Crawford and Wheeler (1921: 137) referred to the '"late Bronze Age" culture characterized by finger tip urns, razors, hoards and square camps', and Fox (1923: 85) spoke of the 'Halstatt culture' and the 'pre-La Tène iron culture' in his study of the archaeology of the Cambridge region. Furthermore, it is not difficult to find some of the basic assumptions embodied in the culture concept elaborated in earlier literature, even though terms such as 'race' and 'area of cultivation' were used in place of culture. For instance, in 1905 Greenwell argued that two early Iron Age burials in Yorkshire belonged to a common group because 'there is so much in common in their principal and more important features, that they must be regarded as the burial places of people whose habits and manner of life were similar' (1905: 306). On this basis he argued that, in the absence of evidence to the contrary, such an 'area of cultivation suggests the existence of people united by affinity of blood' (Greenwell 1905: 307). Indeed, although it is important to note that 'ties of blood' and 'race' had been replaced by brief references to ancestry and common origins, the same emphasis on the correlation of distinctive cultural habits and ways of life with discrete communities or cultural groups is evident in Crawford's (1921) discussion of techniques for the identification of cultures. He stated that 'culture may be defined as the sum of all the ideals and activities and material which characterise a group of human beings. It is to a community what character is to an individual' (ibid.: 79), and also that archaeologists should aim to discover 'homogeneous cultures' through the analysis of a broad range of types and their distribution in space and time (ibid.: 132).

By comparison to these authors, Childe's (1929) early characterization of culture was minimalistic. In the preface to *The Danube in Prehistory*, he defined an archaeological culture as 'certain types of remains – pots, implements, ornaments, burial rites, house forms – constantly recurring together' (1929: v–vi). However, during the 1930s Childe (1933b, 1935) elaborated on the nature of archaeological cultures in two papers that were explicitly engaged with a critique of the correlation of race with archaeological and linguistic groupings:

> Culture is a social heritage; it corresponds to a community sharing common traditions, common institutions and a common way of life. Such a group may reasonably be called a people. . . . It is then a people to which the culture of an archaeologist must correspond. If ethnic be the adjective for people, we may say that prehistoric archaeology has a good hope of establishing an ethnic history of Europe, while a racial one seems hopelessly remote.
>
> (Childe 1935: 198–9)

Similar arguments were reiterated in Childe's later discussions of archaeological methodology, where he stressed that the arbitrary peculiarities of artefacts are 'assumed to be the concrete expressions of the common social traditions that bind together a people' (Childe 1969 [1950]: 2; see also 1956: 16, 31).

In contrast to Kossinna and many others, Childe emphasized the importance of the association of particular artefact types under conditions suggesting their contemporaneous use in the same society (i.e. he considered

material assemblages to be more important than individual artefact types).
Thus, the archaeological culture, for Childe, was a formal, not a geographical or chronological, unit. Its boundaries had to be established empiri-
cally from the delineation of cultures rather than by seriation of individual
types (Trigger 1980: 41–3). Nevertheless, although Childe stressed the
importance of all aspects of the material record in the description of
archaeological cultures, in practice most were defined on the basis of a
small number of diagnostic artefacts (e.g. Childe 1956: 121–3). Such a
reliance on a few diagnostic types became quite extreme in the work of
some archaeologists. For instance, in a re-evaluation of the British Iron
Age, Hodson (1964) identified a single culture, called the Woodbury complex, on the basis of only three widely distributed type fossils – the
permanent round house, the weaving comb and the ring-headed pin (see
Figure 2.1).

The definition of culture areas became the principal means by which
European prehistory was delineated in space and time until at least the
1970s (e.g. Bordes 1968; Burkitt 1933; Childe 1927 [1925]; Erich 1954,
1965; Hawkes 1940; Piggott 1965). This produced a mosaic of peoples and
cultures, as expressed in maps, tables and charts (see Figures 2.2, 2.3 and
2.4). In North America, nineteenth- and early twentieth-century archaeo-

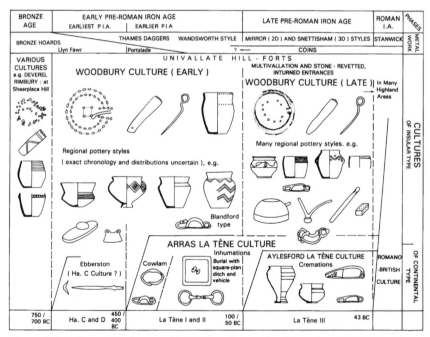

Figure 2.1 Schematic diagram illustrating the main elements of the 'Woodbury
Culture' as defined by Hodson (1964: 108).

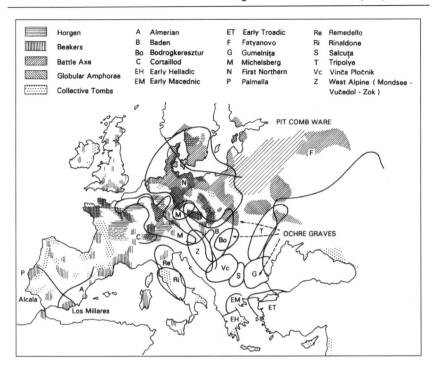

	Horgen	A	Almerian	ET	Early Troadic	Re	Remedello
	Beakers	B	Baden	F	Fatyanovo	Ri	Rinaldone
		Bo	Bodrogkeresztur	G	Gumelniţa	S	Salcuţa
	Battle Axe	C	Cortaillod	M	Michelsberg	T	Tripolye
	Globular Amphorae	EH	Early Helladic	N	First Northern	Vc	Vinča Pločnik
		EM	Early Macednic	P	Palmella	Z	West Alpine (Mondsee -
	Collective Tombs						Vučedol - Zok)

PIT COMB WARE

OCHRE GRAVES

Alcala

Los Millares

Figure 2.2 'Europe in period III: Beaker and Battle-axe cultures', redrawn from Childe (1957 [1926]: 351).

logy also resulted in a culture-historical approach to the past, but the concepts and techniques involved were the product of somewhat different developments.

One of the major distinctions between the development of North American and European archaeology was the perceived relationship between the archaeologist's own cultural history and the archaeological past. In Europe, archaeological material was often assumed to be the ancestral remains of various European peoples, and the rise of various forms of nationalism established a vested interest in the study of national origins and histories; preferably histories illustrating the great antiquity and continuity of the nation concerned. Moreover, evolutionary archaeology provided evidence of the supposed progress and superiority of European peoples. In contrast, the prehistoric remains of North America were clearly not the remains of the forebears of the dominant colonial society, and macro-cultural evolutionary shifts were assumed to be absent in North American prehistory as Native American society was regarded as static and 'primitive' (Trigger 1978: 93–5). Partly as a result of these differences, the initial development of descriptive typology in North American archaeology

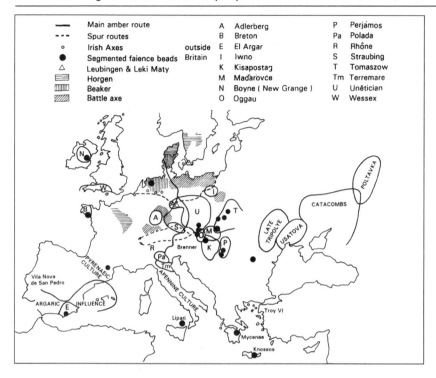

Figure 2.3 'Europe in period IV: early Bronze Age cultures and trade routes', redrawn from Childe (1957 [1926]: 352).

was primarily geographical rather than chronological; in stark contrast to European archaeology, a chronological framework did not begin to become established in American archaeology until the early decades of the twentieth century.

The first culture-historical synthesis in North American archaeology was Kidder's study of archaeological material from nine river drainages in the southwest published in 1924. He defined four successive periods or stages, the Basket Maker, post-Basket Maker, pre-Pueblo and Pueblo. He also defined regional variants of this sequence, referring on occasion to both the periods themselves and the regional variants as cultures. It is clear that Kidder (1962 [1924]: 161) regarded archaeological cultures as equivalent to chronological stages, for instance when he states that 'the investigator must select for study those phenomena which most accurately reflect changes in culture or, what amounts to the same thing, chronological periods'; an approach which was rejected by others (e.g. Childe 1927 [1925]). Nevertheless, his culture-historical scheme represented an important step in the development of the concept of an archaeological culture in North America.

Kidder's study of southwestern archaeology was taken up by other archaeologists who were concerned with its chronological implications, and in 1927 the Pecos conference was called with the aim of developing a general classificatory system for southwestern archaeology based largely on Kidder's scheme (Trigger 1989: 189; Willey and Sabloff 1974: 110). However, other culture classificatory schemes were also being formulated, principally by Gladwin and McKern who each developed hierarchical, dendritic, classificatory schemes in the mid-1930s. The categories in these schemes ranged from very broadly defined units based on superficial trait similarities to very narrowly defined units based on a high degree of trait similarity. For instance, in Mckern's (1939: 308–10) system these categories, ranging from the broadest to the finest units, were termed 'bases', 'patterns', 'phases', 'aspects' and 'foci' (which were further subdivided into 'components'). Although both classificatory systems were based on similar hierarchical schemes, Gladwin's system involved territorial dimensions, and a temporal element is implicit in the dendritic framework (Willey and Sabloff 1974: 111), whereas Mckern's system eschewed spatial and temporal dimensions (McKern 1939: 302–3).

These systems of classification established the systematic use of cultural units for the classification of archaeological data in the United States. Although a specialized terminology was developed in preference to the term 'culture', these categories constituted formal cultural units, rather than chronological stages, and were assumed to represent past tribes, or groups of closely related tribes (e.g. McKern 1939: 302, 308). In comparison to British culture-historical archaeology, American culture-history tended to be dominated by a concern with typological and chronological detail, to the exclusion of more ambitious culture-historical reconstruction and the investigation of past ways of life (Willey and Sabloff 1974: 88–130). Nevertheless, classificatory schemes such as those developed by Kidder, Gladwin and McKern ultimately contributed to the definition of a mosaic of cultures defined in space and time in a similar manner to European culture-history (see Willey and Phillips 1958).

Despite variations in the archaeological traditions of different countries, the culture-historical paradigm, in one form or another, has provided the dominant framework for archaeological analysis throughout most of the world during the twentieth century. European and North American culture-history has been 'exported' around the world, for instance German methodology to Namibia (Kinahan 1995: 86), the Vienna School to Argentina through the work of Imbelloni and Menghin (Politis 1995: 202), North American culture-history to Andean and Central American countries (ibid.: 205), Childe almost everywhere. Yet such 'exports' (or impositions) are also transformed, at least to some extent, by the particular conditions characterizing the new context in which they are introduced (see Ucko 1995b: 2).

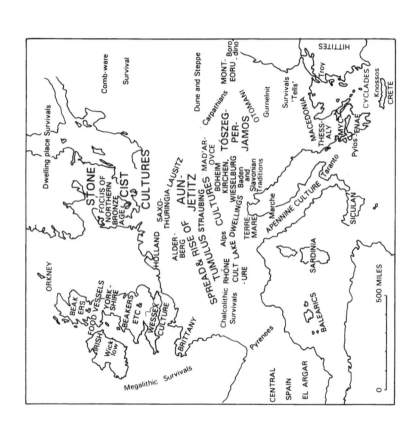

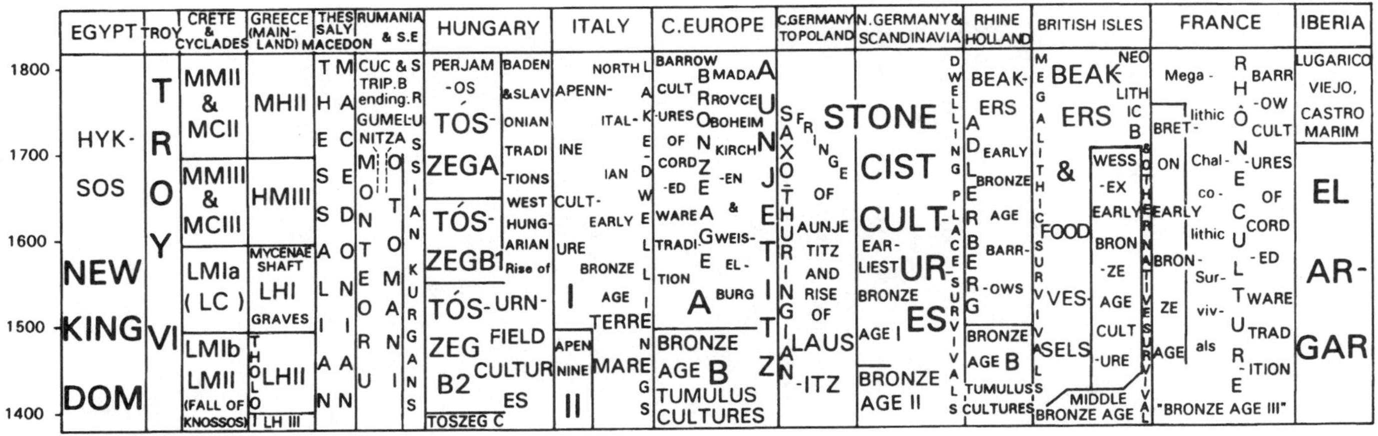

Figure 2.4 'The achievement of the European Bronze Age, 1800–1400 BC', after Hawkes (1940, map VI and table VI).

Trigger (1978: 86) has argued that the widespread adoption of the culture-historical approach in archaeology was stimulated by the need to establish a system for classifying the spatial and temporal variation that was increasingly evident in the archaeological record. Similar arguments continue to be made with relation to 'virgin' archaeological territory:

> In the case of regions which are still archaeologically *terra incognita* the application of the culture-historical approach has enormous significance. In those areas where a skeletal framework is already available, perspectives developed by processual and post-processual archaeologies are particularly useful.
>
> (Paddayya 1995: 139; see also Renfrew 1972: 17)

Such statements seem to imply that culture-history involves the description and classification of variation in material remains without reference to any preconceived concepts or theory. It cannot be denied that human ways of life vary in space and time and that this variation is frequently manifested in some form or another in material culture. However, the particular classificatory framework developed in archaeology in order to deal with such variation was, and still is, based on certain assumptions about the nature of cultural diversity. These assumptions tend to have been largely implicit due to the empiricist nature of traditional culture-history, and statements about the conceptual framework governing the identification of past cultures and peoples were often scarce (exceptions include Childe 1935; Crawford 1921; Tallgren 1937).

As we have seen one of the principal assumptions underlying the culture-historical approach is that bounded, homogeneous cultural entities correlate with particular peoples, ethnic groups, tribes, and/or races. This assumption was based on a normative conception of culture; that within a given group cultural practices and beliefs tend to conform to prescriptive ideational norms or rules of behaviour. Such a conceptualization of culture is based on the assumption that it is made up of a set of shared ideas or beliefs, which are maintained by regular interaction within the group, and the transmission of shared cultural norms to subsequent generations through the process of socialization, which purportedly results in a continuous cumulative cultural tradition. Childe (1956: 8) was explicit about this process, arguing that:

> Generation after generation has followed society's prescription and produced and reproduced in thousands of instances the socially approved standard type. An archaeological type is just that.

It is clear that Childe regarded culture as an essentially conservative phenomenon; a view which was common within a diffusionist and migrationist framework. Internal cultural change and innovation was perceived as a slow and gradual process amongst most cultural groups, with the exception of a few particularly creative groups. These latter groups were considered to be centres of innovation and change, either because of their inherent biological or cultural characteristics, or because of their environmental circumstances. Gradual change was attributed to internal drift in the prescribed cultural norms of a particular group, whereas sudden large-scale changes were explained in terms of external influences, such as diffusion resulting from culture contact, or the succession of one cultural group by another as a result of migration and conquest: 'Distributional changes [in diagnostic types] should reflect displacements of population, the expansions, migrations, colonizations or conquests with which literary history is familiar' (Childe 1956: 135).

Thus, the transmission of cultural traits/ideas was generally assumed by archaeologists to be a function of the degree of interaction between individuals or groups. A high degree of homogeneity in material culture has been regarded as the product of regular contact and interaction (e.g. Gifford 1960: 341–2), whereas discontinuities in the distribution of material culture were assumed to be the result of social and/or physical distance. Consequently, the social/physical distance between distinct past populations could be 'measured' in terms of degrees of similarity in archaeological assemblages.

This conceptualization of culture has been referred to as the 'aquatic view of culture':

> culture is viewed as a vast flowing stream with minor variations in ideational norms concerning appropriate ways of making pots, getting married [and so on]. . . . These ideational variations are periodically 'crystallized' at different points in time and space, resulting in distinctive and sometimes striking cultural climaxes which allow us to break up the continuum of culture into cultural phases.
>
> (Binford 1965: 204)

Continuities in the flow are a product of contact and interaction, discontinuities a product of distance and separation. However, although Binford's 'aquatic' metaphor captures the diffusionist orientation of much of the culture-historical literature, he over-emphasizes the extent to which culture is conceptualized as a vast continuum in culture-historical archaeology. Cultures, with an emphasis on the plural, were often viewed as distinct entities, despite the flow of ideas between them, and were reified as actors on an historical stage. Hence, Childe argued that on the basis of archaeological cultures, 'prehistory can recognize peoples and marshal them on the stage to take the place of the personal actors who form the historian's troupe' (Childe 1940: 2; see also Piggott 1965: 7). Moreover, the 'crystallization' of variation at different points in time and space constitutes the basis of the culture-historian's framework, so that the resulting reconstruction of prehistory comprises a mosaic of cultures; a 'typological' conceptualization of space and time measured in terms of socio-culturally mean-ingful events, such as contacts, migrations and conquests, and intervals between them (cf. Fabian 1983: 23).

SOCIAL ARCHAEOLOGY AND ETHNICITY: AN AMBIVALENT RELATIONSHIP

The demise of culture-history as a dominant paradigm in archaeology, at least in Anglo-American archaeology, was brought about by the establish-ment of processual or new archaeology with its conceptualization of culture as a system, and its emphasis on the functionalist explanation of social process and cultural evolution. To a certain extent the development of processual archaeology was stimulated by disillusionment with the descrip-tive nature of archaeological research. Whilst traditional archaeology had been largely satisfied with tracing what happened in prehistory in terms of cultures and their movements, archaeologists in the 1950s and 1960s became increasingly concerned with how and even why cultural change occurred (e.g. Willey and Phillips 1958: 5–6). For instance, it was empha-sized that the correlation of a distinct cultural break in the archaeological record with migration does not adequately explain the social processes involved. Instead it is necessary to examine why migration occurred and how it operated on past societies.

As part of their 'manifesto', the new archaeologists launched an attack on the normative concept of culture which had dominated traditional archae-ology. It was argued that culture constitutes an integrated system, made up of different functioning sub-systems, and as a corollary archaeological remains must be regarded as the product of a variety of past processes, rather than simply a reflection of ideational norms (e.g. Binford 1962, 1965, Clarke 1978 [1968]). Culture was conceptualized as an adaptive mechanism, and a variety of functionalist-oriented ecological and neo-evolutionary approaches were developed with the aim of analysing various dimensions of past socio-cultural systems. In particular, research focused on the appli-cation of predictive law-like models in the interpretation of technological and economic systems, but other dimensions of society such as ideology, political organization and symbolism, also became distinct foci of analysis within the systemic approach (for an historical review see Trigger 1989).

As a result of these developments descriptive historical reconstructions of past cultures and peoples were pushed into the background of archae-ological interpretation by the establishment of a new hegemony focusing on the functionalist and processual analysis of past socio-cultural systems. Within this new framework the interpretation of ethnic groups remained almost indelibly tied to traditional descriptive culture-history, relegated to a sterile and marginal position in the interpretative agenda; a marginalization which was reflected in a decline in explicit references to ethnic entities in the literature concerned with social analysis and explanation (Olsen and Kobylinski 1991: 10; Moberg 1985: 21). The main exception has been in the field of historical archaeology, where the existence of historical references to specific ethnic groups has resulted in the perpetuation of the 'ethnic labelling' of sites and objects. Straightforward correlations between particular forms and styles of material culture and particular ethnic groups have continued to dominate historical archaeology (e.g. Elston *et al.* 1982; Etter 1980; Staski 1987: 53–4), but the continued interest in ethnicity has also resulted in some innovative theoretical approaches (e.g. Burley *et al.* 1992; Horvath 1983; McGuire 1982, 1983; Praetzellis *et al.* 1987).

Although the identification of archaeological cultures and their distribution in space and time ceased to be regarded as an adequate explanation of the archaeological record, or an end in itself, such concerns were not discarded altogether. Indeed, whilst social archaeology has been committed to the explanation of settlement systems, trade networks, social ranking, political systems and ideology, the traditional culture unit has survived as the basic unit of description and classification, inevitably shadowed by the implicit connotation of a corresponding social or ethnic group, even where such a correlation has been criticized. For instance, Bradley (1984: 89, 94) makes frequent references to the 'Wessex Culture', Renfrew (1972: 187, 191; 1973: 187) to the 'Phylokopi I Culture' and the 'Copper Age cultures of the Balkans', and Sherratt (1982: 17) refers to the 'Szakálhát' and 'Tisza' cultures.

For some (e.g. Binford 1965), the retention of a normative culture concept was justified, because, whilst functional aspects of material culture were no longer considered to be appropriate for the identification of cultures or ethnic groups, such information was still assumed to be held in non-functional stylistic traits (see Chapter 6). However, many people adopted a pragmatic position similar to Renfrew (1972; 1979; see also Hodson 1980), arguing that the archaeological culture and the typological method were still necessary for the basic description and classification of the 'facts' prior to the process of explanation:

> While the simple narration of events is not an explanation, it is a necessary preliminary. We are not obliged to reject Croce's statement (quoted in Collingwood 1946, 192): 'History has only one duty: to narrate the facts', but simply to find it insufficient. The first, preliminary goal of an archaeological study must be to define the culture in question in space and time. Only when the culture has been identified, defined and described is there any hope of 'taking it apart' to try to reach some understanding of how it came to have its own particular form.
>
> (Renfrew 1972: 17)

This statement reveals the distinction between empirical description and classification ('where' and 'when' questions), and social explanation and interpretation ('how' and 'why' questions) which has been, and continues to be, intrinsic to social/processual archaeology. Cultures and ethnic groups remain firmly located at the empirical descriptive level of archaeological research, whilst other aspects of society are seen as components making up a dynamic cultural system (e.g. Renfrew 1972). Furthermore, whilst such a distinction between empirical description and explanation has been the focus of post-processual critiques (e.g. Hodder 1986; Shanks and Tilley 1992 [1987]), these have not, for the most part, been associated with a reconsideration of the interpretation of ethnicity in archaeology, focusing instead largely on symbolic and ideological systems.

There are a number of exceptions to this general picture, all of which involve the transposition of ethnic groups and ethnicity from the domain of description and classification to that of explanation and interpretation as distinguished within processual archaeology. Thus, Olsen (1985: 13) remarks that Odner's (1985) re-analysis of Saami ethnogenesis 'is mainly concerned with the question *why* Saami ethnicity emerged, and *how* it has been maintained' rather than the traditional when and where questions. This shift involves a reconceptualization of ethnicity as an aspect of social organization often related to economic and political relationships, and in particular inter-group competition. Ethnic identity, it is argued, involves the active maintenance of cultural boundaries in the process of social interaction, rather than a passive reflection of cultural norms. Ethnicity thus becomes an aspect of social process, and yet another component in the social system, alongside subsistence, economics, politics, religion and so on, which requires processual analysis, in stark contrast to its previous status as a passive normative backdrop.[1]

Such a reconceptualization of ethnicity as an aspect of social organization has resulted in two main areas of research: (1) Studies that are concerned with the relationship between material culture and ethnic symbolism (e.g. Hodder 1982a; Larick 1986; Haaland 1977; Praetzellis *et al.* 1987; Shennan 1989b; Washburn 1989). For instance, on the basis of ethno-archaeological research Hodder (1982a) has argued that there is rarely a one-to-one correlation between cultural similarities and differences and ethnic groups. He demonstrated that the kinds of material culture involved in ethnic symbolism can vary between different groups, and that the expression of ethnic boundaries may involve a limited range of material culture, whilst other material forms and styles may be shared across group boundaries. (2) Research that is concerned with the role of ethnicity in the structuring of economic and political relationships (e.g. Blackmore *et al.* 1979; Brumfiel 1994; Kimes *et al.* 1982; McGuire 1982; Odner 1985; Olsen 1985; Perlstein Pollard 1994). For instance, Brumfiel (1994) argues that in the Aztec state ethnicity was a tool fashioned to suit the needs of particular political factions. The Aztecs sought to override particularistic ethnic identities within regional elites, but at the same time promoted derogatory ethnic stereotypes which served to reinforce the superiority of the civil state culture (an argument which has parallels with recent explanations of Romanization, see pp. 33–6 below).

However, such studies are sporadic and tend to be confined to specific, isolated case studies. Despite the important implications for archaeology generally, this recent research into ethnicity has not had an extensive impact on the discipline. Consequently, ethnicity, and the relationship between cultures and ethnic groups, remains a problematic area of archaeological analysis. On the one hand, the identification of ethnic groups is based upon implicit assumptions inherited from traditional archaeology, and located in the domain of the supposedly pre-theoretical description of the empirical evidence. On the other, ethnicity has been elevated, in a few instances, to the status of social process, subject to archaeological explanation. Thus an artificial dichotomy between empirical description and social interpretation persists in a great deal of archaeological research, and the position of ethnic groups within this dichotomy is ambivalent. This situation can be further explored through a more detailed consideration of existing interpretations of a particular region and period: the late Iron Age and early Roman period in Britain.

THE CASE OF ROMANIZATION

The historical moment of the Roman conquest has profoundly structured the interpretation of the archaeological remains dating to between 100 BC and AD 200 in northwestern Europe, including a large area of Britain. The incorporation of late Iron Age societies[2] within the Roman Empire has been taken to constitute a temporal boundary between past cultures, and between non-literate and literate societies, and this in turn has provided the basis for a period boundary, and a split between prehistoric and classical archaeology, which can be traced back as far as the eighteenth century (Cunliffe 1988). Recent research has focused on the nature of interaction between late pre-Roman Iron Age and Roman societies, and the persistence and transformation of late Iron Age socio-economic and political structures following their incorporation within the Roman Empire (see pp. 33–6 below). However, throughout much of the history of archaeological research the boundary between the late Iron Age and Roman periods has constituted a rigid framework which has structured the interpretation of cultural identity, as it has other dimensions of past social and cultural organization.[3]

The interpretation of cultural identity or ethnicity in the late pre-Roman Iron Age in Britain has traditionally been subsumed within a culture-historical framework. Hawkes (1931) developed the first standard cultural classification for the entire Iron Age, defining three major archaeological cultures, Iron Age A, B and C, and the scheme was subsequently popularized by Childe (1940). The ABC classification was based upon a migrationist framework in which continental Iron Age societies were regarded as the major source of innovation and change which spread to peripheral areas such as Britain as a result of the movement of peoples. Iron Age A was defined on the basis of Halstatt-style material culture, Iron Age B on the basis of La Tène-style material culture, and Iron Age C on the basis of a distinctive cremation burial rite, wheel-turned pottery, and late La Tène metalwork in restricted areas of Britain.[4] Within these major culture categories distinctive distributions of material culture, such as regional pottery styles, have been interpreted in terms of immigrant peoples, such as the Marnians and the Belgae, who were supposedly derived from different regions of the continent. For instance, Childe regarded the Iron Age A haematite pottery present at All-Cannings Cross, Meon Hill and Hengistbury Head as the cultural manifestation of Jogassian immigrants (1940: 204–6). Similarly, he interpreted burials and stray objects regarded as characteristic of the La Tène tradition in East Anglia as the culture of 'Marnian Chieftains' who established control of the 'Halstatt peasantry' and later founded the Iceni tribe (ibid.: 222).

Such peoples and their cultures provided the framework for the spatial and temporal classification of data and the explanation of culture change throughout the Iron Age. However, as Champion (1975: 128) points out, in their analysis of the Iron Age, 'archaeologists have too readily constructed a "culture" from nothing more than a single pottery type, and invoked the ethnic interpretation for its distribution'. The strict definition of an archaeological culture as a regularly recurring assemblage of artefacts was waived by Childe (1940) in his identification of immigrant peoples and their cultures in Britain on the basis of fine-ware pottery styles alone. He explained the absence of recurring and parallel assemblages as a result of either the invasion of only the elite members of society, or a supposed cultural degeneration due to the stress of migration. The unrestrained application of the culture concept in the identification of immigrant groups of people was subjected to a critique by Hodson (1960; 1962; 1964), who developed an alternative framework based on the definition of a broad indigenous culture, the 'Woodbury complex' which was itself only based on three cultural traits (see Figure 2.1). However, the underlying ideas remained the same; that is the archaeological culture as the basic unit of analysis, and the explanation of culture change in terms of invasion or trade (Champion 1975; 1984 [1979]). Within this framework Iron Age research has been largely preoccupied with typology and chronology and the desire to trace prototypes and parallels between Britain and the European continent (Champion 1984 [1979]: 146).

The identification of cultures and peoples in the archaeological record has been reinforced in the late Iron Age by the existence of historical references to the inhabitants of pre-Roman Britain which have dominated archaeological interpretation. Historically attested peoples have been conceptualized as tribes and chiefdoms, as well as ethnic groups, and it appears that ethnic groups are often implicitly regarded as commensurate with the former two categories, which have also been attributed political dimensions. Stylistic variations in late pre-Roman Iron Age pottery, and the distribution of coin types, have been used in the identification of these tribes or ethnic groups, such as the Dobunni, the Durotrigues, the Iceni, the Catuvellauni, the Belgae and so on (e.g. Cunliffe 1978 [1974]; see Figure 2.5).[5]

Attempts to force archaeological evidence into an historical framework based on the activities of individuals and groups has often proved unproductive. For instance, the appearance of the distinctive wheel-turned pottery and burial rites of the Aylesford–Swarling culture has been associated with the migration of the Belgae into south-eastern England on the basis of Caesar's observations in *Gallic War* (V, 12) (e.g. Hawkes and Dunning 1930). However, Birchall's (1965) chronological reassessment of the Aylesford–Swarling type pottery demonstrated that most of it was later than Caesar's incursion into south-eastern England, undermining assertions that this pottery provides evidence for Belgic invasions around 75 BC.[6]

Nevertheless, these historically attested categories have been maintained, and to some extent integrated within the broader ABC culture-historical framework. The Iceni have been interpreted as descendants of the supposed Iron Age B Marnian invaders (e.g. Childe 1940: 222), whereas the Belgae are associated with Iron Age C, and there is some debate as to which of the Iron Age tribes in south-east England are Belgic and which are not (e.g. Rodwell 1976). However, for the most part the historical evidence for particular named peoples constitutes a distinct superstructure, which is rarely explored in a detailed manner in terms of the nature of such peoples, and the meaning of the stylistic patterns which have been traditionally associated with them. Consequently these abstract cultural and historical categories have persisted alongside, and as a backdrop to, the analysis of Iron Age socio-economic and political organization (e.g. Cunliffe 1978 [1974]). In a few instances the distribution of particular styles of pottery has been re-examined and socio-economic explanations advocated in opposition to the traditional ethnic interpretation (e.g. Peacock 1969; see also the debate between Blackmore *et al.* 1979 and Peacock 1979). Moreover, the nature of late Iron Age stylistic distributions, and their relationship to ethnic groups, has occasionally been critically examined (e.g. Blackmore *et al.* 1979; Hodder 1977a, 1977b; Kimes *et al.* 1982). Nevertheless the ethnic entities themselves remain intact. Whether or not economic explanations are offered for particular styles of material (e.g. Peacock 1969, 1979), or the boundaries of ethnic groups themselves are re-analysed in terms of socio-economic and political factors (e.g. Blackmore *et al.* 1979), the late Iron Age is still conceptualized as a mosaic of bounded monolithic ethnic or tribal units.

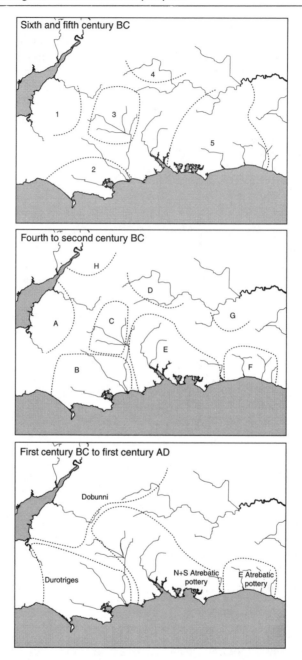

Figure 2.5 A typical representation of late pre-Roman Iron Age tribal/ethnic boundaries based on the distribution of regional pottery styles (redrawn after Cunliffe 1990: 535, where the caption reads 'Ethnogenesis in southern Britain. Distribution of distinctive pottery styles reflecting possible ethnic divisions').

In contrast to the investigation of spatial boundaries marking the supposed territories of discrete groups in the late pre-Roman Iron Age, the analysis of culture and identity following the Roman conquest is reconfigured in terms of a temporal boundary between the broad cultural categories of 'native' and 'Roman'. Close contact between Roman and native societies following the Roman conquest in Britain is assumed to have initiated a brief period of culture change, ultimately resulting in the synthesis of Romano-British culture and society – a process which has been called Romanization.

There are few detailed theoretical statements about what Romanization might have entailed, but several elements can be isolated from the literature. Primarily it is taken to describe the cultural processes which result from the interaction between two supposedly distinct cultures. The nature of this change has been assumed by most to involve the progressive adoption of Roman culture by indigenous populations, including Roman speech and manners, political franchise, town life, market economy, material culture, architecture and so on (e.g. Haverfield 1923 [1912]). Although it has been suggested that Romanization was a two-way process, resulting in the synthesis of both Roman and native culture (e.g. Haverfield 1923 [1912]; Millett 1990a), it is still assumed primarily to involve the adoption of Roman culture by indigenous populations. Moreover, this adoption of Roman culture has also been taken to reflect the adoption of Roman identity. For instance, in *The Romanization of Roman Britain*, Haverfield (1923 [1912]: 22, my emphasis) stated that:

> Romanization *extinguished the difference between Roman and provincial* through all parts of the Empire but the East, alike in speech, in material culture, in political feeling and religion. *When the provincials called themselves Roman or when we call them Roman, the epithet is correct.*

As a form of culture change resulting from the incorporation of one culture by another, the concept of Romanization has many parallels with the concept of acculturation, as used in anthropology and sociology between the 1920s and 1960s (see Chapter 3). Both concepts have been developed within a common framework of thought derived from the colonial era and a widespread interest in the assimilation and modernization of non-western societies (Hingley 1991: 91; 1996; Slofstra 1983: 71; Webster 1996: 4–5). The use of the concept of Romanization in British archaeology was embedded in a framework of nineteenth- and early twentieth-century imperial politics, with particular reference to India (e.g. Haverfield 1911). Anthropological studies of acculturation and culture contact were often related to the practical application of anthropology in colonial areas in the 1920s and 1930s, particularly in British anthropology (Beals 1953: 376–9). Furthermore, as well as sharing a concern with colonial and imperial relations, the study of both Romanization and acculturation tends to consist of the description of cultural traits, with little theoretical discussion or analysis of the dynamics of acculturation (e.g. Beals 1932, Redfield *et al.* 1936).[7]

The concepts of Romanization and acculturation sit easily within a culture-historical framework. The processes of change traditionally associated with both concepts are based on the assumption of a one-to-one correlation between culture and ethnic identity, and the idea that cultural contact and conquest result in the rapid transmission of cultural traits and ideas. Hence, the traditional interpretations of late Iron Age tribal boundaries and Romanization are based upon similar principles, the main difference being that Romanization constitutes an all-encompassing temporal boundary, which seemingly obliterates pre-conquest spatial differentiation.

Recent research into Romanization has attempted to break down the temporal boundary between late Iron Age and Roman society in order to examine the heterogeneous social and cultural processes transcending the Roman conquest. The analysis of cultural change in the early Roman Empire in western Europe is still largely embedded in acculturation theory, for instance, Millet (1990a: 1–2; see also Slofstra 1983) considers Romanization to be a form of acculturation, which he defines as the interaction of two cultures leading to the exchange of information and traits. However, there is a shift in the nature of research away from the description of cultural traits and towards a concern with the economic and political dimensions of Romanization and the nature of Roman imperialism (Millett 1990b: 35). Within this framework greater emphasis is placed upon the analysis of potential variation between the indigenous socio-cultural systems of the peoples involved in Romanization at different times, and in different regions of the western Empire.

It has been argued that the Roman Empire did not have the bureaucratic apparatus to sustain widespread intervention, nor did it follow an active policy of Romanization in the provinces (e.g. Blagg and Millett 1990; Haselgrove 1987a, 1990; Millett 1990a; 1990b). On the contrary it has been suggested that, although the Romans may have encouraged the adoption of Roman practices and cultural styles in some instances, the impetus for such processes was essentially locally driven; the 'motor for Romanization can be seen as internally driven rather than externally imposed' (Millett 1990b: 38). Although there is some variation in theoretical approach, the protagonists of such a position have tended to argue that the development of the western Empire was assisted by underlying similarities in the principles of social reproduction that characterized both the late Iron Age societies of western Europe and the patron–client relationships of the Roman Empire (Haselgrove 1990: 45). It has been suggested that late Iron Age societies were essentially characterized by a hierarchical system of ranking based on competitive emulation and relationships of clientage. Within such a system of social reproduction, power and identity were already dependent upon participation in groupings of increasing scales of inclusion (Haselgrove 1987: 105). The Roman Empire was able to extend this scale of participation and dependency through the establishment of patron–client relationships with the local elite, enabling the Empire to maintain power over the western provinces through existing social structures with minimal military and administrative intervention (Haselgrove 1987; Millett 1990a, 1990b). In this context, it is argued, Roman culture became the focus of the existing system of competitive emulation; access to Roman material items and the adoption of Roman ways of life became the means by which the hierarchical positions of the elite were constituted and maintained (Haselgrove 1987: 117; Millett 1990a: 69). In turn, it is argued that the behaviour of the elite was emulated by other sections of society, providing the impetus for the more widespread changes in architecture and material culture associated with Romanization (Haselgrove 1990: 45; see also Millett 1990a).

This approach suggests that the changing circumstances surrounding the Roman conquest of large areas of western Europe were associated with a shift in the locus of power and status, but at the same time many of these processes represent a continuation, if in a transformed state, of existing pre-conquest structures of social reproduction (Haselgrove 1990: 67). A further important element is that the social and cultural change resulting from the Roman conquest is regarded as the product of the varying social structures and histories that characterized relationships between different late Iron Age societies and the Roman Empire (e.g. Haselgrove 1990; Hingley 1984, 1989). For instance, Haselgrove (1990: 46, my emphasis) argues that however uniform the eventual outcome in material terms, Romanization represents 'the aggregate of processes operating essentially at a local level, people by people. Even within a single province, the form and degree of change varied *between different groups and regions*'.

Such research has contributed to a broader understanding of the social and cultural processes transcending the Roman conquest, and has played an important role in the analysis of socio-political relations and their potential intersection with the process of Romanization. However, this work has been almost exclusively concerned with the emulation of Roman material culture in the legitimation of political power. There has been very little consideration of the ways in which the production and consumption of Roman-style material culture may have become enmeshed in the reproduction and transformation of ethnic identity. In this way recent research into Romanization reflects a general trend in archaeological analysis, in which variation in material culture, which was traditionally perceived in terms of cultural and ethnic relationships, is now interpreted in terms of socio-economic and political relationships. Yet, at the same time, the assumed existence of bounded monolithic ethnic groups or tribes in the late Iron Age remains a part of the interpretative framework of such research (e.g.

Haselgrove 1990: 46), and the boundaries of these groups are still identified on the basis of stylistic variation (e.g. Millett 1990a, esp. ch. 2). Furthermore, the adoption of Roman-style material culture is still assumed, implicitly at least, to reflect an identification with the Roman Empire. There have been very few attempts to explore critically the relationship between cultural variation and ethnic identity. For the most part, assumptions about the relationship between culture and ethnicity remain part of a received implicit framework, rather than the subject of analysis.

An examination of a number of late Iron Age and early Roman sites in Essex and Hertfordshire (see Figure 2.6) reveals that assumptions about the bounded monolithic nature of cultural and ethnic entities also continue to underlie the chronological and spatial classification of material culture. In general, the detailed description and interpretation of particular artefact assemblages and site histories, in addition to the interpretation of Romanization, is ultimately based upon 'reading from style to history' (Davis 1990: 23). That is, a stylistic grouping, whether in a single class of artefact or an assemblage of artefacts, is held to be 'co-extensive with some other grouping of historical data or with actual historical entities – with artists, workshops, "periods" or "phases" of cultural and social history' (ibid.: 24). Furthermore, it is often the case that, whereas the traditional culture-historical narrative has been abandoned, the associated classificatory framework has been maintained, reinforcing an empiricist tendency in archaeology to substitute the mere identification of material entities in place of the interpretation of social entities (Miller 1985: 2–3).

For instance, the categories 'late Iron Age', 'Roman', and, to a lesser degree, 'Romanized', play an important role in the description and interpretation of material remains. Of the locally produced pottery, grog-tempered wheel-turned pottery is classified as 'native', whereas sand-tempered kiln-fired pottery which increases in incidence throughout the first and second centuries AD is classified as 'Roman' (e.g. Hawkes and Hull 1947: 157; Parminter 1990: 178, 181; Partridge 1981: 351). Changes in architectural style are generally regarded as a reflection of Romanization (e.g. Partridge 1981: 52) and classified as such in site reports. For instance, timber, rectilinear buildings of sill-beam construction are usually categorized as a 'Roman' architectural style (e.g. Neal et al. 1990: 34, 91). Such categories, which accommodate a heterogeneous set of artefacts and architectural styles and tend to compress them into a neat temporal and spatial framework, are maintained at the expense of a detailed analysis of variation in the material remains incorporated within them. For instance, Hawkes and Hull (1947: 257) argue that, whilst it is possible to define a variety of types of 'pure native' and 'Romano-British or Roman' pottery, the mass of fine-ware pottery 'exhibits intermediate Romanizing character in such a variety of gradations that any attempt at close definition would be misleading'. Moreover, a similar, although less explicit, ethos appears to under-

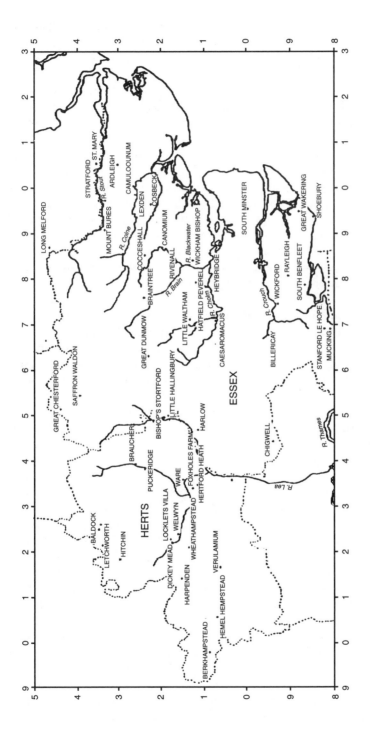

Figure 2.6 Location map showing the main archaeological sites dating to the late pre-Roman Iron Age and early Roman period in Essex and Hertfordshire.

lie the neglect of so-called Romanized locally produced pottery in the more recent excavation reports for the sites in Essex and Hertfordshire, both in terms of publication and detailed classification (e.g. Rodwell 1988, Parminter 1990).

Even the dating of material on the sites considered here is structured by preconceived ideas about the nature of reified historical entities such as cultures and peoples. Dating is almost entirely achieved through a combination of the historical association of artefacts, such as Samian pottery and coinage, relative typological chronologies, and the stratigraphic sequences of particular sites. In practice there tends to be a heavy reliance on dating by historical association and the seriation of types. The assignation of calendar dates to Romano-British (and late Iron Age) sites depends upon a chain of association which ultimately stops with the Classical texts. However, this historical method relies upon the assumption that artefacts of a similar style and/or known date of manufacture were deposited at the same time, thus disregarding potential fluctuations in the production, circulation and consumption of artefacts (Going 1992: 96, 111).

The dating of much of the material on the sites, such as brooches and locally produced pottery, tends to be based on relative typological sequences, which are also ultimately tied into calendrical dates by association with Samian and coinage chronologies. The basic principle underlying relative typological sequences is that 'the genealogy of objects [can] be established by inspecting them and by arranging them in an appropriate order, so that like goes with like' (Renfrew 1979: 14). Such a principle when used as an indicator of temporal progression is based upon two crucial assumptions: (1) that change is a gradual, regular process which occurs in a uniform manner, usually throughout a spatially homogeneous area, and (2) that a prime cause in variation in design is date of manufacture (Spratling 1972: 279–80; see also Davis 1990). These assumptions are enshrined in techniques of seriation in archaeology and are derived from ideas about culture and cultural change within traditional culture-historical archaeology. Namely, that dissimilar assemblages reflect social and or physical distance and are either the product of different peoples or of different periods, whereas similar artefacts and assemblages are a product of the same group of people at a particular period of time. In the case of both historical and typological dating these ideas are taken as given and used in the construction of temporal frameworks, with the result that assumptions about the bounded monolithic nature of culture and identity are substantiated and reinforced (e.g. Partridge 1981: 51–2; Butcher 1990: 115).

The case of Romanization illustrates that abstract cultural and ethnic categories remain a fundamental part of the conceptualization of the past in archaeology despite critiques of culture-history. Such categories provide a basic framework for the classification and description of the evidence, and their assumed existence continues to underlie the analysis of other aspects of socio-cultural organization. Hence, in many instances an essentially culture-historical framework persists, disguised by the recent explicit concern with social relations and social process.

It is only through such an examination of a particular body of archaeological knowledge that it is possible to dissect the complex matrix of preconceived ideas concerning cultures and peoples which are perpetuated within the discipline. The extent to which such ideas inform various dimensions of archaeological theory and practice highlights the need to make explicit the nature and origins of these ideas, and to re-evaluate them in the light of current theories of ethnicity. All too often concepts such as 'ethnic group' and 'culture' are regarded as natural categories, and it is important to consider the historical contingency of these concepts within the human sciences.

Chapter 3

Taxonomies of difference

The classification of peoples in the human sciences

In the social sciences, the progress of knowledge presupposes progress in our knowledge of the conditions of knowledge. That is why it requires one to return persistently to the same objects . . .; each doubling-back is an opportunity to objectify more completely one's objective, subjective relation to the object.

(Bourdieu 1990: 1)

In the history of the 'western' human sciences, a concern with human physical and cultural diversity has been primarily located in the realm of anthropology, where diversity has been a central motif. Indeed, Stocking (1988: 3) has retrospectively characterized the history of anthropological thought as 'the systematic study of human unity-in-diversity'. However, despite this enduring concern with diversity, the concepts that have been used in the classification of difference have not remained static, and their meaning and orientation have been influenced by different questions at different times during the history of anthropology. In the last two to three decades there has been a rapid growth in the study of ethnicity, and the term 'ethnic' has been applied to a wide range of socio-cultural groups formerly defined as racial, cultural, tribal, linguistic and/or religious. The adoption of the concept of ethnicity did not merely represent a change in terminology, it also embodied one of a number of theoretical shifts in the way in which human groups have been conceptualized and understood within the history of the human sciences. Concepts such as 'ethnic', 'race', 'tribe' and 'culture' do not reflect universal and unchanging divisions of humanity. On the contrary, they represent specific, historically contingent ways of looking at the world, which intersect with broader social and political relations. Furthermore, earlier approaches to the classification of human diversity often constrain, influence and persist alongside more recent perspectives.

RACE, CULTURE AND LANGUAGE IN NINETEENTH-CENTURY THOUGHT

The early nineteenth century witnessed the re-emergence of a concern with human diversity *per se*, and consequently the classification of human groups.

Prior to this period, an interest in diversity had been side-tracked by the Enlightenment concern with the universal development of civilization (Stocking 1987: 19). Although knowledge of 'exotic' customs had been increasing throughout the eighteenth century, philosophers such as Locke, Fergusen and Kames were largely interested in diversity with relation to defining the temporal stages of human progress. The concepts of 'civiliza- tion' or 'culture' related to a singular process through which all of humanity progressed. There was 'no real notion of culture as the constituting med- ium of different worlds' (ibid.). Thus, the early nineteenth century marks a significant shift in the study of humanity with the emergence of the idea that human groups were essentially distinct, primordial entities, character- ized by specific physical qualities – a transformation primarily embodied in the concept of 'race' (Banton 1977: 18; Biddiss 1979: 11; Stocking 1968: 21–41).[1]

There was considerable disagreement about the nature of race during the nineteenth century (see Hunt 1863), and a complex relationship existed between cultural and historical conceptions of race, and biological and hereditary notions of race. To a certain extent these different conceptions of race coincided with the development of the concept within two distinct traditions of thought, which persisted, if in different forms, throughout the nineteenth century: (1) a physical 'anthropological' tradition which was closely aligned with comparative anatomy (Stocking 1988: 4–5); (2) an 'ethnological' tradition, which was closely related to comparative linguistics (philology) and existing national traditions of Christian chronology dating from the sixteenth century (Stocking 1973: xi–xli; 1987: 50).[2]

In the earlier part of the nineteenth century the conceptualization of race within these two traditions differed in a number of important respects. The anthropological tradition can be traced to the work of early anatomists, such as Cuvier, who produced racial classifications on the basis of physio- logical and anatomical studies (see Banton 1977; Stocking 1968).[3] Cuvier himself did not challenge the Biblical paradigm of the essential unity of the human species (Kennedy 1973: 143), but others, such as Knox in Britain, and Nott and Gliddon in America, used the rigidity of anatomically defined racial types to argue that different races had distinct origins – a theory known as polygenism.[4] In support of their claim, polygenists placed con- siderable emphasis on the permanent nature of racial types, arguing that hybrid offspring were infertile (Banton 1977: 51). Furthermore, the con- cept of race came to be used in a deterministic fashion, in that mental and cultural characteristics were seen to be a direct reflection of physical structure (Biddiss 1979: 12; Odum 1967: 7).

The concept of race was also central to the ethnological tradition, but the emphasis was placed on philology and national genealogy, an approach which was reinforced by the Romantic movement of the late eighteenth and early nineteenth centuries. Linguistic characteristics were considered to be the most reliable indicators of race, and ethnologists, such as Prichard (1973 [1813]), used linguistic similarities to trace historical relationships between different races (Poliakov 1974 [1971]: 258; Stocking 1987: 51). In contrast to the anthropological tradition, the ethnologists endorsed the monogenistic theory that all human groups possessed a common origin. In support of this view, they emphasized the fluidity of racial categories over time, and usually argued that races had diverged as a result of different environmental conditions (Stocking 1987: 50–1).

The forms of classification and explanation which characterized physical anthropology and ethnology during the earlier part of the nineteenth century were structured by the debate between the monogenists and the polygenists about the question of a single versus multiple human origins (see Banton 1977; Odum 1967; Stocking 1987). However, the basis of this debate was destroyed during the 1860s and 1870s following the acceptance of palaeontological evidence for the deep antiquity of humanity and the impact of Darwinian evolutionary theory (Odum 1967: 14; Stocking 1968: 45). Together these developments served to establish the essential unity of the human species (see Harris 1968; Hurst 1976) and further stimulated a tradition of social evolutionary thought which had started to emerge in the 1850s.[5]

The development of ideas about socio-cultural evolution in the 1860s and 1870s, in the context of a radically altered temporal framework, resulted in the formulation of a different mode of classifying human diversity. In contrast to the existing racial classifications of humanity, which resulted in historical or abstract hierarchical classifications of *physical* types, socio-cultural evolutionism involved the classification of *cultural* stages within a developmental and evolutionary framework (e.g. Morgan 1974 [1877]; Tylor 1873 [1871]).[6] Furthermore, in contrast to the preceding ethnological tradition, the socio-cultural evolutionists were no longer primarily concerned with tracing the history of *particular* races or nations, but rather with the classification of the universal stage or condition of development which such races or nations were assumed to represent.[7]

Nevertheless, whilst race was a subsidiary issue for the socio-cultural evolutionists, this did not lead to the abandonment of the concept. Rather, the establishment of an evolutionary framework led to a reconfiguration of existing racial categories within a spatial and temporal hierarchy of progress, often explained in terms of the evolutionary notions of competition, 'natural selection' and 'survival of the fittest' (see Haller 1971; Stocking 1987: 224; Trigger 1989: 116). Even in the work of E. B. Tylor, who did not attribute any hereditary value to the notion of race (Tylor 1873 [1871]: 7), the establishment of a hierarchy of races is evident: 'Few would dispute that the following races are arranged rightly in [ascending] order of culture: – Australian, Tahitian, Aztec, Chinese, Italian' (ibid.: 27). Other socio-cultural evolutionists went further, using ideas about the inheritance of acquired cultural characteristics to develop biosocial theories of race within the new evolutionary framework. The anthropologist Herbert Spencer was particularly influential in this area (Bowler 1989: 154). Like Tylor, he accepted the 'psychic unity' of humanity, but at the same time placed much greater emphasis on variation in the mental makeup of different races. Drawing on Lamarkian ideas, he claimed that the utility of certain modes of socio-cultural behaviour resulted in the transformation of the mental makeup of the individual and that this was then inherited by subsequent generations (Bowler 1989: 153–4; Stocking 1968: 240–1).

Socio-cultural evolution and Lamarkian theories of change allowed for considerable fluidity in racial categories over time, as did the long-standing traditions of philology and national genealogy which persisted alongside evolutionary thought in the later nineteenth and early twentieth century (e.g. Beddoe 1885; Fleure 1922). However, a rigid conception of race, and the explanation of cultural diversity and inequality on the basis of physical, biological diversity, also persisted and became even more entrenched within the Social Darwinist milieu of the later nineteenth century (Biddiss 1979: 20; Stocking 1968: 42–68). For instance, Galton (1865: 68), who was the founder of the eugenics movement, argued for a deterministic view of hereditary processes and a fixed hierarchy of inherited mental and physical talents largely unmodified by social circumstance and nurture.

Thus, throughout the nineteenth century the concept of race, albeit in diverse forms, remained the dominant mode of conceptualizing human groups, and it was used as a synonym for national, cultural and linguistic groups in much of the literature (Huxley and Haddon 1935: 20). Moreover, explanations for cultural, social and moral diversity were often subordinated to the concept of hereditary, physical racial types (e.g. Jackson 1866). In this sense, Barth's (1969a: 13) generalization that traditional modes of classifying peoples in the human sciences can be characterized by the equation race = language = culture appears to be valid. Yet it has to be emphasized that the conflation of culture and language with notions of biological race in the nineteenth century was the combined product of a number of quite different theoretical approaches: (1) the linguistic notion of race which was central to the 'ethnological' and comparative philological traditions; (2) the racial determinism of the physical 'anthropological' tradition which assumed a direct, fixed correlation between physical form and structure, and mental and cultural capabilities; (3) the widespread adoption of the Lamarkian proposal that acquired cultural characteristics could become inherited, which served to reinforce a vague correlation of race with national, cultural and linguistic groups; (4) the Social Darwinist conception of a parallel relationship between cultural and physical evolution. Although all these theoretical approaches did contribute to a dissolution of the boundaries between physical and cultural diversity in the classification of peoples, it is evident that the relationship between race, language and culture in nineteenth-century thought was far from straight-forward.

Despite contemporary critiques of prevailing nineteenth-century ideas about race (e.g. Babington 1895; Freeman 1877; Huxley 1870; Müller 1877), the concept persisted into the twentieth century as an all-encompassing form of classification and explanation in the face of empirical evidence and theoretical argument to the contrary.[8] The role of racial classifications in broader social and political contexts provides some indication as to why the concept of race was so powerful, and why it became so entrenched towards the end of the nineteenth and the beginning of the twentieth century. Modes of racial classification and explanation penetrated many aspects of social life, and were certainly used to mediate and justify relationships between groups of people in the context of European colonialism, and nationalist and class unrest within Europe (see Biddiss 1979; Gossett 1975 [1963]; Montagu 1945; Stocking 1987). With the emergence of Romantic nationalism in the early nineteenth century, the idea that race and nation naturally coincided with one another and that the state should represent a homogeneous racial-cum-national unit became widely accepted, leading to divisive and exclusive forms of nationalism by the mid to late nineteenth century (see Huxley 1870 for a critical discussion). Racial theories were also enmeshed in various debates about slavery, colonial policy and the social status of groups belonging to the supposed 'lower' races and classes (e.g. Cairnes 1865; Farrar 1867; Jackson 1866; Mackay 1866). However, the relationship between political doctrines and particular forms of racial classification and explanation was complex. For instance, in the mid-nineteenth century, monogenists argued both for and against the institution of slavery (Gossett 1975 [1963]: 62–3). Furthermore, rigid racial typologies and associated notions of racial determinism were used to endorse the worst of colonial exploitation and subordination (e.g. Jackson 1866), as well as to support the need for western philanthropy (e.g. Farrar 1867).

The ambiguity of the relationships between particular ideas about race and specific political arguments suggests that the persistence of race as a taxonomic category and mode of explanation cannot be interpreted in a simplistic manner solely in terms of the legitimation of political aims. However, the role that nineteenth-century ideas about race played in the construction of instrumental social categories, both in the 'western' and 'non-western' worlds, was undoubtedly a significant force in the development and perpetuation of the concept of race as a means of classifying and explaining the variability of peoples. Moreover, the interrelationships between the category of race and broader nationalist and imperialist discourses in the nineteenth century have, in part, set the agenda for subsequent modes of classifying human groups. Initially, during the earlier twentieth century, the social and ideological purposes which the concept of race served contributed to a reaction against the concept itself, and a concerted attempt to separate the analysis of cultural and biological diversity in the human sciences.

FROM RACE TO CULTURE: THE CONCEPTUALIZATION OF DIFFERENCE IN THE EARLY TO MID-TWENTIETH CENTURY

During the late nineteenth and early twentieth centuries a concern with the study of culture and society, as distinct from the study of the physical, so-called racial divisions of the human species, resulted in the classification of peoples on a cultural as opposed to a racial basis. This shift away from an all-encompassing notion of race and the reorientation of social thought around the concepts of 'culture' and 'society' drew upon a long tradition of ideas about custom and civilization (see Gruber 1973). However, it was the formulation of the concept of culture by anthropologists such as Tylor and Boas, and the institutionalization of the disciplines of social anthropology and sociology, which provided the basis for the shift in emphasis from race to culture.

The work of the socio-cultural evolutionists in the later nineteenth century was important in the establishment of social and cultural anthropology (traditionally known as ethnology), a discipline which has been defined as 'the science which deals with the "cultures" of human groups' and is 'not primarily concerned with races as biological divisions of *Homo Sapiens*' (Lowie 1937: 3). However, as already noted, the socio-cultural evolutionists tended to see culture as a universal process of development, which was measured in terms of cultural stages, rather than a plurality of cultures representing the patterned ways of life of distinct peoples (see Harris 1968; Honigmann 1976; Stocking 1968, 1987). For instance, the idea of culture as a universal process of development is evident in the work of Tylor who formulated the classic anthropological definition of culture: 'Culture, or civilization . . . is that complex whole which includes knowledge, belief, art, law, morals, custom, and any other capabilities and habits acquired by man as a member of society' (Tylor 1873 [1871]: 1). Although such a definition could be used in the analysis of a plurality of discrete cultures, it is clear that Tylor was concerned with the definition of cultural stages. As Stocking (1968: 73; emphasis in original) points out,

> The concept of a plurality of civilizations had existed since the early nineteenth century, and is at least implicit in portions of Tylor's work; but when he went on to . . . speak of the 'civiliz*ation* of the lower tribes' as related to the civiliz*ation* of the higher nations,' it is clear that he meant the degree rather than the type or style of civilization.

Tylor referred to a plurality of 'races', 'tribes' and 'nations', but not to cultures in the sense of the organized and patterned ways of life of particular peoples. Furthermore, the concept of race was still an important aspect of social evolutionary thought, providing the basic unit of human differentiation and in many instances an explanation of developmental inequalities between peoples, as in Spencer's biosocial theory of evolution.

It was not until the late nineteenth century that the concept of culture in the plural sense was established, and there were concerted attempts to separate cultural and racial classifications (see Stocking 1968, 1988). The German anthropological tradition was important in terms of the rejection of the idea of unilinear evolution in favour of an emphasis on cultural contacts and diffusion (Heine-Geldern 1964: 411). In his book, *Völkerkunde*, published in 1885–8, the German geographer and ethnologist, Friedrich Ratzel, sought to show that diffusion created 'culture areas' – relatively homogeneous, organically integrated cultural complexes, which became conceptualized as *Kulturkreise* (culture circles) in the work of Froebenius and Graebner. Taking the *Kulturkreis* as the primary analytical concept they established an elaborate *Kulturhistorische Methode* (culture-historical method) in an attempt to ascertain historical sequences on the basis of the contemporary geographical distribution of culture complexes; an approach which characterized the so called 'Vienna School' of the early 1900s (Heine-Geldern 1964: 411–12; see also Zwernemann 1983).

The work of the German-American anthropologist, Franz Boas, which was undoubtedly influenced by the German *Kulturkreise* School, was particularly important in the development of the concept of culture in the sense of a plurality of historically conditioned, distinct cultural wholes in opposition to a sequence of cultural stages (Stocking 1968: 213). As part of his critical stance against evolutionism, Boas (e.g. 1974 [1887], 1974 [1905]) developed a particularistic, historical approach to the study of the cultures of diverse tribes and the diffusion of traits and ideas between such cultures. Furthermore, his work was also instrumental in undermining prevailing ideas about racial determinism in the early decades of the twentieth century (see Barkan 1988; Stocking 1968, 1974). Much of Boas's research was concerned to illustrate that neither race nor language were barriers to the diffusion of ideas, and that human behaviour is determined by a habitual body of cultural traditions passed on from one generation to another through processes of learning (Stocking 1968: 214–33). That is, he maintained that human behaviour is culturally determined, an idea which became one of the central tenets of twentieth-century anthropology.

Boas's work was particularly influential in the North American tradition of cultural anthropology (Singer 1968: 529; Stocking 1974: 17–19). Here, culture was the core concept and it was taken to be composed of implicit and explicit patterns of behaviour which constituted the distinctive achievement of human groups – their material culture, beliefs, myths, ideas and values (see Kroeber and Kluckhohn 1952; Singer 1968). The primary research task of the cultural anthropologist was to 'delineate cultural patterns and, beyond that, to compare and classify types of patterns' (Singer 1968: 530). The study of the cultural patterns of a given region also involved the reconstruction of its cultural history in terms of diffusion, culture contact and acculturation (see Honigmann 1976).

Both the American historical tradition and German culture-history also bear some resemblance to the diffusionist approach which was formulated in Britain in the late nineteenth and early twentieth century, as in the anthropological works of Rivers, Elliot-Smith and Perry (Honigmann 1976; Zwernemann 1983). There were important differences between the three traditions, for instance Boas (1974 [1905]) emphasized the complexity of processes of diffusion and acculturation, whereas Elliot Smith (e.g. 1928: 17, 35–6) and Perry (e.g. 1924: 2, 64–7) adopted a more extreme position, suggesting that ultimately processes of diffusion could be traced to one source – Egypt – the 'fount of civilization'. Nevertheless, all three were characterized by their opposition to unilinear socio-cultural evolution and in particular the idea of independent invention. In countering this idea they focused on demonstrating the importance of diffusion between cultures from an historical perspective.

It is in the context of this interest in the geographical and historical dimensions of cultural variation, and the conceptual framework it provided, that archaeologists began to classify spatial variation using the culture concept (Daniel 1978 [1950]: 242; Trigger 1989: 150–5). Kossinna and Childe were influenced by the German ethnological tradition, and Boas himself certainly saw a role for archaeology in tracing the historical movements of distinct tribal units (Gruber 1986: 179–80). Indeed, some of the earliest systematic stratigraphic excavations were carried out by his students (Willey and Sabloff 1974: 89). Thus, as in the case of socio-cultural evolution, anthropologists (ethnologists) and archaeologists worked in close association with one another, particularly in North America, using both anthropological and archaeological data in the reconstruction of culture histories ranging from a local to a worldwide scale.

In North American cultural anthropology a concern with the classification of cultures and the reconstruction of culture-histories persisted during the first half of the twentieth century. However, in British anthropology extreme diffusionism and social evolutionism were both superseded rapidly by functionalist and structural-functionalist theories of society. In contrast to culture-historical and diffusionist traditions of anthropology, British structural-functionalist anthropology was strongly influenced by Durkheimian sociology and was anti-historical in character. Furthermore, the concepts of 'society' and 'social structure' rather than culture have tended to be the central focus of research. Society was regarded as an organic, coherent system made up of interdependent social institutions (Malinowski 1944; Radcliffe-Brown 1952), and the study of social structure involved 'the ordered arrangement of parts or components' within a social system

(Radcliffe-Brown 1952: 9). The social relationships and institutions of 'tribal society' were the primary focus of research, and the notion of 'tribal society' constituted one of the main classificatory concepts (see Lewis 1968; Kuper 1988).[9] Tribal societies were assumed to be isolated, homogeneous, autonomous units based on kinship, territorial ties, a shared set of values and an awareness of a common social and cultural identity (see Lewis 1968; Rosaldo 1993 [1989]: 31–2).[10]

Nevertheless, despite variations in the classification of socio-cultural entities within different anthropological traditions during the first half of the twentieth century, there were a number of underlying similarities in the abstract concepts employed. The need to counter racial determinism has constituted an important agenda in the social sciences throughout the twentieth century.[11] The separation of the concepts of race and culture which is evident in the work of Boas was reinforced between the 1920s and 1940s in response to the use of racialist doctrines for political purposes (e.g. Huxley and Haddon 1935), and in particular in reaction to the Holocaust. To a certain extent the concept of culture emerged as a liberal alternative to racist classifications of human diversity (Clifford 1988: 234), and the notions of 'a culture' and 'a society' became used in place of 'a race' as synonyms for a group of people.

However, although the emergence of the concept of culture reflects a shift away from racial classifications of human diversity, the concept carried over many assumptions which were central to nineteenth-century classifications of human groups (ibid.: 234, 273). In particular, there remains an overriding concern with holism, homogeneity, order and boundedness, which has been attributed to the development of ideas concerning human diversity in the context of nineteenth- and twentieth-century nationalist thought (Handler 1988: 7–8; Spencer 1990: 283, 288–90; Wolf 1982: 387). The perpetuation of these concerns in twentieth-century conceptions of culture and society resulted in a general representation of the world as divided up into discrete, homogeneous, integrated cultures (and societies), which were implicitly equated with distinct peoples or 'tribes' (Clifford 1988: 232–3; Rosaldo 1993 [1989]: 31–2; Wolf 1982: 6–7). Group identity, or 'peoplehood', was assumed to be a passive reflection of cultural similarities.

Such a picture is the combined product of various kinds of analysis in the human sciences. As Rosaldo (1993 [1989]) has shown in his critique of social analysis, the norms of a specific culture (or society) have been determined through the generalization of particular, localized observations in the idiom of classic ethnography. Such a mode of analysis is based on the *a priori* assumption 'that stability, orderliness and equilibrium characterized traditional societies' (Rosaldo 1993 [1989]: 42), and that therefore cultural practices and beliefs are likely to be uniform throughout society. As a result of such assumptions, which should themselves be the subject of analysis, the society in question becomes represented as an homogeneous unit, unchanging through time. This view of culture (or society) as a discrete, homogeneous entity has been reinforced through empiricist syntheses of cultural and political geography, and literature adopting the *Human Area Relations Files* style of comparison (Fardon 1987: 168, 184). The results of normative modes of ethnographic description have also been elevated to general principles in abstract theoretical statements of various types (e.g. Radcliffe-Brown 1952), producing 'ideal systems' in contrast to 'empirical' ones (Leach 1964 [1954]: 283).

A similar picture of discrete, homogeneous cultural entities is generated through archaeological theory and practice. At a methodological level, the same kind of objectification of specific localized traits takes place in the definition of cultures as in ethnographic contexts. Such a process is epitomized by the phenomenon of the 'type site', which supposedly contains the archetypal traits of a particular 'archaeological culture'. The concept of the 'type site' is based on the assumption that material cultural traits reflect the mental makeup or cultural norms of the people who produced them, and that these norms would have been homogeneous throughout a bounded socio-cultural group. Moreover, this assumption is then reinforced by the tendency to focus on similarities and continuities, rather than differences and discontinuities, between the 'type site' and other sites within a particular region. At a broader level, traditional, empiricist reconstructions of particular periods or regions have been concerned with the distribution of cultures in space and time and the interaction between them. Furthermore, although such reconstructions are no longer the ultimate aim of recent research in archaeology, bounded socio-cultural units still provide the basic framework for the analysis of past social processes in much of the research carried out in the last three decades (see Chapter 2).

As a result of the way in which different kinds of analysis intersect with, and reinforce, one another, assumptions about the holistic, monolithic nature of cultures and societies have persisted stubbornly in the face of evidence to the contrary. It has been clear for some time that reality is more heterogeneous and untidy than such concepts acknowledge. For instance, in ethnographic studies, where researchers have been faced with defining the boundaries of 'their group', the concepts of culture, society and tribe raised methodological problems even at the height of their authority (Cohen 1978: 380–2; Narroll 1964: 283–4). Consequently, it has long been acknowledged that, as analytical units, concepts such as culture and tribe are not absolute, but arbitrary:

> The lines of demarcation of any cultural unit chosen for description and analysis are in a large part a matter of level of abstraction and of convenience for the problem at hand. Occidental culture, Graeco-Roman culture, German culture, Swabian culture, the peasant culture of

the Black Forest of 1900 – these are all equally legitimate abstractions if carefully defined.

(Kroeber and Kluckhohn 1952: 367)

Nevertheless, specific case studies of named groups of people required justification as well as careful definition. For instance, in his study of the Tallensi, Fortes (1969 [1945]: 14–29) argued that it was difficult to distinguish the Tallensi from other 'so-called "tribes"' on the basis of any political, cultural or linguistic unity and singularity. In order to overcome this problem, he suggested an alternative abstract concept as the basis for the definition of the unit of study:

> For the concept of a society as a closed unit . . . we must substitute the concept of the *socio-geographic region*, the social elements of which are more closely knit together among themselves than any of them are knit together with social elements of the same kind outside of that region.
>
> (Ibid.: 231; my emphasis)

A great deal of anthropological fieldwork carried out between the 1920s and 1960s was concerned with similar situations, in that there was a distinct lack of coincidence between the boundaries of cultural, linguistic and socio-structural phenomena, but the concept of a unit culture served to obscure the significance of such facts (Leach 1964 [1954]: 282). The inevitable methodological problems concerning boundary definition were overcome by conceptual modifications, such as Fortes's (1969 [1945]) 'socio-geographic region', without fundamentally challenging the anthropological concepts of tribe, culture and society. In British structural-functionalism at least, the definition of group boundaries tended to be merely an initial step in the analysis of the internal structural interrelationships of the social system. In other areas, such as American cultural anthropology, a concern with diffusion and acculturation meant that cultural boundaries were a more prominent aspect of analysis. However, even here, cultural traits were assumed to be passed between autonomous discrete cultures as a result of instances of 'contact', or in the case of acculturation, to lead to amalgamation of one culture with another ultimately resulting in a single homogeneous bounded entity. Discontinuity and heterogeneity were considered to be fleeting exceptions, abnormalities which are 'destructive of law, logic and convention' (Wilson 1945: 133, cited in Leach 1964 [1954]: 287), and, except in a few instances (e.g. Fortes 1969 [1945]: 16; Leach 1964 [1954]: 17), they were certainly not regarded as a focus of overarching social relations and interaction.

Thus, in the context of the notion of 'primitive society' (Kuper 1988), an abstract and idealized concept of 'tribal society' has prevailed in the anthropological literature at least throughout the early to mid-twentieth century. Although the concept of race had been vehemently attacked, the idea of a bounded, holistic social unit defined by language, culture and political autonomy remained intact, seemingly close enough to many empirical situations to serve the purposes of most anthropologists. It is this general picture that provided the backdrop to critiques of the concepts of tribe culture and society, and to the emergence of the concept of ethnicity as a central category in the classification of peoples.

THE EMERGENCE OF ETHNICITY AS A PRIMARY TAXONOMIC CATEGORY

The surge of interest in the phenomenon of 'ethnicity' during the late 1960s and 1970s was initially evident in the increasing number of journal articles and index entries devoted to the subject, and was eventually transformed into a major academic and political enterprise, with journals, conferences and research units devoted entirely to the subject.[12] The sudden interest in ethnicity represented both a further shift in classificatory terminology due to the pejorative connotations of existing taxonomic categories, and a significant change in the theoretical conceptualization of cultural groups. However, it is not possible to describe a coherent series of 'discoveries' which culminated in the conceptual and theoretical shifts embodied in the notion of ethnicity. Rather, the emerging concern with ethnicity in the late 1960s and 1970s resulted from attempts to deal with a variety of empirical, theoretical and ideological problems with existing anthropological and sociological categories, alongside an increase in the political salience of ethnic self-consciousness in various regions of the world.

In anthropology, growing dissatisfaction with concepts that had traditionally formed the basis of research in the humanities – notably 'culture', 'society' and 'tribe' – was a significant factor in the development of an interest in ethnicity. Methodological problems with such concepts were particularly acute in anthropology as the discipline was largely concerned with the study of individual tribal societies in their entirety, and consequently the society, culture or tribe constituted the basic unit of research. In contrast, the problem of defining 'society' was not of such immediate methodological concern in sociology, as sociologists were traditionally involved with the analysis of particular elements of what was assumed to be an essentially monolithic society. Furthermore, the nature of anthropological fieldwork, involving long-term participant observation, meant that anthropologists were often confronted with inconsistencies between the general models they used and particular empirical situations, in contrast to sociologists who tended to deal with 'ideal' models based on generalizing comparative analysis (Leach 1964 [1954]: 283).

During the 1950s and 1960s anthropological critiques of the concepts of culture, society and tribe emphasized the non-correlation of different boundary phenomena, and in some instances the very existence of discrete socio-cultural entities was questioned (e.g. Jaspan 1964: 298; Leach 1964 [1954]: 299; Moerman 1965: 1215). For instance, in his influential study of the Kachin and Shan of Burma, Leach (1964 [1954]: 17) argued that

> there is no intrinsic reason why the significant frontiers of social systems should always coincide with cultural frontiers. . . . the mere fact that two groups of people are of different cultures does not necessarily imply – as has always been assumed – that they belong to two quite different social systems.

Such studies stimulated demands for the development of theoretical frameworks enabling the analysis of the interrelation of social systems and the relationships between social and cultural boundaries (e.g. Leach 1964 [1954]: 284).

At the same time, the demise of formal colonialism between the 1950s and 1970s provided the background to further critiques of anthropological concepts, in particular the concept of 'tribe', which was attacked for its pejorative connotations of 'primitiveness' and 'backwardness', and dismissed as a construct of colonial regimes (e.g. Colson 1968; Fried 1968; Ranger 1983: 250). Furthermore, ideas about 'primitive society', embodied in the concept of the tribe as a bounded, homeostatic, integrated and essentially static whole, became difficult to sustain in the light of the large-scale change brought about by colonialism that was so visibly demonstrated by growing national liberation movements.

In the context of such internal and external critiques of the discipline and its concepts, the development of theories of ethnicity in anthropology embodied both a terminological and a theoretical shift. On the one hand, the concept of an 'ethnic group' became regarded as an acceptable substitute for the concept of tribe by a number of anthropologists (e.g. Arens 1976).[13] On the other hand, the concept of ethnicity was for the most part embedded in a theoretical approach which seemed much more appropriate to the social phenomena being studied. Focusing on the processes involved in the construction of group boundaries in the context of social interaction, new theories of ethnicity accommodated the broader colonial context, which could no longer be ignored with ease. Moreover, the ethnic categories used by the people being studied started to be taken into consideration, partly in response to increasingly active demands from colonized minority groups for self-determination. Consequently, whilst traditional definitions of 'tribes' or 'peoples' involved the enumeration of various traits, relating to language, material culture, beliefs and values, research increasingly focused on the self-definitions of particular ethnic groups in opposition to other groups (e.g. Barth 1969a; Gulliver 1969; Moerman 1965). In effect, there was a reorientation of research focusing on the role of ethnic phenomena in the organization of social groups and social relations in contrast to the traditional concern with cultures and their historic boundaries; a reorientation that was consolidated by Barth (1969a) in his introduction to *Ethnic Groups and Boundaries* (see Chapter 4).

In sociology and psychology the recognition of ethnicity as a major topic of research was a product of somewhat different problems. The concept of an ethnic group had already been incorporated within sociological and psychological terminology during the early twentieth century, as it was believed to have fewer political and derogatory connotations than the concept of race (e.g. as argued by Montagu 1945; UNESCO 1950). However, in classical sociology of the early to mid-twentieth century, ethnic and racial groups were generally considered to be secondary sociological phenomena in contrast to what were assumed to be central aspects of society, such as class divisions. Thus, the study of race or ethnicity was considered a peripheral area of research in sociology:

> ethnicity was never really regarded by early sociologists as one of the defining attributes of the social system – that is, as a necessary and universal feature – the possibility, or even the need for, a general theory of ethnic conflict was not seriously considered.
>
> (Parkin 1978: 621; see also Lockwood 1970)

In countries with a high immigrant population, such as the United States, ethnic groups constituted a significant area of applied research in both sociology and psychology. However, an underlying assumption was that continuous contact between cultural groups would result in a decrease in cultural diversity (e.g. Gordon 1964), and that as a result ascriptively based identities 'would progressively give way under the homogenizing influence of the modern industrial order' (Parkin 1978: 621).[14] The process of homogenization was a central assumption underlying notions such as the 'melting pot' and 'Anglo-conformity' in the United States, and, in the context of such ideas, research tended to focus on the pace and extent of assimilation (Bash 1979: 80).

To a certain extent such assumptions about the nature of ethnic differences and the inevitability of acculturation and assimilation were a product of a similar kind of conceptualization of 'culture' and 'society' to that which dominated anthropology throughout much of this century. Society was assumed to be essentially homogeneous in culture and, as in anthropology, continuous culture contact was assumed to lead to a reduction in cultural difference and the assimilation of originally discrete groups. Another important element in the assimilationist model was the liberal, modernist myth that the development of 'advanced', complex societies characterized by large-scale industrialism, democracy, integrated education and mass media would lead to the dissolution of ethnic differences. As Smith (1981: 2) points out:

> Liberals have generally taken the view that, as mankind moved from a primitive, tribal stage of social organization towards large-scale industrial societies, the various primordial ties of religion, language, ethnicity and race which divided it would gradually but inexorably loose their hold and disappear.

During the 1960s and 1970s sociologists became increasingly aware that the situation was more complex than acknowledged by such theories of assimilation and development. Ethnic groups had not disappeared, even in the heartlands of the modern industrial west (see Glazer and Moynihan 1975; Gordon 1975), and whilst a degree of acculturation had occurred, cultural distinctiveness had been maintained, and in some instances new elements of cultural diversity introduced (Roosens 1989: 9). In response to these observations there has been a vast increase in research on ethnic groups, and, as in anthropology, a concerted attempt to develop theoretical explanations for the phenomenon of ethnicity. As with recent anthropological theories of ethnicity, sociological theories have tended to emphasize the subjective construction of ethnicity in the process of social interaction. However, there is a greater tendency in sociology to conceptualize ethnic groups as economic and political interest groups, a position which is intimately linked to the mobilization of ethnicity as a basis for political action in the last three decades.

Indeed, the development of an interest in ethnicity across a number of disciplines was not solely a product of internal empirical and theoretical problems within the human sciences; broader social and political trends played an important role. In western societies minority ethnic groups gained increasing power and voice in the context of the civil rights movement and a developing national and international discourse on cultural relativism and self-determination. Furthermore, the demise of formal colonialism, and the establishment of independent nation-states in regions previously under colonial rule, created new contexts for the articulation of national and ethnic identities (see Sharp and McAllister 1993: 18–20). In these diverse contexts ethnic alliances and interests became increasingly salient in the domain of national and international politics, stimulating greater attention from disciplines such as anthropology and sociology in response to what has been hailed as an 'ethnic revival' or the development of a 'new ethnicity' (Glazer and Moynihan 1975; Smith 1981; see also Chapter 5).

Throughout the history of the human sciences the transformation of the taxonomic categories involved in the classification of peoples has been a product of both internal and external developments. A dialectical relationship exists between the classification of groups in the human sciences and the organization of human diversity. The emergence of the concept of ethnicity as a major taxonomic category in the classification of peoples was partly stimulated by a theoretical shift away from the fixed, reified categories of 'race', 'culture', 'society' and 'tribe' towards a processual analysis of ethnicity as a form of social interaction. Yet other factors have been involved, including the meanings which concepts such as race, tribe and ethnicity have accumulated within the context of a number of different functioning ideological discourses, and the increasing salience of ethnicity in the realm of national and international politics in the last two to three decades.

Chapter 4

Ethnicity

The conceptual and theoretical terrain

THE CONCEPTUALIZATION OF ETHNICITY

The prolific use of the term ethnicity to refer to diverse socio-cultural phenomena in the last two to three decades has resulted in considerable disagreement about the nature of ethnic groups. What is ethnicity, and how should it be defined? In the human sciences, definitions of ethnicity have been influenced by a variety of factors which intersect with one another. These include:

- the impact of different theoretical and disciplinary traditions (such as neo-Marxism or phenomenology, psychology or anthropology);
- the particular aspects of ethnicity being researched (ranging from the socio-structural dimensions of ethnicity in a plural society, to the cultural construction of ethnic difference, to the effects of ethnic identity on individual performance in education, and so on);
- the region of the world where research is being conducted (e.g. the highlands of Papua New Guinea, American inner cities, the former Soviet Union);
- the particular group that is the subject of research (e.g. the Australian Aborigines, migrant Turkish workers in Europe, or the Jewish people (see Bentley 1983; Isajiw 1974)).

This picture is further complicated by the fact that few people explicitly define what they mean by the terms ethnicity and ethnic group. In a survey of sixty-five sociological and anthropological studies of ethnicity, Isajiw (1974: 111) found only thirteen that included some kind of definition of ethnicity, and the remaining fifty-two had no explicit definition at all. However, despite the distinct lack of explicit definitions of ethnicity in much of the literature, it is possible to identify two central issues which cross-cut different conceptualizations of ethnicity:

(1) The classic anthropological debate concerning the prioritization of etic or emic perspectives[1] has been reconfigured in the form of a distinction

between 'objectivist' and 'subjectivist' definitions of ethnicity (Burgess 1978; Isajiw 1974; Ross 1980). In a generic sense, 'objectivists' regard ethnic groups as social and cultural entities with distinct boundaries characterized by relative isolation and lack of interaction, whereas 'subjectivists' regard ethnic groups as culturally constructed categorizations that inform social interaction and behaviour. Hence, in practice, the 'objectivists' tend to take an etic perspective, and define ethnic groups on the basis of the analyst's perception of socio-cultural differentiation. In contrast, the 'subjectivists' give precedence to the emic perspective, and define ethnic groups on the basis of the subjective self-categorizations of the people being studied.

It has long been recognized that such a simplistic distinction between 'objective' and 'subjective' definitions of ethnicity is problematic as it entails the naive pre-supposition of a value-free objective viewpoint located with the researcher, versus the subjective culturally mediated perceptions of the people being studied. The ideal of objectivity has been extensively critiqued in the human sciences for the past forty years at least, and a variety of positions which acknowledge the subjectivity of research have been developed.[2] As a result, it is generally accepted that the categories of the social scientist and the people being studied are equally subjective, and constitute different, although sometimes overlapping, taxonomies embedded within diverse frameworks of meaning. However, the situation is more complex because the distinction between 'objectivist' and 'subjectivist' definitions of ethnicity also relates to a difference of opinion about the nature of ethnicity itself. Are ethnic groups based on shared 'objective' cultural practices and/or socio-structural relations that exist independently of the perceptions of the individuals concerned, or are they constituted primarily by the subjective processes of perception and derived social organization of their members? At this level the opposition between 'objectivism' and 'subjectivism' continues to plague the definition of ethnicity, as it does broader studies of society and culture, where it is inherent in oppositions between different theories of society and culture – structuralist and phenomenological, and materialist and idealist (see Bourdieu 1977).

(2) Definitions of ethnicity are also characterized by a tension between specificity and generality; that is between generic definitions which are considered to be too broad to be of any analytical use in the analysis of particular cases, and definitions that are so narrow that their comparative potential is minimal and their principal function is descriptive. The formulation of an adequate comparative definition of ethnicity is thwarted by the lack of a developed theory of ethnicity and the tendency to elevate observed regularities in ethnic behaviour to the level of causal principles in the conceptualization and explanation of ethnicity. For instance, to assume

that because ethnic identity is manipulated for economic gain in some instances, ethnic groups should be defined as interest groups.

The disparity that results from the application of the 'objectivist' and 'subjectivist' approaches to the definition of ethnic groups is clearly highlighted by a debate between Narroll (1964, 1968) and Moerman (1965, 1968) about the definition of the Lue people of northern Thailand. In a critique of Narroll's (1964) definition of the 'cultunit', Moerman (1965) argued that the Lue cannot be defined on the basis of objective, coterminous discontinuities in language, culture, polity and territory, and that such discontinuities are rarely discernible in ethnographic situations. The Lue share a wide range of cultural traits with their neighbours in northern Thailand and are only distinguished by a small number of cultural traits (Moerman 1965: 1217–21; 1968: 157). Yet identification as Lue, and the validation of this identity in social life, is an important aspect of social organization, in contrast to many aspects of cultural variation that are irrelevant to group organization and the mediation of inter-group relations. Moerman concluded that the self-identification of ethnic groups should be taken into account in anthropological definitions, and that ethnic groups, such as the Lue, can only be understood in a broader social context in interaction with other groups:

> the Lue, at least, cannot be viewed in isolation if one is to define their "Lueness", identify them as a tribe, and understand how they survive in modern Thailand. . . . The Lue cannot be identified – cannot, in a sense, be said to exist – in isolation.
>
> (Moerman 1965: 1216)[3]

In response to Moerman's analysis, Narroll (1968) defined the Lue as part of a broader cultunit, 'Northern Thai', on the basis of a number of cultural traits, primarily focusing on language. With relation to the use of the label 'Lue' by the inhabitants of Ban Ping, he argued that 'the Lue are the Lue. But to us, for global comparative purposes, perhaps they are not the *real* Lue' (Narroll 1968: 78), rather, they are 'post-Lue' or 'ex-Lue', as they no longer possess *all* the cultural traits that *originally* defined the group. Moreover, he also uses this argument with relation to other ethnic groups:

> Many so-called Basque communities today consist of people who call themselves Basques and who have many Basque characteristics and who are the biological and cultural descendants of true Basques. However they lack one essential Basque characteristic. They no longer speak the Basque language. Such people might well be called 'post-Basques'.
>
> (Ibid.)

It is clear that the purpose of Narroll's classification of the Lue is very different from that proposed by Moerman. His concept of the cultunit was developed within the traditional anthropological framework of cross-cultural research, which requires the definition of comparable socio-cultural units. In this context ethnic groups are not the primary focus of research, rather their definition is a means to an end. In contrast, although Moerman is also concerned with defining a unit for the purposes of analysis, his research involved a detailed study of social systems in the region of Bang Ping. Hence, he was primarily concerned with formulating a definition of the Lue that was meaningful in terms of the ascription of ethnic identity and the mediation of social relations in that region.

Classificatory systems quite rightly vary depending on the issues they are supposed to address, and Moerman and Narroll are attempting to classify the Lue people for quite different purposes. Nevertheless, Moerman's analysis does question the kind of universal system of cross-cultural classification Narroll is proposing by illustrating the significance of ethnic categories, such as that of the Lue, in the structuring of social relations and social practices in northern Thailand. For how useful is the category, 'Northern Thai', even as a basis for the cross-cultural comparison of social and cultural practices, if it holds very little importance in ongoing social life in this region? Furthermore, Narroll's notions of 'true' Lue and 'post' Lue assume that culture-bearing units are relatively permanent entities that have an original 'pure' culture. This concern with static, pristine cultural entities is symptomatic of an essentially synchronic perspective of human societies embedded in western notions of cultural continuity and tradition (see Clifford 1988; Williams 1989).[4] As argued in Chapter 3, the representation of 'tribes' and 'societies' as abstract static entities each with an unchanging 'primitive' culture was commonplace between the 1920s and the 1960s, particularly in British anthropology. However, such an approach has proved inadequate in the face of the complexity revealed by many ethnographic situations (Jaspan 1964: 298; Messing 1964: 300), and the challenge presented by the political mobilization of ethnic groups that were formerly the focus of such studies (see Chapter 3).

Moerman's (1965, 1968) approach to the definition of the Lue anticipated the main direction of subsequent research on ethnic groups. During the 1960s and 1970s a straightforward 'subjectivist' approach to the definition of ethnicity prevailed in the literature. Yet Moerman, like many others, was primarily concerned with the detailed ethnographic analysis of a particular group, and it was Barth (1969a) who was the first to incorporate a 'subjective' approach to ethnicity into a programmatic theoretical model in his introduction to *Ethnic Groups and Boundaries*.

Barth's primary objective was to investigate the social dimensions of ethnic groups and in particular the maintenance of ethnic boundaries, which he distinguished from the traditional investigation of isolated cultural units (Barth 1969a: 9–11). In keeping with this emphasis on the social dimensions of ethnicity he argued that ethnic groups should be defined on the basis of the actor's own categorizations of themselves and others. Furthermore, a categorical ascription

> is an ethnic ascription when it classifies a person in terms of his basic, most general identity, presumptively determined by his origin and background. To the extent that actors use ethnic identities to categorize themselves and others for the purposes of interaction they form ethnic groups in this organizational sense.
>
> (Ibid.: 13–14)

From this perspective, cultural variation is not endowed with a determining role and Barth (1969a: 14) suggests that whilst 'ethnic categories take cultural differences into account, we can assume no one-to-one relationship between ethnic units and cultural similarities and differences'. For instance, the Pathans of Afghanistan and Pakistan constitute a self-aware ethnic group despite considerable social and cultural differences within the group (Barth 1969b: 118–19). Barth argues that Pathan identity is based on the organization of social relations in certain key areas; hospitality, public affairs and the seclusion of domestic life, which provide the basis for shared values and judgements (ibid.: 120–2). It is through the performance of accepted modes of behaviour in these social domains that Pathan identity is reconfirmed and validated (ibid.: 123).

Barth's approach to the definition of ethnic groups based on the actor's own perceptions of ethnicity was not new in itself. For instance, as early as 1947 Francis argued that the ethnic group constitutes a community based primarily on a shared 'we-feeling' and that 'we cannot define the ethnic group as a plurality pattern which is characterized by a distinct language, culture, territory, religion and so on' (Francis 1947: 397).[5] However, Barth's reiteration of the subjective and ascriptive aspects of ethnic identity within a programmatic theoretical framework is widely recognized as a turning point in the anthropological analysis of ethnic groups (e.g. Buchignani 1982: 5; Eriksen 1993a: 37; Vermeulen and Govers 1994: 1). Subsequently, the definition of ethnic groups as 'self-defining systems' (Just 1989: 74), placing primary emphasis on the cognitive categories of the people concerned, has been pervasive in academic research.

Such a definition has also played an important role in legislation and public policy since the late 1960s. For instance, for certain (Federal) government purposes during the early 1970s Australian Aboriginal people were defined on the basis of self-identification by an individual and acceptance of that identity by an Aboriginal community (Ucko 1983a: 31). The definition of ethnic groups as self-defining systems has also permeated social policy in Britain through policy-oriented research institutions such as the Research Unit on Ethnic Relations (University of Bristol), established in 1970, and maintained by the government-funded Social Science Research

Council. In the Unit's ethnicity programme, which initially focused on the sphere of work, Wallman (1977: 532) states that:

> 'Ethnicity' refers here to the perception of group difference and so to the social boundaries between sections of the population. In this sense ethnic 'difference' is the recognition of a contrast between 'us' and 'them'.

Yet there are a number of problems with 'subjectivist' definitions of ethnicity. The insistence that all social phenomena involving the ascription of culturally based collective identity and the maintenance of group boundaries should be considered as 'ethnic', regardless of other differentiating characteristics, has led to the incorporation of a wide range of groups within the category of ethnic group (e.g. see Hunt and Walker 1974; Roosens 1989). These groups include: minority groups; indigenous groups; ethno-nationalist groups; groups based primarily on religion, language, political organization, racial categorizations; groups formerly regarded as 'nations', 'tribes', 'minorities', 'cultures', 'racial groups' and/or 'religious groups'. In effect the concept of ethnicity has been used in the analysis of a wide range of groups subject to different kinds of classification, embedded in different forms of social organization, and constituted in diverse social and historical contexts. Moreover, as pointed out earlier, the concept of ethnicity has been influenced by different disciplinary traditions, and used in the analysis of diverse areas such as the political mobilization of ethnic groups, the psychological aspects of ethnicity and the social stratification of ethnic groups.

This expansion of the category of ethnicity in social scientific research has resulted in doubts about the analytical utility of the concept (e.g. Blu 1980; Fardon 1987; Hinton 1981; Just 1989). On the basis of a processual 'subjectivist' definition of ethnicity there is little to distinguish it from other forms of group identity such as gender, class and caste groups, and consequently there is a risk that ethnicity will disappear as a separate field of enquiry. Defined as the social reproduction of basic categories of group identity on the basis of self-definitions and definitions by others, ethnicity is 'devoid of any substantial content' as a comparative analytical concept (Eriksen 1992: 8–9). For instance, in an analysis of the Greek 'ethnos', Just (1989: 75) argues that social entities, such as ethnic groups, are self-defining systems, but he concedes that:

> Though my definition of the criteria for defining the Greek 'ethnos' is, I trust, formally sound, it is also essentially empty. In practice empirical criteria are referred to: and however vague, fuzzy-edged and inconsistent, historically misleading, or scientifically invalid these criteria may be, they are what give substance to the claim of ethnic identity.

In reaction to this problem, the 'empirical criteria' that Just refers to have been reincorporated into processual definitions of ethnicity, in order to qualify the character, quality or condition of belonging to an ethnic group. For instance, de Vos (1982 [1975]: 9) defines an ethnic group as a group that is 'self-consciously united around particular traditions', which include common territory, language, religion and racial uniqueness, but emphasizes that none of them is an essential criterion. Such a definition differs from the traditional definition of ethnic groups on the basis of the enumeration of supposedly objective cultural traits, because the 'traditions' de Vos (1982 [1975]) refers to are not 'given', fixed traits, but rather those traits that he considers to be most salient in peoples' consciousness of ethnicity. However, as the importance of specific aspects of culture in the definition of ethnicity varies between ethnic groups, the character of ethnicity as an abstract phenomenon is still elusive. Consequently de Vos (1982 [1975]: 16, my emphasis) concedes that, 'the ethnic identity of a group of people consists of their subjective, symbolic or emblematic use of *any* aspect of culture, in order to differentiate themselves from other groups'. Ultimately, as Blu (1980: 224) points out, it is still difficult to pin down exactly 'just what it is that sets "ethnic" groups apart from other symbolically differentiated groups with a strong sense of identity'.

Despite these problems, others have also attempted to produce a narrower definition emphasizing the primacy of specific cultural criteria, such as language or a consciousness of common descent/history, in emic classifications of ethnicity (e.g. see Cohen 1978: 385–7; de Vos 1982 [1975]: 19). However, it is clear that there is very little agreement as to what particular aspects of culture are essential to the category of ethnicity, and narrow, substantive definitions are likely to hinder the analysis of any common processes underlying various culturally based identity groups. Furthermore, social scientific approaches that combine a subjectivist definition of ethnicity with an emphasis on particular aspects of cultural differentiation have a tendency to conform to the ideologies of cultural difference prevailing in the particular social and historical contexts that are the focus of study.

Aside from the cultural content of ethnicity, socio-structural and political factors have also been used in an attempt to distinguish ethnic groups from other kinds of grouping, and to distinguish different kinds of ethnic groups. Many such definitions combine different elements in the conceptualization of ethnicity. For instance, Yinger (1983: ix, my emphasis) defines ethnic groups broadly as part of a multi-ethnic society:

> An ethnic group . . . *is a segment of a larger society* whose members are thought, by themselves and/or others, to have a common origin and to share important segments of a common culture and who, in addition, participate in shared activities in which the common culture and origin are significant.

Vincent (1974) prefers a more specific regional definition and argues that ethnic groups in the United States should be distinguished from minority groups on the basis of political mobilization. Minority groups, she argues, are subject to economic, social and political subordination by the categorizations of the dominant society, whereas ethnic groups are characterized by political mobilization and a re-appropriation of the definition of self.[6] Still others have attempted to develop various sub-categories based on empirical variations in the social context of ethnicity, in addition to an overarching processual 'subjectivist' definition. For instance, Eriksen (1993a: 13–14) divides ethnic groups into 'urban ethnic minorities', 'indigenous peoples', 'proto-nations' (i.e. those aspiring to nationhood) and 'ethnic groups in plural societies'. He argues that such empirical categories may be useful in defining forms of ethnicity that are more readily compared than others, but nevertheless he is adamant that it is necessary to maintain a broad 'subjectivist' definition for the purposes of analysis.

Notwithstanding the dominance of 'subjectivist' definitions, some have maintained a more essentialist and internally oriented, 'objectivist' conceptualization of ethnicity in terms of fixed cultural and historical traits. In the 'western' social sciences such an emphasis on the primacy of cultural and historical traits is related to the idea that ethnicity is a primordial given ascribed at birth, which exerts overwhelming coercive ties on members of the group due to the deep-seated psychological desire for rootedness in human nature (e.g. Connor 1978; Isaacs 1974). It is claimed that such a 'basic group identity' (Isaacs 1974) is an essential aspect of an individual's identity, and ethnicity is often conceptualized as an ineffable, static and inherent identity (see pp. 65–8 below).

The conceptualization of ethnicity in the former Soviet and Eastern European intellectual traditions also places considerable emphasis on the cultural and historical continuity of the ethnic unit – the 'ethnos' (Shennan 1991: 29). Although self-identification is generally recognized as an important element, it is argued that the essence of the ethnos is constituted by very real cultural and linguistic components which constitute the 'inner integrity' of a group's identity (Bromley 1980: 153). For instance, in the Soviet discipline of ethnic cartography, self-awareness, usually as obtained from population censuses, is considered to be an important criterion for identifying ethnoses (e.g. Brook 1983: 39, 51). However, it is assumed that this self-awareness is something that has developed over long periods, and is a reflection of other 'objective' components of identity such as language, beliefs and values, the material culture of everyday life, and so on (e.g. see contributions to Kochin 1983). Ethnicity is not considered to be primarily a relational construct in the sense of a 'we'/'they' opposition between groups in a plural society (Fortes 1980). Furthermore, ethnic identity is regarded as distinct from socio-structural and economic circumstances; it pertains to the social life of people, regardless of these conditions, and has greater continuity than such phenomena.

Nevertheless, as in 'western' intellectual traditions, there is considerable diversity of opinion about the nature of ethnicity, and in particular its relationship to socio-economic formations. For instance, Dolukhanov (1994: 23), in contrast to traditional Soviet theory, considers the ethnos to be more integrally linked to economic relations, such as the spatial division of labour, and also to environmental adaptation. Whereas others, such as Brook (1983: 39), argue that ethnic groups pass through different evolutionary stages in a parallel fashion to the socio-economic organization of societies:

> [The] eariest type – the tribe – is typical of the primitive communal system. In slave-owning and feudal social formations a new type of ethnic entity – the nationality (*narodnost*) – made its appearence. The development of capitalist relations and the intensification of economic contacts gave rise to ethnic entities – nations – which stood at a higher level of development.

Irrespective of the many permutations discussed here, a conceptualization of ethnic groups as self-defining systems, and an emphasis on the fluid and situational nature of both group boundaries and individual identification, has prevailed in the last two to three decades. Within this broad generic definition, the analysis of particular ethnic groups has been largely concerned with the perception and expression of group boundaries; ethnicity is considered to be a consciousness of identity *vis-à-vis* other groups – a 'we'/'they' opposition. The incorporation of a definition of ethnic groups as self-defining systems within a theoretical framework focusing on boundary maintenance, the situational aspects of ethnic identification, and the movement of personnel across boundaries, has facilitated the analysis of the social dimensions of ethnic groups and filled a theoretical void in the analysis of inter-group relations. Up until the 1950s anthropologists (and social scientists generally) did not have an analytical vocabulary to examine the ongoing interrelations between socio-cultural groups. As Leach (1964 [1954]) convincingly demonstrated there was an urgent need to develop such a vocabulary, and the formulation of the concept of ethnicity by Barth and others served that purpose, implying contact and interrelationship, as well as ambiguity and flexibility.

At the same time, the extensive application of the concept of ethnicity to a wide range of socio-cultural phenomena in the social sciences has raised questions about the analytical validity of such a broad category. In response, tighter definitions of ethnicity have been developed, either in terms of a narrower definition of the concept itself, or a sub-classification of different kinds of ethnicity. Such definitions generally involve an elaboration of the 'subjectivist' definition of ethnicity on the basis of cultural content and/or socio-structural organization. However, attempts to amalgamate 'subjective' and 'objective' elements within a single definition of ethnicity have largely failed due to the absence of an adequate theoretical framework; a theoretical framework that addresses the relationship between peoples' perceptions of ethnic identity (their own and others'), and the cultural practices and social relations in which they are engaged.

THE PRIMORDIAL IMPERATIVE

[M]an's essential tribalism is so deeply-rooted in the condition of his existence that it will keep cropping out of whatever is laid over it, like trees forcing their way through rocks on mountainsides a mile high.

(Isaacs 1974: 16)

The 'primordial' perspective is one of two theoretical approaches which have dominated the literature on ethnicity in the last two to three decades, the other being known as the 'instrumentalist' perspective. The concept of primordial attachments was developed by Shils (1957) in order to describe the particular relational qualities inherent in kinship ties. He claimed that the significance of these primordial qualities is not merely a function of interaction, but lies in the '*ineffable significance* attributed to ties of blood' (Shils 1957: 122; my emphasis). The concept was then applied to social groups of a larger scale than those based on immediate kin relations by Geertz (1963: 109), who argued that primordial attachment stems from

the 'givens' . . . of social existence: immediate contiguity and kin connection mainly, but beyond them the givenness that stems from being born into a particular religious community, speaking a particular language . . . and following particular social practices. These congruities of blood, speech and custom, and so on, are seen to have an ineffable, and at times overpowering, coerciveness in and of themselves. One is bound to one's kinsman, one's neighbour, one's fellow believer, *ipso facto*; as the result not merely of personal affection, practical necessity, common interest, or incurred obligation, but at least in great part by virtue of some unaccountable absolute import attributed to the very tie itself.

Hence, it is argued that primordial bonds between individuals result from the givens of birth – 'blood', language, religion, territory and culture – which can be distinguished from other social ties on the basis of the 'ineffable and unaccountable' importance of the tie itself. Following Shils and Geertz, primordial attachments are involuntary and possess a coerciveness which transcends the alliances and relationships engendered by particular situational interests and social circumstances.

Both Shils and Geertz use the concept of primordialism as a means of describing certain kinds of social attachment, rather than as an explanatory concept (Scott 1990: 150). However, Isaacs develops the concept of primordial ties as a means of *explaining* the power and persistence of ethnic identity which he calls 'basic group identity'. He describes basic group identity as:

> the identity made up of what a person is born with or acquires at birth. It is distinct from all the other multiple and secondary identities people acquire because unlike all the others, its elements are what make a group, in Clifford Geertz' phrase, a 'candidate for nationhood'.
>
> (Isaacs 1974: 15)

Isaacs (ibid.: 27) follows Shils and Geertz in identifying the primordial bonds of basic group identity with a range of characteristics that are ascribed at birth; for example, the individual acquires names (individual and group); the history and origins of the group; nationality (or other national, regional or tribal affiliation); language; religion; and value system. However, Isaacs also draws on psychological theories of identity in order to explain the strength and endurance of 'tribal'/'ethnic' sentiments and attachments in the modern world. He argues that individuals acquire such primordial bonds through early processes of socialization, and that such attachments have an overwhelming power because of a universal, human, psychological need for a sense of belongingness and self-esteem (ibid.: 29–30). The manifestation of this human condition according to Isaacs (ibid.: 16) can be seen in the

> . . . massive re-tribalization running sharply counter to all the globalizing effects of modern technology and communications. . . . great masses are retreating and withdrawing in the face of the breakdown or inadequacy of all the larger coherences or systems of power and social organization.

Similar explanations are adopted by other authors, who argue that ethnic identity has its roots in human nature. It is claimed that as ethnic identity is based on primordial attachments that are 'given' at birth, it is a more natural and fundamental form of identity than other forms of social identity (e.g. Connor 1978; Isaacs 1974; Keyes 1976). The cultural characteristics ascribed at birth are important elements in the definition of ethnic groups, and serve to distinguish ethnicity from other forms of group identity (see Keyes 1976). The appeal to basic psychological needs constitutes a further dimension of the primordialist approach, particularly with relation to the perceived ethnic revival in modern industrial nation-states (e.g. Connor 1978; Isaacs 1974; Stack 1986). Ethnicity, and its relation, tribalism, are regarded as deep-seated destructive tendencies leading to inter-group hostilities and conflicts which are suppressed by liberal democratic social structures, but which always threaten to break through this supposedly tranquil and harmonious existence. It is in many ways part of the myth of civilization overcoming the barbarian in all of us, which is so pervasive in popular culture and in media representations of conflict and social strife.

Further elaborations on the primordialist thesis have focused on the psychological and biological explanation of conflict which is seen in terms of ingroup amity and outgroup emnity. For instance, drawing on social psychological research Kellas (1991: 12–13) argues that humans have a propensity for communal sentiments within a defined group and hostility towards members of an outgroup, and that these psychological processes underlie ethnic phenomena. It has also been suggested by those adopting a socio-biological approach that ethnic groups and inter-ethnic competition have a biological basis (e.g. Kellas 1991; Reynolds *et al.* 1987; van den Berghe 1978). For instance, within an overarching socio-biological framework van den Berghe (1978: 403) argues that both race and ethnicity represent an extended or attenuated form of kin selection (see also Reynolds *et al.* 1987). As such, ethnicity has a biological basis, not because

> we have a gene for ethnocentrism, or for recognising kin; rather . . . that those societies that institutionalised forms of nepotism and ethnocentrism had a strong selective advantage over those that did not (assuming that any such ever existed), because kin selection has been the basic blueprint for animal sociality.
>
> (van den Berghe 1978: 405)

Within the socio-biological framework kinship sentiments form the basis of the primordial component of ethnicity and cultural criteria are merely proximate explanations: 'Just as in the smaller kin units, the kinship was real often enough to become the basis of these powerful sentiments we call nationalism, tribalism, racism and ethnocentrism' (ibid.: 404).

Socio-biological theories of ethnicity raise their own specific problems. They are essentially based on the notion of kin selection, which has been criticized at a number of levels. At an evolutionary level it is predicated on the claim that throughout most of the history of the human species, people have lived in small endogenous groups with some degree of isolation and a tendency towards inter-group hostility in the context of resource stress – resulting in fairly distinct gene pools. However, whilst it seems likely that early *Homo sapiens* lived in small groups, the other claims have been questioned, undermining the evolutionary dimension in the socio-biological argument (Reynolds 1980: 312). At another level, the connection between kin selection and the primordial basis of ethnic groups can also be challenged.[7] If ethnic groups are often based on 'putative rather than real' (van den Berghe 1978: 404) kin relations then the logic of the socio-biological argument breaks down, unless 'primordial inter-group theory based on sociobiology can explain why the new non-genetic transmission of kinship and group affiliation has to follow the logic of the old genetic one' (Reynolds 1980: 311). The mechanism of kin selection is concerned with the survival of closely related genetic material into the next generation and if this is not the outcome of ethnic chauvinism, because ethnic ties often consist of putative rather than real kinship, then it is difficult to see how societies that have institutionalized ethnocentrism will be 'selected' for in terms of biological evolution (as argued by van den Berghe 1978: 405). The only way out of this impasse is to posit a genetic basis for ethnocentrism as a result of thousands of years of biological evolution; an idea which van den Berghe (1978: 405) himself explicitly rejected.

To return to the overall primordial perspective, its main advantage is that it focuses attention on the strong emotions often associated with ethnic and national attachments, and the potency of the cultural symbols involved; aspects which are not adequately addressed by many recent instrumentalist approaches to ethnicity. Primordialist approaches also offer an explanation for the persistence of some ethnic groups over considerable periods of time, when it appears to be to their own social disadvantage (McKay 1982: 397). However, a number of serious problems can be identified with the basic primordialist argument:

(1) Primordialist theories result in a romanticization and mystification of ethnic identity. It is argued that ethnic identity is based on the ineffable coerciveness of primordial attachments, such as name, territory, language and culture, but the psychological potency of such attachments is only vaguely explored. Ultimately, primordial ties or ethnic sentiments are posited as primitive and atavistic attributes which gain power from an instinctive predisposition in human nature (e.g. Isaacs 1974; Connor 1978; Kellas 1991). For instance, Kellas (1991: 18–19) claims that 'human nature and human psychology provide the "necessary conditions" for ethnocentric and nationalist behaviour, and such behaviour is universal', and also that 'the biological and psychological characteristics of humans have not evolved greatly since the "hunter-gatherer" society of several thousand years ago' (ibid.: 14). Although Kellas elaborates on the psychological and biological basis of ethnicity to a greater extent than many advocates of the primordial perspective, his consideration of these areas is vague and general. For others, primordialism itself is a mystical psychological disposition, almost by definition 'shadowy and elusive' (e.g. Connor 1978: 379). Consequently, primordial approaches are either too general or too obscure to possess a great deal of explanatory power: 'the intangible aspects of the primordial approach constitute at best an *ex post facto* argument. In searching for the givens of social existence, the primordial approach explains everything and nothing' (Stack 1986: 2).

Despite such problems, Stack (1986) and others argue that primordial approaches capture an essential aspect of ethnicity – the psychological and emotional strength of ethnic attachments. Yet there is no reason why such psychological dimensions should be shadowy or atavistic, leaving the analysis of this aspect of ethnicity devoid of any rigour or explanatory power.

For instance, de Vos (1982 [1975]: 17) argues that ethnic identity often constitutes a significant dimension of an individual's concept of self:

> Ethnicity . . . is in its narrowest sense a feeling of continuity with the past, a feeling that is maintained as an essential part of one's self-definition. Ethnicity is also related to the individual need for collective continuity. The individual senses to some degree a threat to his own survival if his group or lineage is threatened with extinction.

De Vos (1982 [1975]) goes on to examine the psychological dimensions of the imposition of pariah and outcast status on some ethnic groups, of changes in group status, of individual passing and social mobility, and the forms of sanctioning, alienation and withdrawal that these processes may engender. There is nothing particularly mystical about the need to maintain a sense of self that is not completely at odds with one's cultural and social circumstances, and hence to avoid assimilation into ethnic or national groups in order to limit the psychological stress engendered by such processes. The transformation of ethnicity in multi-ethnic societies is a complex process mediated by the articulation of psychological needs as well as socio-economic interests (see de Vos 1982 [1975]; de Vos and Romanucci Ross 1982a [1975] and 1982b [1975]).

(2) Primordial approaches suggest that ethnic identity is a determining and immutable dimension of an individual's self-identity, because the primordial attachments that underlie ethnicity are involuntary and coercive (Scott 1990: 151). The cultural traits that represent these sentiments, such as language, descent, place of birth, are also often viewed as fixed and involuntary. However, such an approach cannot explain the fluid nature of ethnic boundaries; the situational quality of ethnic identity at the level of the individual; or the fact that the importance of ethnicity itself varies significantly in different social contexts and between different individuals.[8]

A number of people have attempted to accommodate the fluid and instrumental aspects of ethnicity within a primordialist framework (e.g. Keyes 1981; Stack 1986). For instance, Keyes (1981: 5) argues that ethnic identities entail a primordial relationship between people – principally involving a cultural interpretation of descent. At the same time, he suggests that cultural symbols that represent the identity of a particular group are often transformed in the context of social change (ibid.: 14–15), and that individuals may draw upon differing representations of their ethnicity in different social circumstances (ibid.: 10). Nevertheless, the relationship between the psychological dimensions of ethnicity and the cultural symbols that signify it is still largely unexplored.

(3) From a primordial perspective ethnicity becomes an abstract natural phenomenon which can be explained on the basis of 'human nature' with

little, if any, analysis of the social and historical contexts in which particular ethnic groups are formulated. In a simplistic form, primordial explanations suggest that ethnic groups are formulated in a social and political vacuum. A classic example is the naturalization of ethnic and national conflict:

> Citizens are expected to be ready to die for their 'Fatherland'/'Motherland', and it may even be natural to want to do so. One would hardly die willingly for one's job, one's social class, or even one's state, if that is not seen as the 'Fatherland'.
>
> (Kellas 1991: 9)

However, class, religious and political disputes, which are not related to ethnicity in a straightforward manner, can also lead to violent conflict. The explanation of ethnic and national conflict as a romantic and instinctive response to primordial alliances given through birth, or simply as an innate reaction to cultural diversity, obscures analysis of the economic and political interests that are often a central aspect of such conflicts (Lloyd 1974: 223). It should be asked why ethnic relations are amicable in some situations and lead to conflict in others, and whether conflicts would disappear if inequality were eradicated (McKay 1982: 399). The way in which primordial approaches treat the issue of conflict reflects a general neglect of the role of socio-structural factors in the formulation of ethnicity. Ethnicity becomes situated as a transcendental essence which persists through time irrespective of diverse and changing social and historical contexts.

In the light of research that highlights the relationship between ethnicity and political and economic relations a number of authors have attempted to incorporate these aspects within a primordial framework (e.g. Bell 1975; Kellas 1991; Keyes 1981). The primordial dimensions of ethnic identity are placed as a baseline for the construction of particular forms of ethnicity and for the mobilization of ethnic groups with relation to political and economic interests:

> Identity and behaviour are partly genetic, but they are also shaped by context and choice. In politics they are resources waiting to be used by politicians and their supporters to their own advantage. Human nature provides the necessary conditions for ethnocentric behaviour, but politics converts this into the 'sufficient conditions' for nationalism as we understand it today.
>
> (Kellas 1991: 19).

Nevertheless, the relationship between the psychological and cultural dimensions of ethnicity and the instrumental aspects of ethnicity remains largely unexplored in such attempts to add a superficial instrumental dimension to the primordialist model.

(4) In addition to a neglect of the historical and social grounding of particular ethnicities, primordialist approaches also fail to consider the

historically situated and culturally constructed nature of the very concepts that are central to their argument – most notably 'ethnic group' and 'nation'. The national or ethnic unit becomes situated as *the* natural and universal unit of human organization and collectively oriented emotional attachment (e.g. Kellas 1991),[9] despite historical studies that patently contradict such an assumption.[10]

Moreover, in a broader sense, the primordialist approach itself is part of a much older intellectual current associated with the romanticization and naturalization of the ethnic or national unit. Representations of national and ethnic groups which have emerged within such academic traditions are not far removed from the conceptualization of the nation inherent in many nationalist discourses. For instance, Connor elevates the ideology of nationalism to the very essence of the nation through his argument that kinship and blood lineage are the central dimensions of nationhood:

> Bismarck's famous exhortation to the German people, over the heads of their particular political leaders, to 'think with your blood' was . . . [an] attempt to activate a mass psychological vibration predicated on an intuitive sense of consanguinity.
>
> (Connor 1978: 380)

He claims that such discourses implicate the true nature of the nation, because people invariably *think* that descent and blood lineage are the basis of their national identities, irrespective of anthropological and biological evidence to the contrary (ibid.: 380–1). On this basis the American people are

> not a nation in the pristine sense of the word . . .. [The] unfortunate habit of calling them a nation, and thus verbally equating American with German, Chinese, English, and the like, has seduced scholars into erroneous analogies. Indeed, while proud of being 'a nation of immigrants' with a 'melting pot' tradition, the absence of a common origin may well make it more difficult, and conceivably impossible, for the American to appreciate instinctively the idea of the nation in the same dimension and with the same poignant clarity as do the Japanese, the Bengali, or the Kikuyu. It is difficult for an American to appreciate what it means for a German to be German or for a Frenchman to be French, because the psychological effect of being American is not precisely equatable.
>
> (Ibid.: 381)

Connor's argument embodies many of the flaws in the primordialist approach: the complexities of particular nationalisms are ignored; a notion of 'pristine' nationalism (or ethnicity) is reinforced, raising the spectre of deviance from this seemingly 'natural' unit of human social life (cf. Williams

1989); and the historical specificity of the notion of a homogeneous nation based on descent or 'blood relations' is disregarded through a naive attribution of validity to a particular formulation of the concept derived largely from 'western' nationalist discourses. Clearly, the complex relationship between social-scientific concepts and broader discourses of identity requires a more critical analysis than that embodied in the primordialist approach (see Chapter 5).

To summarize, primordialist approaches to ethnicity and related phenomena attempt to explain the psychological dimension of ethnicity and the potency of particular symbols, which are inadequately addressed by many instrumentalist theories of ethnicity. However, at present, knowledge about the purported psychological and/or biological bases of primordial attachments is vague, and the level of explanation fails to address the dynamic and fluid nature of ethnicity in varied social and historical contexts. Moreover, primordialist approaches often incorporate ideas derived from nationalist ideologies without adequately historicizing these ideas.

INSTRUMENTAL ETHNICITIES

> In a fairly short time we have moved from metaphors of blood and stone to clay and putty.
>
> (Horowitz 1977: 7, cited in McKay 1982: 399)

The last two to three decades have witnessed a large-scale shift towards the conceptualization of ethnicity as a dynamic and situational form of group identity embedded in the organization of social behaviour and also in the institutional fabric of society. Research focusing on these dimensions has been broadly defined as the 'instrumentalist' theoretical approach (Bentley 1987: 25) – being characterized by a concern with the role of ethnicity in the mediation of social relations and the negotiation of access to resources, primarily economic and political resources.[11] However, despite their common ground, studies focusing on these aspects of ethnicity also reflect a wide range of theoretical perspectives, for instance, ranging from neo-Marxism (e.g. Hechter 1976), through cultural ecology (e.g. Barth 1969a, 1969b), to social interactionalism (Eidheim 1969). They also accommodate a general division in the human sciences between those approaches that emphasize the primacy of individual behaviour (e.g. Patterson 1975), and those that focus on social structures or cultural norms (e.g. Cohen 1974); or put more simply, a contrast between emphasizing freedom or constraint in the interpretation of social behaviour, and in particular human agency (Eriksen 1993a: 57). As noted earlier, the former approach tends to be associated with a subjectivist approach, whilst the latter tends to involve an objectivist approach.

In anthropology, the works of Barth (1969a) and Abner Cohen (1974) are generally regarded as having played a pivotal role in the development of the instrumental approach. The starting point for Barth's theoretical framework was that ethnic groups are not the result of geographical or social isolation, and, importantly, they are not merely the bearers of discrete cultural entities. Instead, he argued, ethnic boundaries are often the very foundations of embracing social systems (Barth 1969a: 10). As a result, interaction between members of different ethnic groups does not always lead to the loss of cultural differences due to processes of acculturation. Cultural diversity can persist despite inter-ethnic contact and interdependence (ibid.).

Much of Barth's argument was then taken up with the explanation of boundary persistence; for if ethnic groups are not the passive product of cultural differentiation there must be some other explanation for the formation and persistence of organizationally relevant ethnic categories. Focusing on the interaction and interdependence of ethnic groups, Barth (1969a) argued that the persistence of boundaries can be explained as adaptation to a particular social or ecological niche. Furthermore, he argued that the interdependence of groups occupying different niches can take several forms: ethnic groups may occupy distinct niches or territories in a natural environment with minimal competition for resources except along the boundaries; they may occupy the same niche and be in competition for resources; or they may occupy different but reciprocal niches in close interdependence (ibid.: 19–20). For instance, the Fur and the Baggara occupy separate niches in the Darfur region of Sudan; the Fur engage in sedentary hoe agriculture relying mainly on the production of millet, whilst the Baggara are nomadic cattle pastoralists. In terms of subsistence the Fur and Baggara provide complementary resources and there is little competition between them except when the cattle invade the irrigated gardens of the Fur during the dry season (Haaland 1969: 58–9). In other cases, where groups compete for the same resources, hierarchical ethnic relationships can develop between the groups, as in the case of Italian and Turkish 'guestworkers' and the Walloons and Flemings in Belgium (see Roosens 1989), the Sami and the Norwegians in Norway (see Eidheim 1969), and the Ndendeuli and the Ngoni in Malawi (see Cohen 1978).

As well as suggesting that ethnic categories are a function of participation in particular social niches, Barth (1969a: 24) argued that changes in individual ethnic identity, leading to a flow of personnel across ethnic boundaries, are related to the economic and political circumstances of the individuals concerned. For example, some of the hoe-agricultural Fur of Sudan have adopted the lifestyle and identity of the nomadic cattle Arabs, the Baggara (see Barth 1969a: 25–6; Haaland 1969); a shift in identity which is explained by both Haaland and Barth as a function of the limited opportunities for capital investment in the Fur economy in contrast to the opportunities presented by Baggara cattle pastoralism.

Barth, along with a number of others (e.g. Eidheim 1969; Haaland 1969; Salamone and Swansom 1979), adopts an approach which can be seen as an extension of pre-existing social theories, such as phenomenology and social interactionalism, and the classic emphasis on 'status' and 'role' in sociology (Calhoun 1994: 13). Such an approach is conducive to looking at ethnicity as an individualistic strategy. For instance, Barth (1969a: 22–3) argues that individuals pass from one categorical identity to another in order to advance their personal economic and political interests, or to minimize their losses. Similarly, Eidheim's (1969) study of Lapp identity suggests that people suppress their identity in some situations and emphasize it in others depending on the social advantages and disadvantages which a particular identity engenders in different situations. In contrast, Cohen (1969, 1974), who also interpreted ethnic groups as interest groups, has argued that it is necessary to take into account the normative effects of culture and its power in constraining individual actions:

> An ethnic group is not simply the sum total of its individual members, and its culture is not the sum total of the strategies adopted by independent individuals. Norms and beliefs and values are effective and have their own constraining power only because they are the collective representations of a group and are backed by the pressure of that group.
>
> (Cohen 1974: xiii)

As a result Cohen placed greater emphasis on the ethnic group as a *collectively* organized strategy for the protection of economic and political interests. He argued that in the course of social life a variety of groups emerge whose members share common interests. In order to pursue these interests collectively such a group has to develop 'basic organizational functions: distinctiveness (some writers call it boundary); communication; authority structure; decision making procedure; ideology; and socialization' (ibid.: xvi–xvii). It is possible for these organizational functions to be developed on a formal basis; however, Cohen (ibid.: xvii) argues that in many instances formal organization is not possible and under these circumstances the group will articulate its organization by drawing on existing cultural practices and beliefs, such as kinship, ritual, ceremony and cultural values. According to Cohen (ibid.: xxi) this use of culture to systematize social behaviour in pursuit of economic and political interests constitutes the basis of ethnicity.

There are a number of similarities in the work of Cohen (1974) and Barth (1969a): they both focus on the organizational features of ethnicity, and ethnicity is regarded as constituting the shared beliefs and practices that provide a group with the boundary maintenance and organizational dimensions necessary to maintain, and compete for, socio-economic resources. They can both then be defined as instrumentalists. However, they also reflect two persistent positions within instrumental approaches to ethnicity:

those who focus on the socio-structural and cultural dimensions of ethnicity and adopt a more objectivist approach; and those who focus on the interpersonal and behavioural aspects of ethnicity and take a more subjectivist stance.

During the 1970s and 1980s the instrumentalist perspective came to dominate research on ethnicity, often following on from the work of Barth (1969a) and Cohen (1974). For example, in his analysis of the strategic use of ethnic solidarity in American urban society, Hannerz (1974) draws upon Cohen's (1969) characterization of ethnic groups as interest groups. As research on the instrumental dimensions of ethnicity flourished, it also diversified, focusing on various different aspects of ethnicity such as inter-ethnic competition (e.g. Despres 1975; Otite 1975), the political mobilization of ethnicity (e.g. Bell 1975; Roosens 1989; Ross 1980; Vincent 1974), or the stratification of ethnic relations within multi-ethnic societies (e.g. Shibutani and Kwan 1965). For instance, Glazer and Moynihan (1975) have focused on the political dimensions of ethnicity in contemporary western societies (especially the United States), and claim that ethnicity has gained strategic efficacy since the 1960s as a basis for asserting claims against governments (Glazer and Moynihan 1975: 10; see also Roosens 1989).

Research in the 1970s and 1980s has also placed considerable emphasis on the fluid and situational aspects of both individual and group identity (e.g. see Cohen 1978; Handelman 1977; Horowitz 1975). These are dimensions of ethnicity that were neglected by writers such as Barth (1969a), who regarded ethnic categories as all-encompassing and relatively fixed, despite the movement of individuals across the boundaries. The group, as an integrated fixed entity, is even further reified by a continued emphasis on ethnicity as a reflection of shared norms (e.g. Cohen 1974), or the socio-structural basis of ethnicity. As Vincent (1974: 376) has argued,

> We tend to seek the embodiment of ethnicity in overly corporate forms. Possibly, as we move further away from holistic, organismic, systems models – from descent to alliance, from group to non-group, from a 'cookie-cutter' concept of culture to a finer understanding of the ephemerality and inconsistency of social relations – this concept of ethnicity will be clarified.

In order to avoid such reification of the group, Vincent and others (e.g. Cohen 1978; Handelman 1977; Wallman 1977) have suggested that it is important to explore the perception and negotiation of ethnicity by individuals in different contexts of interaction. In doing so they have shown that the perception and expression of a person's ethnic identity can vary in different situations depending on the context and scale of interaction, resulting in a series of nesting dichotomizations (Cohen 1978: 378). For instance, Gulliver (1969: 22–3) points out that the Kikuyu of Kenya have been regarded as one tribe, but in pre-colonial times they were made up of a large number of overlapping more or less autonomous communities distinguished in varying degrees by residence, dialect, organization, customs and so on. For certain purposes they amalgamated into larger groupings known as 'sub-tribes' which were then consolidated under colonial rule. In order to defend old and new interests, and in opposition to colonial rule, these sub-tribes also joined up to form the group known as the Kikuyu, a unity that was central to the Mau Mau revolt, and yet again with other groups to form what has been referred to as the northeastern Bantu block. All the time the constituent segments of such groupings may remain active in certain spheres whilst suppressed in other spheres of social life.

Furthermore, ethnic identity may be suppressed in situations where it possesses a social stigma, and in still other situations it may be irrelevant as a basis for interaction (Cohen 1978: 395–7). Thus, in addition to its segmentary and fluid character, ethnicity itself is a variable and its salience changes in different contexts depending upon whether it is a meaningful element in the structuring of social interaction. Recognition of the shifting and segmentary nature of ethnicity has also revealed the way in which culture and tradition are drawn upon in the construction of ethnicity, often being transformed in the process. The invention and re-invention of history and tradition in the mobilization and legitimation of ethnicity have been a particular focus of attention in recent literature (e.g. see contributions to Hobsbawm and Ranger 1983; Tonkin et al. 1989).

The rapid growth of what can be broadly termed instrumentalist approaches to ethnicity has contributed to an understanding of the common processes and structures underlying the formation of ethnic groups and the politicization of ethnic identity. By breaking away from essentialist perspectives, such as those involving a one-to-one correlation between culture and ethnicity, or the biological/psychological determinism of the primordial perspective, instrumentalist approaches have contributed to the description and explanation of the dynamic and situational aspects of ethnicity which are clearly evident in many cases. However, there are also a number of problems with aspects of this perspective:

(1) Many instrumentalist approaches fall into a reductionist mode of explanation whereby ethnicity is defined in terms of the observed regularities of ethnic behaviour in a particular situation:

> Thus analysts' mental models are transformed into causal principles located in the (conscious or unconscious) minds of the people whose behaviour is being studied. In ethnicity studies this meant that if ethnic groups act in ways that appear strategically advantageous, then strategic advantage must be the raison d'être of these groups.
>
> (Bentley 1987: 48)

Thus, the essence of ethnicity is frequently reduced to the mobilization and politicization of culture in the organization of interest groups (e.g. Cohen 1974; Ross 1980; Vincent 1974). However, as Epstein (1978: 310, cited in McKay 1982: 399) points out, 'to describe an ethnic group as having interests is one thing, to define it in these terms is something quite different'.

Whilst the analysis of the economic and political dimensions of ethnicity has been productive in revealing and explaining the dynamic and situational aspects of ethnic organization, the reduction of analysis to these factors alone can lead to an overly deterministic argument. For instance, the ultimate implication of some instrumental approaches (e.g. Cohen 1974) is that ethnicity comes into existence in order to serve the purposes of interest groups. There are many examples which patently contradict such an argument, where ethnicity cannot be explained in terms of the pursuit of temporary economic and political interests. For instance, as in the continued recognition of Aboriginal identity by the indigenous population of Australia, at least prior to the 1970s, in the context of severe negative discrimination in Australian society. The construction of Aboriginal identity following European colonization of Australia indicates that the manifestation of ethnicity is the product of a range of processes embedded in relations of power between groups which are reproduced and transformed in the communication of cultural difference (see contributions to Beckett 1988b; Keen 1988).

(2) The reduction of ethnicity to economic and political relationships frequently results in a neglect of the cultural dimensions of ethnicity (Deshen 1974: 281–4). This neglect is a consequence of the idea that ethnic categories provide an 'empty vessel' into which various aspects of culture may be poured:

> one cannot predict from first principles which [cultural] features will be emphasized and made organizationally relevant. In other words, ethnic categories provide an organizational vessel that may be given varying amounts and forms of content in different socio-cultural systems. . . . . The cultural features that signal the boundary may change, and the cultural characteristics of the members may likewise be transformed, indeed even the organizational form of the group may change – yet the fact of continuing dichotomization between members and outsiders allows us to specify the nature of continuity, and investigate the changing cultural form and content.
>
> (Barth 1969a: 14)

From this perspective, culture plays a secondary role in the formation and transformation of ethnic identity: if an individual's lifestyle becomes transformed to the extent that it is incompatible with existing ethnic categorizations s/he will adopt a more appropriate ethnic identity based on different cultural diacritica and value orientations (e.g. Barth 1969a: 25); or if interest groups coalesce they will use existing cultural practices and beliefs, or even create new ones, in order to provide the organizational features of the group, such as the monopoly of particular socio-economic domains, modes of appropriate social interaction and behaviour and so on (e.g. Cohen 1974; and see Williams 1989: 409 for a critique).

The distinction made by Barth between culture and ethnicity, and the emphasis that he and others have placed on the organizational aspects of ethnicity, has maintained a central position in subsequent theories. Encompassed within this framework, most instrumental studies take the existence of group identity, and the cultural diacritica which symbolize that identity, for granted, and proceed to describe the socio-structural and instrumental dimensions of ethnicity. For instance, in an analysis of ethnic identity amongst migrant and urban-born Mossi in Kumasi, Nigeria, Schildkrout (1974: 187, 216–17) claims that culture is irrelevant to the persistence of ethnicity as a basis for personal and group identity and that ethnic categories are maintained by structural factors. Consequently, ethnic identity and cultural symbols become conceptualized as detached attributes washed on the tides of economic and political relations.

A few instrumentalists do grant culture a significant, if secondary, role in the organization of ethnic groups; however, the relationship between culture and the instrumental dimensions of ethnicity is not adequately explored. For instance, Barth acknowledges that whilst there is not a one-to-one relationship between culture and ethnic units, 'ethnic groups only persist as significant social units if they imply marked difference in behaviour, i.e. persisting cultural differences' (Barth 1969a: 15–16). Moreover, he defines ethnic identity as an ascriptive identity 'presumptively determined by . . . origin and background' (ibid.: 13). How then do people such as the Fur adopt a Baggara lifestyle and identity to suit their economic aspirations, when Baggara identity is presumably defined on the basis of origin and shared cultural knowledge? Barth (1969a: 28–9) does recognize this 'anomalous . . . feature of ethnic identity', and the ambiguity engendered by changes in ethnic categorization; however, he does not confront this problem, or the problematic status of culture in his theoretical approach.

(3) The reductionist mode of analysis in many instrumentalist studies also results in the neglect of the psychological dimensions of ethnicity. Research has suggested that cultural ascriptions of ethnic identity may comprise an important aspect of an individual's sense of self, creating conflict for people whose social relations and cultural practices become removed from their sense of identity (see Bentley 1987; Keyes 1981; de Vos 1982 [1975]). Consequently, psychological factors may have a significant

influence on the instrumental manipulation of ethnicity and need to be taken into account in studies that tend to reduce human agency to rational self-interest.

(4) The assumption, in many instrumentalist approaches, that human behaviour is essentially rational and directed towards maximizing self-interest results in an oversimplification of the perception of interests by culturally situated agents, and disregards the dynamics of power in both intra-group and inter-group relations. Membership in a particular ethnic group (or nation) does not confer a homogeneous perspective on the individuals concerned (Asad 1980: 645), and it cannot be assumed that members of an ethnic group will agree as to what is in their 'interests'. The perception of appropriate or possible gains and desires is culturally mediated, engendered by the dispositions that individuals possess as a result of their experience of the 'objective' structures that define their socio-cultural practices (Bourdieu 1977; see also Chapter 5). Consequently members of different ethnic groups, and to some extent members of the same ethnic group, will perceive their interests and their identities differently and follow different courses of action (Sharp and McAllister 1993: 20).

(5) Finally, as a result of the tendency to define ethnicity as a politicized or mobilized group identity, and the neglect of the cultural and psychological dimensions of ethnicity, it is difficult to distinguish ethnic groups from other collective-interest groups (Hechter 1986: 19). Consequently, within some instrumental perspectives ethnic identity is regarded as a variant of class (e.g. Patterson 1975). As McKay (1982: 340) points out, it is important to explore the complex interrelationships between different social identities, such as class, ethnic and gender identity, rather than conflate such identities within the framework of a crude economic or cultural determinism.

Overall, instrumentalist approaches have contributed to the comparative analysis of ethnic groups – their relation to socio-economic and political relations, boundary maintenance, and inter-ethnic relations; aspects which are neglected by primordialist approaches. However, instrumentalist approaches tend to be reductionist and fail to explain the generation of ethnic groups. Moreover, like the proponents of the primordial perspective, instrumental approaches do not provide an adequate theory of the relationship between culture and ethnicity.

AN INTEGRATED THEORETICAL APPROACH?

The primordial and instrumental approaches have often been positioned by their proponents as diametrically opposed, alternative explanations of the emergence and persistence of ethnic behaviour. As causal explanations of ethnic behaviour, the two approaches are contradictory:

we are told, on the one hand, that the continued salience of ethnic factors is because they are deep-seated, irrational, atavistic allegiances incapable of being altered and, on the other hand, because they are peripheral loyalties which can be readily manipulated in a rational way for pursuing political and economic goals.

(McKay 1982: 396)

However, the instrumental and primordial perspectives concentrate on potentially complementary aspects of ethnicity, and a number of people have indicated the sterility of this debate.[12] As McKay (1982: 401–2) points out,

ethnic tension or conflict which is *purely ideal or purely material* constitutes a minority of all cases. It is surely the case that all polyethnic societies are characterized by a *combination* of instrumental and affective bonds. . . . it seems pointless to bifurcate 'theories' into primordial *or* mobilization camps, when it is obvious that *both* dimensions are involved.

In an effort to transcend the opposition between primordial and instrumental perspectives, a number of people have attempted to incorporate both perspectives within a single theoretical framework (e.g. Doornbos 1972; McKay 1982; Smith 1981; Stack 1986). For instance, McKay (1982: 403; my emphasis) reformulates the two perspectives into a matrix model, whereby, rather than 'asking *which* approach – primordialist or mobilizationist – has more explanatory power, it is now possible to enquire about the *extent* to which both are operative to *varying degrees*'. His model leads to the formulation of a typology of different types of ethnic behaviour, involving varying degrees of primordial and instrumental factors. For example, he identifies 'ethnic traditionalists', such as the Jews, whose primordial interests are, he suggests, more salient than material ones; 'pseudo-ethnics', such as Appalacian Americans, and other 'white ethnics' in the US, whose primordial and material interests are both low; and 'ethnic militants', such as Basque militant groups, whose primordial and instrumental interests are both very prominent (McKay 1982: 403–7).

However, McKay (1982: 408) himself notes that his model is purely descriptive and empirical, making no attempt to explain why groups emerge, persist or disappear or why the salience of primordial and instrumental dimensions varies. Others, such as Smith (1981, 1984), who also suggest that the intensity of ethnic behaviour varies along a continuum attempt to develop an explanatory model rather than just a descriptive one. Smith's (1981) theory is grounded in an analysis of the socio-historical contexts in which ethnicity is constructed, and he argues that the economic conditions associated with modern industrial nation-states have exacerbated ethnic movements, leading to greater intensity of sentiment and the mobilization of groups. However, Smith (1981: 87) claims that the

importance of economic factors lies only in their ability to activate historically rooted cultural communities which have been an important element in
human social life throughout recorded history:

> Economic deprivation, economic exploitation, economic growth, are all
> grist to the nationalist mill; but in themselves they do not generate ethnic
> sentiments or nationalist movements. The uneven development of indus-
> trialisation, which roughly coincided with the development of national-
> ism, has undoubtedly sharpened ethnic tensions and contributed to a new
> store of national grievances; but the cleavages and antagonisms so accen-
> tuated, together with the aspirations and ideals based upon them, have
> their roots and inspiration elsewhere.
>
> (Smith 1981: 44)

Ultimately, Smith's explanation of ethnicity remains within the primordialist framework (see Smith 1981: 66–7), and the instrumental dimensions of
ethnicity are situated as secondary phenomena, which emerge in particular
social and historical situations – one being the development of industria-
lization. As a result, a chronological continuum is created between long-
standing ethnic traditions that can be understood in terms of primordial
ties, and those that have been transformed by present interests and strategies and have only a dimly remembered heritage (Douglass 1988: 199).
Whilst such an approach enables the analysis of primordial and instrumental aspects as variables, it situates them as distinct but mutually influencing
processes, along a temporal scale. This scale progresses from natural,
primordial entities in the misty depths of history to the instrumental and
seemingly arbitrary manipulation of ethnicity in pursuit of economic and
political resources in the modern society.

An alternative response to the need to break down the opposition
between instrumental and primordial perspectives can be found in theoretical approaches that attempt to account for the interaction between psychological and socio-structural aspects of ethnicity in the context of social
change (e.g. de Vos 1982 [1975]; de Vos and Romanucci-Ross 1982b [1975];
Keyes 1976, 1981). For instance, Keyes (1976, 1981) emphasizes the need to
look at both cultural and social aspects of ethnic identity in dialectical
relation to one another, particularly when they are rendered problematic
in situations of change. The basis of his analysis of change is the premise that
a tension exists 'between cultural meanings that people construct to differentiate their primordial identities from those of others, and the patterns that
emerge in social interactions as individuals and groups seek to pursue their
interests' (Keyes 1981: 14). In relatively stable social situations mechanisms
to resolve these tensions, such as sanctions, may be maintained. However, a
radical shift in the social context may bring about changes in the form and
pattern of social interaction resulting in the construction of new cultural
meanings and a reassessment of ethnic identities.

In many respects Keyes's theoretical approach is similar to the 'psycho-cultural' approach put forward by de Vos. De Vos (1982 [1975]) argues that in order to understand why certain peoples maintain symbolic forms of social differentiation over long periods, despite a lack of political autonomy and often to their own disadvantage, it is necessary to give priority to the emotional and even irrational psychological features underlying social identity. However, he also claims that both the instrumental and primordial dimensions of ethnic phenomena are present, and it is this that creates an essential tension for the individual. De Vos advocates a conflict approach to the analysis of change very similar to that proposed by Keyes, and maintains that the locus of change lies in the tension between the cultural and instrumental dimensions of ethnicity (see also de Vos and Romanucci-Ross 1982b [1975]).

It is evident that most attempts to develop an integrated theoretical approach for the analysis of ethnicity involve the assertion of some kind of primordial basis for ethnicity which is then articulated with epiphenomenal social stimuli, such as economic and political competition. As noted above, such an approach often leads to the construction of a diachronic model of ethnic groups and their relation to specific economic and political contexts. However, the primordial and socio-political aspects of ethnicity are still situated as discrete, although mutually influencing, processes, with causal explanations specifying the source and direction of ethnic change.

This superficial articulation of the primordial and instrumental perspectives within an overarching framework overlooks a fundamental difference between them, which undermines the formulation of a general theory of ethnicity. Primordial and instrumental perspectives tend to be based on conflicting notions of human agency manifested in an unproductive opposition between rationality and irrationality, and the economic and symbolic domains of social practice. Many of the integrated theoretical approaches discussed above implicitly accept such dichotomies between different modes of human behaviour as a baseline for their analysis, and proceed to try to identify the different forms of ethnicity which are engendered by these conflicting modes of behaviour. Hence, ethnic groups are considered to be the product of both the rational pursuit of economic and political interests in the mode of '*Homo economicus*', and the forces of coercive and atavistic primordial affinities. Such a distinction is oriented around a restricted ethnocentric definition of rational economic interest which, as Bourdieu (1977: 177) points out,

> can find no place . . . for the strictly symbolic interest which is occasionally recognised (when too obviously entering into conflict with 'interest' in the narrow sense, as in [some] forms of nationalism or regionalism) only to be reduced to the irrationality of feeling or passion.

In addition to the absence of a coherent theory of human action that can transcend the primordial–instrumental dichotomy, both perspectives share a critical gap in their explanatory logic: they fail to address the question of how people recognize commonalities of interest or sentiment underlying claims to a common identity. As Bentley (1987: 27) points out, 'ethnic identity claims involve a symbolic construal of sensations of likeness and difference, and these sensations must somehow be accounted for'. In order to address such issues it is necessary to reconsider the relationship between culture and ethnicity without resorting either to the idea that culturally determined ethnic affinities possess an innate primordiality or to a teleological, functionalist argument which assumes that cultural boundaries and associated ethnic identities come into being on an arbitrary basis in order to serve instrumental purposes.

Chapter 5

Multidimensional ethnicity
Towards a contextual analytical framework

A WORKING DEFINITION OF ETHNICITY

As we saw in Chapter 4, the definition of ethnicity, both in a generic sense and in the case of particular ethnic groups, has been beset by difficulties. Nevertheless, from the late 1960s onwards the dominant view within 'western' social scientific traditions has been that ethnic groups are 'self-defining systems' and consequently particular ethnic groups have been defined on the basis of self-identification and identification by others. Such a definition has largely been set within a theoretical framework focusing on the construction of ethnic boundaries in the context of social interaction and their organizational properties. Ethnicity has been regarded as essentially a consciousness of identity *vis-à-vis* other groups; a 'we'/'they' opposition.

In what follows, a similar processual and relational approach to the definition of ethnicity is adopted. *Ethnic groups are culturally ascribed identity groups, which are based on the expression of a real or assumed shared culture and common descent* (usually through the objectification of cultural, linguistic, religious, historical and/or physical characteristics). As a *process* ethnicity involves a consciousness of difference, which, to varying degrees, entails the reproduction and transformation of basic classificatory distinctions between groups of people who perceive themselves to be in some respect culturally distinct (Eriksen 1992: 3). The cultural differences informing ethnic categories are, to varying degrees, systematic and enduring, because they both inform modes of interaction between people of different ethnic categories, and are confirmed by that interaction; that is, ethnic categories are reproduced and transformed in the ongoing processes of social life.

This processual approach to the definition and analysis of ethnic groups has a number of advantages over the traditional, 'objectivist' definitions, and the associated view of cultures as fixed and monolithic entities. It enables the analysis of the processes involved in the construction of ethnicity and their role in the mediation of social interaction and social relations, thus providing a basis for the comparative study of ethnicity, whilst avoiding the problems derived from the reification of ethnic groups as discrete, integrated social entities. As Eriksen (1992: 28) indicates, a focus on social process as opposed to group characteristics enables 'students of ethnicity to discard unsatisfactory strategies of empiricist "butterfly collecting", to replace substance with form, statics with dynamics, property with relationship and structure with process'.

Yet despite such analytical advantages, there have been a number of critiques of processual approaches to the definition and analysis of ethnicity, which warrant further consideration:

(1) The use of ethnicity as a central concept for the comparative analysis of a wide range of socio-cultural phenomena has been questioned (e.g. Blu 1980: 219; Chapman *et al.* 1989: 16–17; Fardon 1987: 175). For instance, it has been argued that processual definitions of ethnicity, whatever their theoretical orientation, are 'essentially empty' (Just 1989: 75), and could be applied to any 'symbolically differentiated groups with a strong sense of identity' (Blu 1980: 224), such as gender, class and kin-based groupings. The essence of this critique is the legitimate claim that, at a basic level, the processes entailed in the construction of ethnicity are essentially similar to the processes involved in the construction of gender, class and kinship in that they are all culturally constructed categories based on the communication of real or assumed difference.

However, ethnicity can be distinguished from other forms of social grouping on the basis of the constituents of such categories of group identity, and the kind of interpersonal relationships and formal organization they entail. For instance, gender categories are cultural constructs that inscribe aspects of sexual differentiation and inform the cultural practices and social relations of, and between, men and women (although not necessarily in a binary opposition) (see Moore 1988). Classes are categories of people differentiated on the basis of their unequal access to economic, political and cultural resources, resulting in the division of society into horizontal strata (Seymour-Smith 1986). Thus, in contrast to ethnic groups, class and gender divisions do not entail the reproduction of classificatory differences between people who perceive themselves to be *culturally distinct*, instead they generally relate to divisions *within* a broad cultural grouping (cf. Eriksen 1992: 6–7, 50). However, the boundaries between these different forms of identity are not clear-cut, and ethnic differences are frequently enmeshed in gender and class divisions in a complex manner. For instance, in plural social contexts, ethnic groupings may become embedded in hierarchical power relationships, characterized by differential access to economic resources in a similar manner to class (see Cohen 1969; Gluckman 1971; Roosens 1989). Consequently, in any particular analysis it is necessary to consider the intersection of different kinds of identity – ethnic, class, gender and so on – and the ways in which they become institutionalized in different societies (see Eriksen 1992: 173–9).

(2) A number of critics have also argued that formal/processual definitions of ethnicity are ahistorical and fail to take into account wider social and historical contexts (e.g. Fardon 1987: 175; Khan 1992: 173–4; Muga 1984: 10–14). Having excluded substantive characteristics, such as linguistic and cultural traits, from the definition of ethnic groups, there is a tendency to ignore the differences between them in varying social and historical contexts; ethnicity, it is suggested, becomes a unitary socio-cultural phenomenon present in vastly different situations – both modern and premodern. Thus, Fardon (1987: 171) argues that

> Once there was a large vocabulary to describe types of differences (of race, of language, of nation (in its old sense) and so on). These categories were often ill-defined and sometimes pejorative, but they did preserve the important, and I think justifiable, sense that not all of these differences were of the same type. Since ethnicity gobbled up these distinctions and regurgitated them as variants of a single type of 'ethnic' difference, it seems that many notes on the scale of difference have become muted if not lost.

Blu (1980: 219) makes a similar point:

> When ethnicity has come to refer to everything from tribalism to religious sects, from City men in London to the shifting identities of the Shan and Kachin, from regionalism to race, it is difficult to see that it has any universal utility either as an analytical tool or a descriptive one.

There are likely to be important distinctions between different ethnic groups, which are not accommodated within the processual definition proposed above. For instance there are obviously differences between indigenous ethnic groups such as the Australian Aborigines, immigrant minorities such as Bengali communities in Britain, and ethno-nationalist groups such as the Basques. Furthermore, there may be considerable variation between ethnic groups in pre-modern societies as opposed to modern societies, and non-state societies as opposed to state societies. The potential differences between such groups, as well as the similarities between them, need to be explored. Nevertheless, attempts to restrict the application of processual definitions of ethnicity by reinstating a number of substantive criteria, have largely resulted in teleological reasoning. Regularities in the behaviour and characteristics of a particular ethnic group are attributed to ethnicity in general, and are frequently seen as causal (functional) principles (Bentley 1987: 48). Hence, if the regularities of ethnic behaviour appear to be related to particular socio-structural positions, such as a segment of a broader multi-ethnic society (e.g. Yinger 1983: ix), or fundamental changes in the organization of society, such as the emergence of world capitalism (Muga 1984: 17–19), then ethnicity becomes defined and explained in these terms. Such teleological definitions of ethnicity do not facilitate the explication and analysis of the general processes involved in the formation and transformation of ethnic groups as they are restricted to the form that ethnic phenomena take in particular social and historical contexts. Furthermore, attempts to incorporate substantive content, such as specific cultural characteristics, or particular socio-structural relations, into the definition of ethnicity risk the reification of ethnic groups, and obscure the multidimensional, contested and situational nature of ethnicity.

It is possible to carve up socio-cultural phenomena along various lines for the purposes of analysis, and inevitably the particular definition adopted must be evaluated with relation to the purposes of the classification. The aim here is to produce a theoretical framework facilitating the analysis of the formation and transformation of ethnic groupings in various social and historical contexts. In order to achieve such an analysis it is necessary to adopt a formal processual definition of ethnicity of the most general kind, rather than produce a detailed classification of various kinds of group identity and culturally constructed idioms of difference. An unashamedly broad formal definition of ethnicity can be used as an analytical tool to explore diverse expressions of ethnicity in different cultural contexts, whereas a minutely detailed substantive or historical classification can reify *types* of ethnic group and in so doing actually close down appreciation of the differing manifestations of ethnicity, in particular social and historical contexts (see Eriksen 1992: 3, 17; 1993a: 12–13). Nevertheless, in using such a broad processual definition in the analysis of any particular ethnic group it will be necessary to examine the kinds of cultural difference involved in the communication of ethnicity, and the way in which ethnicity is institutionalized in particular social and cultural contexts.

TOWARDS A PRACTICE THEORY OF ETHNICITY

The opposition between 'objectivist' and 'subjectivist' definitions highlights a fundamental problem in the analysis of ethnicity which needs to be addressed – that is, the relationship between agents' perceptions of ethnicity and associated modes of interaction, and the cultural contexts and social relations in which they are embedded. What is missing is an adequate theory of the relationship between ethnicity and culture, including culturally inscribed relations of production and reproduction.

The absence of such a theory, bridging the objectivist/subjectivist dilemma, is evident in both primordial and instrumental explanations of ethnicity. In primordial theories the importance of cultural symbols is stressed, but there is little consideration of the relationship between culture and ethnicity. Primordialists simply claim that the enduring significance of particular aspects of culture in the ascription of ethnicity is due to the psychological importance of ethnic identity. In contrast to primordial approaches, instrumental theories of ethnicity rightly place greater emphasis on the distinction between culture and ethnicity. However, having dismissed the idea of a one-to-one relationship between culture and ethnicity, instrumentalists tend to focus on the organizational aspects of ethnicity and take the cultural differences on which it is based for granted. Culture is reduced to an epiphenomenal and arbitrary set of symbols manipulated in the pursuit of changing group interests:

> The most common (tacit) reduction of culture has consisted in showing how ethnic signifiers may change due to changes in context, thereby indicating that the signifiers themselves are really arbitrary, and that the fundamental aspect of ethnicity is the very act of communicating and maintaining cultural difference.
>
> (Eriksen 1991: 129; see also Bentley 1987: 26, 48)

The lack of a developed theory of culture addressing the relationship between objective conditions and subjective perceptions, underlies a critical gap in both primordial and instrumental theories of ethnicity in that neither approach adequately addresses 'how people come to recognize their commonalities in the first place' (Bentley 1987: 27).

Bourdieu's theory of practice transcends the dichotomy between objectivism and subjectivism,[1] and associated oppositions such as determinism and freedom, conditioning and creativity, society and individual, through the development of the concept of the *habitus*:

> The structures constitutive of a particular type of environment (e.g. the material conditions of existence characteristic of a class condition) produce *habitus*, systems of durable, transposable *dispositions*, structured structures predisposed to function as structuring structures, that is, as principles of the generation and structuring of practices and representations which can be objectively 'regulated' and 'regular' without in any way being the product of obedience to rules.
>
> (Bourdieu 1977: 72)

Thus, for Bourdieu, the *habitus* is made up of durable dispositions towards certain perceptions and practices (such as those relating to the sexual division of labour, morality, tastes and so on), which become part of an individual's sense of self at an early age, and which can be transposed from one context to another (ibid.: 78-93). As such, the *habitus* involves a process of socialization whereby new experiences are structured in accordance with the structures produced by past experiences, and early experiences retain a particular weight. In this way, structures of power become embodied, resulting in certain dispositions (cognitive and motivating structures) which influence practice often at an unconscious level. For instance, Bourdieu (ibid.: 77) argues that:

> the practical evaluation of the likelihood of the success of a given action in a given situation brings into play a whole body of wisdoms, sayings, commonplaces, ethical precepts ('that's not for the likes of us') and, at a deeper level, the unconscious principles of the *ethos* which, being the product of a learning process dominated by a determinate type of objective regularities, determines 'reasonable' and 'unreasonable' conduct for every agent subjected to those regularities.

The dispositions of the *habitus* are generated by the conditions constituting a particular social environment, such as modes of production or access to certain resources (ibid.: 77–8).[2] However, Bourdieu's theory differs from normative and structural theories of culture where the practices produced with relation to certain conditions are assumed to involve the mechanistic enactment of a system of rules existing outside of individual and group history. Instead, he suggests that structural orientations only exist in the form of the embodied knowledge and dispositions of the *habitus*, and their very substance depends on the practices and representations of human agents, which in turn contribute to the reproduction and transformation of the objective conditions constitutive of the *habitus* (ibid.: 76–8). Consequently, the dispositions of the *habitus* 'are at once "structuring structures" and "structured structures"; they shape and are shaped by social practice' (Postone *et al.* 1993: 4). In this respect Bourdieu's theory of practice bears some similarity to other practice theories developed in the late 1970s and 1980s, such as Giddens's (1984) theory of 'structuration' and Sahlins's (1981) exploration of 'cosmological dramas', which seek to locate the existence, and therefore the reproduction and transformation, of social or cultural structures in the domain of practice (see Ortner 1984 for an overview).

It has been argued that Bourdieu's conceptualization of the processes involved in the reproduction of social structures and the relationship between social structure and human agency is conservative and deterministic (e.g. DiMaggio 1979: 1470; Jenkins 1982: 272–3, 278). Certainly, there are passages in Bourdieu's work which suggest that societies have a tendency towards stasis and the reproduction of established modes of domination. For instance, he argues that peoples' 'subjective' perceptions have a tendency towards correspondence with the structural conditions of social existence, and they fail to recognize the real nature of the social order, i.e. the structures of domination, thus reproducing the structures of their own subordination (Bourdieu 1977: 164). However, Bourdieu's account of cultural reproduction does accommodate the possibility of strategic agency within the limits of the *habitus*, and the possibility of social change in terms of continuous transformations in the structured dispositions of the *habitus* within changing contexts of social practice (ibid.: 78).[3] Furthermore, he also explores the possibility of active resistance to prevailing modes of domination as a result of exposure to the arbitrariness of taken-for-granted, subconscious (*doxic*) knowledge in the context of radical social and economic change (ibid.: 168; see also pp. 94–5 below).

Extrapolating from Bourdieu's theory of practice, Bentley (1987: 27) has employed the concept of the *habitus* as a means of providing an objective grounding for ethnic subjectivity which involves 'the symbolic construal of sensations of likeness and difference'. The subliminal dispositions of the *habitus*, derived from the conditions of existence, provide the basis for the perception of shared sentiment and interest which ethnicity entails:

> According to the practice theory of ethnicity, sensations of ethnic affinity are founded on common life experiences that generate similar habitual dispositions. . . . It is commonality of experience and of the preconscious habitus it generates that gives members of an ethnic cohort their sense of being both familiar and familial to each other.
>
> (Ibid.: 32–3)

Such a practice theory of ethnicity facilitates the analysis of the relationship between ethnic consciousness and social structures, and more generally ethnicity and culture; as such it has the potential to transcend the 'objective/subjective' dichotomy. Ethnicity is not a *passive reflection* of similarities and differences in the cultural practices and structural conditions in which people are socialized, as traditional normative and primordial approaches assume. Nor is ethnicity, as some instrumental approaches imply, produced entirely in the process of social interaction, whereby epiphenomenal cultural symbols are consciously manipulated in the pursuit of economic and political interests. Rather, drawing on Bourdieu's theory of practice, it can be argued that the intersubjective construction of ethnic identity is grounded in the shared subliminal dispositions of the *habitus* which shape, and are shaped by, objective commonalities of practice: '[a] shared habitus engenders feelings of identification among people similarly endowed. Those feelings are consciously appropriated and given form through existing symbolic resources' (Bentley 1987: 173).

Moreover, these 'symbolic resources' are not essentially arbitrary. The cultural practices and representations that become objectified as symbols of ethnicity are derived from, and resonate with, the habitual practices and experiences of the people involved, as well as reflecting the instrumental contingencies and meaningful cultural idioms of a particular situation. As Eriksen (1992: 45) argues, ethnic symbols

> are intrinsically linked with experienced, practical worlds containing specific, relevant meanings which on the one hand contribute to shaping

interaction, and on the other hand limit the number of options in the production of ethnic signs.

Thus, just as ethnic sentiments and interests are derived from similarities in the *habitus*, so is the recognition of certain cultural practices and historical experiences as symbolic representations of ethnicity.

The application of Bourdieu's concept of the *habitus* to the development of a theory of ethnicity also provides a means of integrating the so-called primordial and instrumental dimensions of ethnicity within a coherent theory of human agency. As the recognition of ethnicity is to some extent derived from commonalities of *habitus*, it can be argued that the strong psychological attachments often associated with ethnic identity and ethnic symbolism, are generated by the critical role that the *habitus* plays in inscribing an individual's sense of social self (see Bourdieu 1977: 78–93). However, this is not to suggest that ethnic identifications, or associated symbolic representations, are fixed and determinative. Drawing on the logic of the *habitus*, Bentley (1987: 35) argues that different dimensions of ethnicity will be activated in different social contexts:

> Since ethnic identity derives from situationally shared elements of a multidimensional habitus, it is possible for an individual to possess several different situationally relevant but nonetheless emotionally authentic identities and to symbolize all of them in terms of shared descent.

Furthermore, ethnicity is also influenced by economic and political interests, resulting in changes in the perception and expression of ethnic identity by individuals, and also in the representation of group identity as a whole. As the instrumentalists have pointed out, ethnic identities are continuously reproduced and transformed within different contexts as individual social agents act strategically in the pursuit of interests. Nevertheless, the manipulation of ethnic categories does not, as instrumental theorists imply, take place in a vacuum whereby individual agents maximize their interests. Rather, such processes are structured by the principles of the *habitus* which engender perception of the possible and the impossible. As Bourdieu (1977: 76) has maintained, human agency is defined by the intersection of the

> socially constituted system of cognitive and motivating structures [which make up the *habitus*], and the socially structured situation in which the agents' *interests* are defined, and with them the objective functions and subjective motivations of their practices.

Ethnicity is also embedded in economic and political relations at a collective level in that the shared dispositions of the *habitus* which underlie ethnic affinities tend to result, at least to some extent, in the recognition of common sentiments and interests in a given situation, providing the basis for the political mobilization of an ethnic group. However, such mobilization does not represent a form of communal consensus, and in many instances it is clear that members of an ethnic group possess different experiences and divergent interests (see Devalle 1992: 237; Roosens 1989; Sharp and McAllister 1993: 19–20). To some extent these divergent positions may be based on relations of domination embedded in the shared dispositions of the *habitus*, and as a result leaders 'whose personal identity myths resonate with evolving configurations of habitus, practice and experience' (Bentley 1987: 47) will gain support despite the fact that their interests do not correspond with those of the entire group (see also Bourdieu 1977: 81). However, in other instances the politicization of ethnicity may involve the active use of force within the group in an attempt to fix an authoritative representation of the group's identity (Sharp and McAllister 1993: 20).

DIFFERENTIAL LOCI OF ETHNICITY

Grounding ethnicity in a coherent theory of cultural production and reproduction, a practice theory affords the explanation of a number of different dimensions of ethnicity which have been rendered incompatible through their opposition as causal explanations of ethnic behaviour, for instance as in the primordial/instrumental debate. A similar theoretical argument is developed by Eriksen, who draws on both Bourdieu's concept of the *habitus* (Eriksen 1992: 167–8), and Wittgenstein's concept of language-games (ibid.: 33–4, 47) as a way of conceptualizing the system of internalized orientations of thought and behaviour that constitute particular modes of practice and provide the basis for the construction of ethnic categories. Developing this idea Eriksen (1992: 28), like Bentley, argues that ethnicity is constituted in a similar manner to culture; it is both 'an aspect of concrete ongoing interaction *and* . . . a meaning-context for the very same interaction'.

However, such an understanding of the relationship between culture, or the *habitus*, and ethnicity is not far removed from the traditional model of ethnicity as a passive reflection of the normative behaviour of a discrete group of people. Bentley's (1987: 170) theory differs from traditional models primarily because the notion of the *habitus* enables a separation between surface cultural expressions and deep structural dispositions, and as a result he is able to accommodate disjunctions between ethnic boundaries and the distribution of objective cultural traits. Nevertheless, his theory of the relationship between the *habitus* and ethnicity results in a partial resurrection of the idea that ethnic groups constitute bounded social entities internally generated with reference to commonality rather than difference; an idea that was central to traditional models of the ethnic group.

As it stands, there are two significant limitations to Bentley's practice theory of ethnicity, which are derived from the way in which he employs the concept of the *habitus*, and from Bourdieu's concept itself. (1) Bentley does not explore the relationship between the shared subliminal dispositions of the *habitus* and the communication of cultural difference leading to the reproduction of ethnic categories. As a result the relationship between the *habitus* and ethnicity remains obscure and there is little consideration of qualitative variation in the kinds of cultural difference that signify ethnic identity. (2) Bentley does not critically examine the comparative value of Bourdieu's concept of *habitus*; he seems to accept that it is a discrete, uniform set of dispositions, possessing a high degree of homology across separate, but highly integrated, social domains.

Throughout Bentley's discussion of ethnicity the precise relationship between the *habitus* and ethnicity remains ambiguous (see the debate between Bentley (1991) and Yelvington (1991)). In his initial paper Bentley acknowledges that it is difficult to account for the institutional boundedness and internal complexity of ethnic groups in the modern world in terms of shared sentiment alone:

> If members of an ethnic group hold different positions in systems of production and distribution, and therefore possess different experiences and divergent interests, this raises the question of why these differences do not undermine ethnic solidarity.
>
> (Bentley 1987: 40–1)

However, rather than following up the possible implications of these problems in terms of a partial break between the *habitus* and the construction of ethnicity, Bentley (ibid.: 43–4) attempts to accommodate the complexity engendered by intra-ethnic differential relations of power and interest within the workings of the *habitus*. In reply to Yelvington's claim that his argument is based upon an insupportable correlation between ethnicity and culture (Yelvington 1991: 158–60), Bentley (1991: 170–1, 175) defends himself by reiterating the argument that, whilst the deep structures of the *habitus* provide the basis for the recognition of shared identity, these structures may produce a wide variety of surface cultural expressions.

Overall, it appears that Bentley does see ethnic identity as a reflection of the *habitus* of the group, and this identity is generated by a subliminal awareness of *likeness* with others of similar *habitus*. As Yelvington (1991: 168) points out, such a theory of ethnicity ignores the fact that, 'sensations of ethnic affinity and common experience are not necessarily covarient: Similarities in habitus do not guarantee ethnic sensations, and differences in habitus do not preclude identification.' There are many examples where it seems highly implausible that the people brought together by the expression of a common ethnic identity share equally in a common *habitus*;

ironically, for instance, Bentley's (1987) own example of black American ethnicity.

Bentley's failure to explore the processes involved in the appropriation of sensations of familiarity in the construction of ethnicity constitutes a critical gap in his argument, which is related to his neglect of the role of 'ethnic others' in the construction of ethnicity. He disregards a number of important insights derived from recent research, most notably the organizational aspects of ethnicity and the contrastive dimension of ethnicity – that ethnicity is a consciousness of difference *vis-à-vis* others. The recognition that ethnicity is not primarily constituted by a subliminal recognition of similarities, but is *essentially a consciousness of difference*, requires further consideration of the relationship between the *habitus* and the construction of ethnicity.

It can be argued that the kind of social experience and knowledge involved in the emergence of a consciousness of ethnicity, and the formulation of ethnic categories, is founded on a fundamental break with the kind of experience and knowledge that constitutes a substantial part of the *habitus*. According to Bourdieu (1977: 164), the workings of the *habitus* are such that the subjective principles of organization and associated modes of knowledge, such as systems of classification relating to gender and class, tend towards a correspondence with the conditions of existence. This correspondence results in a level of social experience, called *doxa*, which entails a misrecognition and naturalization of the real divisions of the social order leading to the reproduction of that order and consequently the modes of domination inherent in it (ibid.: 164–5). The political function of such classifications tends to go unnoticed because agents are not aware of rival or antagonistic schemes of thought or perception.

However, the *doxic* mode of knowledge is not the only form of social knowledge. When a particular mode of living is brought into question practically, for instance as a result of 'culture contact', or political and economic crisis, the field of *doxa* undergoes a transformation:

> The critique which brings the undiscussed into discussion, the unformulated into formulation, has as the condition of its possibility objective crisis, which, in breaking the immediate fit between the subjective structures and the objective structures, destroys self-evidence practically. It is when the social world loses its character as a natural phenomenon that the question of the natural or conventional character . . . of social facts can be raised.
>
> (Ibid.: 168–9)

The result is the establishment of *orthodox* or *heterodox* forms of knowledge which involve an awareness and recognition of alternative beliefs; *orthodoxy* attempting to deny the possibility of alternatives at a conscious level, and *heterodoxy* acknowledging the existence of a choice between different forms of knowledge and their evaluation through explicit critiques. Bourdieu develops this distinction between *doxic* knowledge and other forms of knowledge (*orthodox* and *heterodox*) in an analysis of the emergence of class consciousness, which can also be applied to ethnicity.

Social interaction between agents of differing cultural traditions engenders a reflexive mode of perception which contributes to a break with *doxic* forms of knowledge. Such exposure of the arbitrariness of cultural practices, which had hitherto been mastered in a doxic mode, permits and requires a change 'in the level of discourse, so as to rationalize and systematize' the representation of such cultural practices, and, more generally, the representation of the cultural tradition itself (ibid.: 233). It is at such a discursive level that ethnic categories are produced, reproduced and transformed through the systematic communication of cultural difference with relation to the cultural practices of particular 'ethnic others'. The recognition of shared sentiments and interests which ethnicity involves may be derived, at least in part, from *doxic* experience and knowledge in certain spheres of the *habitus*; similarities that cannot really be grasped in discursive form. However, the emergence of an ethnic consciousness, and the categories and symbols it entails, involves a break with *doxic* knowledge, due to the objectified representation of cultural difference involved in the expression of ethnicity (Eriksen 1993b: 3). In effect, a set of cultural practices and beliefs which had previously formed part of the domain of *doxa* becomes reified as a coherent and concrete object in opposition to specific 'others'.[4]

This process can be illustrated by reference to a specific example, that of the construction of Tswana ethnicity in the context of European colonialism (see Comaroff and Comaroff 1992: 235–63). In the process of interaction and communication between Tswana people and evangelist missionaries, both groups began to recognize distinctions between them; 'to *objectify* their world in relation to a novel other, thereby inventing for themselves a self-conscious coherence and distinctness – even while they accommodated to the new relationship that enclosed them' (Comaroff and Comaroff 1992: 245). This objectification of culture is not a fabrication, an entirely instrumental construction. Tswana ethnicity is based on the perception of commonalities of practice and experience in *Setswana* (Tswana ways) in opposition to *Sekgoa* (European ways). Yet the form Tswana self-consciousness takes in this context is different from the cultural identities that prevailed in pre-colonial times when they were divided into political communities based on totemic affiliations. In both pre-colonial and colonial/post-colonial times the construction of (ethnic) identity has involved the marking of contrast – the opposition of selves and others – but colonialism provided a new context in which Tswana tradition was objectified as a coherent body of knowledge and practice uniting the Tswana people.

Many other cases illustrate similar processes, for instance, amongst others, the formation of Tsonga ethnicity in southern Africa (see Harries 1989), Kayapo ethnicity in Brazil (see Turner 1991) and pan-Aboriginal ethnicity in Australia (see Jones and Hill-Burnett 1982; Tonkinson 1990). Each example has its own particularities and European colonialism as a whole is arguably characterized by certain specific concrete historical conditions in contrast to other periods. However, despite variations in the particular conditions in which ethnic identity is constructed, and in the form that ethnicity takes, it can be argued that similar, although in some cases less radical, processes of objectification are involved in the construction of a consciousness of ethnicity within diverse socio-historical contexts.

The objectification of cultural difference in the construction of ethnicity involves the opposition of different cultural traditions. The particular form such oppositions take is a product of the intersection of the *habitus* of the people concerned with the conditions making up a particular context of interaction. These conditions include the prevailing modes of domination and the relative distribution, between the different 'groups', of the material and symbolic means necessary for imposing dominant modes of ethnic categorization. For example, in many colonial contexts ethnic or tribal categories were imposed by colonial regimes (see Colson 1968; Fried 1968). As a product of the dialectical opposition of different cultural traditions, which are almost invariably characterized by different social and environmental conditions, ethnic categories encode relations of power. However, ethnicity does not merely, as argued by Diaz-Polanco (1987), reproduce the very social conditions that gave rise to it in the first place, thus sustaining relations of domination and subordination, and dividing groups who are similarly disadvantaged. It can also form the basis of political mobilization and a source of resistance when dominated groups have the material and symbolic means to reject external definitions of their identity, and, importantly, when ethnic classifications in one form or another become the object and instrument of political struggle (see Devalle 1992: 233, 239). During the later twentieth century in liberal, democratic societies, ethnic categories have become politicized in this way, resulting in the mobilization of ethnicity – the so-called 'ethnic revival' (see pp. 100–2 below). This mobilization is often mistakenly taken to imply that ethnicity has only recently become embedded in power relations (e.g. Glazer and Moynihan 1975: 8). However, ethnic categories are almost always embedded in power relations of varying degrees of inequality; the difference is that in some cases the social order that they constitute forms part of an established *doxa* or orthodoxy, whereas in others they become objects of debate and critique.

In contrast to Bentley, I suggest that the extent to which ethnicity is embedded in pre-existing cultural realities represented by a shared *habitus* is

highly variable. The degree of contiguity depends upon the cultural transformations brought about by the processes of interaction and the nature of
the power relations between the interacting 'groups'. In some instances, for
example as in some colonial situations, ethnic groups are formed in the
context of large-scale urban migration and associated social and cultural
dislocation (see Comaroff and Comaroff 1992). As a result of such processes minority ethnic groups may be composed of people of diverse
origins, and 'the substance of their identities, as contrived from both within
and outside, is inevitably a *bricolage* fashioned in the very historical processes
which underwrite their subordination' (Comaroff and Comaroff 1992: 57).
Yet even when ethnicity is as much a product of the historical relations of
inequality between 'groups' as it is a reflection of pre-existing cultural
realities, the reproduction of these emergent forms of cultural difference
and relations of inequality over time will lead to their incorporation as part
of the structured dispositions of the *habitus*.[5] As Comaroff and Comaroff
(ibid.: 60) point out:

> ethnic consciousness enters a dialectical relationship with the structures
> that underlie it: once ethnicity impinges upon experience as an (appar-
> ently) independent principle of social organization, it provides a power-
> ful motivation for collective activity. And this, by turn, must perforce
> realize an everyday world dominated by ethnic groups and relations,
> thereby reproducing the very social conditions that gave rise to ethnic
> consciousness in the first place.

Thus, manifestations of ethnicity are the product of an ongoing process
involving the objectification of cultural difference and the embodiment of
those differences within the shared dispositions of the *habitus*. Such processes will lead to fluctuations over time in the correspondence between
the representation of a particular ethnic identity, in terms of objectified
cultural difference, and the cultural practices and historical experience of
the people involved. In some situations there may be a high degree of
contiguity between ethnicity and the *habitus*, whereas in other situations
characterized by social dislocation and subordination there may appear to
be very little.

The actual manifestation of any particular ethnic identity may also vary in
different social and historical contexts. The communication of cultural
difference depends upon the particular cultural practices and historical
experience activated by any given context of social interaction as well as
broader idioms of cultural difference, resulting in substantive differences in
the cultural content of ethnicity in different situations. Moreover, as Eriksen (1991, 1992) argues, the importance of cultural differences in the
articulation of ethnicity may vary in different contexts – cross-culturally,
intra-culturally, and interpersonally:

Ethnicity as a source of cultural meaning and as a principle of social differentiation, is highly distributive within any society or set of social contexts involving the same personnel. Its varying importance, or varying semantic density, can only be appreciated through a comparison of contexts, which takes account of differences in the meanings which are applied by those acts of communicating cultural distinctiveness which we call ethnicity.

(Eriksen 1992: 33)

In an analysis of ethnicity in Trinidad and Mauritius, Eriksen (1991, 1992) argues that, in differentiated societies, the *kind* of cultural difference involved in the communication of ethnicity varies qualitatively in different social domains/fields.[6] For instance, ethnicity is an important signifier in the institutional politics of both Trinidad and Mauritius; since the postwar period most parties have been organized along ethnic lines and derive their support from an ethnic base (Eriksen 1992: 34). However, there is a shared understanding of the meaning of ethnicity, and a wide consensus over values and modes of discourse and interaction:

In other words, *cultural differences are in themselves unimportant in these contexts*; their importance lies in the creation of options for politicians and parties to draw upon such differences in their quest for popularity and power. The formal congruence of ethnicity among politicians of different ethnic membership is complete: the political culture, or language game, is homogeneous as it is being confirmed in ongoing institutionalized political life; . . . in so far as ethnicity is relevant in these contexts of politics, cultural difference is communicated through a shared cultural idiom.

(Ibid.: 36; original emphasis)

In contrast with institutional politics, inter-ethnic interaction in other social domains, such as the labour market, may be characterized by only partial overlap between the relevant meaning systems (or *habitus*) of the people involved (ibid.: 37–40). Moreover, in some social domains such as family life and sexual relations the recognition and articulation of ethnicity may be characterized by discrete, even incommensurable, habitual dispositions and systems of meaning, which inform the social practices of people in different groupings (ibid.: 41). For instance, in Trinidad and Mauritius gender, sexuality and ethnicity intersect with one another. Black male sexual ideology encourages promiscuity and the public expression of sexual prowess (ibid.: 42). In contrast, the articulation of Mauritian Indian identity in the domain of gender relations is inscribed in the value placed on the sacred character of matrimony and the sexual purity of women. The claimed sexual prowess of black men is perceived by Indian men in terms of the supposed weakness of Indian women in the face of sexual advances, and the threat which this poses to their own domestic supremacy (ibid.: 42). Eriksen (ibid.: 42) argues that in this instance the representation of ethnicity in the domain of gender relations is based upon the reproduction of discrete, incommensurable schemes of meaning.

The communication of ethnicity in these different social domains is not isolated and discrete. As Eriksen (ibid.: 43) argues, 'ethnic distinctions are rooted in perceptions of differences between lifestyles', and in order to explain the mobilization of ethnicity in contexts characterized by a unitary language game it is necessary to understand 'the reproduction of discrete socially discriminating language games' (ibid.: 42) in other social domains. Nevertheless, his analysis indicates that the kinds of communication involved in the reproduction and transformation of ethnic categories may vary qualitatively, as well as substantively, in different social domains characterized by different forms of individual and institutional agency, and different regimes of domination and resistance. For instance, the institutionalization of ethnicity in the modern nation-state and its representation in national politics, is likely to be qualitatively different from the activation of ethnicity in the process of interaction between members of a local community or neighbourhood.

Overall, the theoretical approach formulated in this chapter suggests that whilst Bentley's practice theory of ethnicity provides a useful starting point for a comparative analytical framework, it is necessary to develop a broader conceptualization of the *habitus*. Bentley's notion of the *habitus* is taken from Bourdieu's (1977) study of cultural production and reproduction in Kabyle society, and this particular conceptualization of the *habitus* reflects the highly integrated, uniform system of dispositions, which, Bourdieu argues, are characteristic of a small-scale society, where the same agents are linked to one another in a variety of social fields. As Calhoun (1993) points out, it is necessary to take into account the dislocation of different social domains/fields, which is typical of highly differentiated complex societies, in order to develop a valid comparative concept of the *habitus*. Highly differentiated, 'complex' societies are characterized by an 'uncoupling of fields' which

> manifests itself first of all as a reduction in the extent to which the same agents are linked to each other in a variety of fields – say kinship, religion, and economic production – in other words a reduction in the 'multiplexity' of relationships, to use Max Gluckman's (1962) concept. But the uncoupling also manifests itself in a growing heterogeneity among fields, a reduction in the extent to which each is homologous with others.
>
> (Calhoun 1993: 77)

Moreover, this uncoupling of fields results in the rupture and transformation of informal *doxic* knowledge, and consequently a higher degree of codification of tradition than in small-scale societies. For instance, in Trinidad and Mauritius such forms of codification are aspects of the institutionalized representation of ethnic difference in the context of national politics.

Ethnicity is a multidimensional phenomenon constituted in different ways in different social domains. Representations of ethnicity involve the dialectical opposition of situationally relevant cultural practices and historical experiences associated with different cultural traditions. Consequently there is rarely a one-to-one relationship between representations of ethnicity and the entire range of cultural practices and social conditions associated with a particular group. From a 'bird's eye view' the resulting pattern will be one of overlapping ethnic boundaries constituted by representations of cultural difference, which are at once transient, but also subject to reproduction and transformation in the ongoing processes of social life. As Eriksen (1992: 172, emphasis in original) points out,

> *ethnic oppositions are segmentary in character*, the group created through a common cause expands and contracts situationally, and it has *no absolute existence in relation to unambiguous principles of inclusion and exclusion*. This mechanism of segmentation does not always create a neat system of concentric circles or 'Chinese boxes of identities', or an otherwise internally consistent segmentary classificatory system.

Such a view of ethnicity undermines conventional methodological approaches which telescope various spatially and temporally distinct representations of ethnicity onto a single plane for the purposes of analysis and attempt to force the resulting incongruities and contradictions into an abstract conceptualization of the ethnic group as a discrete, internally homogeneous entity characterized by continuity of tradition. The theoretical approach developed here suggests that such a methodological and conceptual framework obliterates the reality of the dynamic and creative processes involved in the reproduction and transformation of ethnicity.

THE 'PURE PRODUCTS GO CRAZY'? HISTORICAL MODELS OF ETHNICITY[7]

> a new word reflects a new reality and a new usage reflects a change in that reality. The word is 'ethnicity' and the new usage is the steady expansion of the term 'ethnic group' from minority and marginal subgroups at the edges of society – groups expected to assimilate, to disappear, to continue as survivals, exotic or troublesome – to major elements of society.
>
> (Glazer and Moynihan 1975: 5)

Glazer and Moynihan's (1975) position represents just one of many recent theoretical arguments which situate ethnic groups as the product of particular social and historical conjunctures. Along with a number of others (e.g. Bell 1975: 141–2; Banton 1977: 145–6), they have argued that the recent increase in the political salience of ethnic and sub-national groups in national and international contexts represents a new form of ethnicity in that ethnic groups are acting as economic and political interest groups. For many, this political mobilization has been brought about by increasing recognition at both a national and international level of principles of cultural and political self-determination in the second half of the twentieth century.

Others (e.g. Clifford 1988; 1992: 108; Comaroff and Comaroff 1992; Friedman 1992: 837) take a different frame of reference and locate the emergence of ethnicity in the context of European colonialism which has resulted in the displacement and fragmentation of pre-existing communities and the imposition of new categories of difference. Furthermore, it is suggested that the subsequent deterioration in the hegemony of the western, modernist world order since the 1960s has contributed to a further proliferation and politicization of 'subaltern' or ethnic identities (e.g. Clifford 1988; 1992).

For still others, the increasing salience of ethnic groups is the product of the specific conjunctures between ethnic and racial categories and relations of production intrinsic to the capitalist world system (e.g. Muga 1984: 17–19). Meanwhile, moving deeper into the past, it has also been suggested that ethnic groups are the product of specific transformations in social organization which took place towards the end of the European Bronze Age (e.g. Renfrew 1995: 57).

The proliferation of arguments concerning the specific socio-historical contexts of ethnicity are potentially boundless, and to some extent purely a question of whether a highly specific or highly generalist definition is adopted. However, historical models of ethnicity merit further exploration here as they are of particular significance to archaeologists if we wish to use contemporary concepts and theories of ethnicity in the analysis of past societies. To what extent can it be assumed that processes involved in the construction of ethnic identities in the contemporary world resemble those that took place in the past? Has there been a relative shift from homogeneity to heterogeneity as many theories suggest? Are the pure products of the past going crazy?

The so-called 'ethnic revival' (Smith 1981) has been connected with a number of different, but in many instances interrelated, macro sociohistorical developments which impinge on local contexts in various ways. Clearly, many of these developments have contributed to a disintegration of pre-existing forms of cultural identity and domination, and subsequently the reconfiguration of relations of identity and power. For instance, European colonialism undoubtedly provided the context (one that is particularly prominent in the theoretical discourses of the human sciences) for radical transformations and cultural confrontation in which new forms of ethnic self-consciousness were inscribed. Furthermore, in the context of the demise of colonial regimes and the disintegration of the dominant western, modernist culture, ethnic groups have drawn upon existing ideologies of nationalism and cultural relativism in the legitimation of their identity, and the articulation of political and economic rights. The most important elements in this ideological complex are generally felt to be the right to cultural autonomy, 'of ethnic self-respect, and . . . continued experience as a people' (Roosens 1989: 150), and the right to political and economic self-determination, many aspects of which are enshrined in international law (see Michalska 1991; Nettheim 1992: 21). It is with relation to such rhetoric that ethnic groups such as the Quebecois (see Handler 1988) and the Canadian Assembly of First Nations (see Moody 1984: 149–51) have made secessionist demands for political and cultural self-determination and autonomy. In other instances, ethnic groups have insisted on varying degrees of autonomy within the nation-state and sought special cultural, economic and political rights (see Bell 1975; Glazer and Moynihan 1975; Smith 1981).

However, whilst such recent developments may have brought about important transformations in the manifestation of ethnicity they do not merit the restriction of ethnicity to specific social and historic contexts. For instance, the mobilization of ethnicity as a basis for political action since the 1960s has resulted in an apparent increase in ethnic consciousness, and numerous transformations in the meaning and practical salience of ethnicity in certain social domains. Yet it does not constitute a completely different form of group identity from that which existed before, one based on politics rather than culture, as suggested by Glazer and Moynihan (1975: 8). Such a distinction between instrumental ethnicity and cultural ethnicity is based on a false dichotomy between culture and socio-political relations. The communication of cultural difference both structures, and is structured by, the distribution of material and symbolic power between communities (see pp. 96–7 above). Thus, recent mobilizations of ethnicity in the negotiation of political rights may involve a transformation of the material and symbolic conditions in which ethnic relations are embedded, and the emergence of new 'styles' of cultural self-consciousness. However, ethnicity is just as likely to have been embedded in socio-political relations in the past as in the present; what have changed, and are always changing, are the historical conditions and the idiomatic concepts in which ethnicity is embedded.

Moreover, there is no reason why ethnicity should be restricted to the context of European colonialism, or to any other macro socio-historical developments, if it is seen as the kind of group consciousness that is based on the dialectical opposition of different cultural traditions in the process of social interaction. In these terms, the cultural categories intrinsic to the

formation of the Aztec state (see Brumfiel 1994), and Aboriginal mytho-
logical representations concerning interaction, exchange and relations of
power between themselves and the Maccassans prior to European colonialism (see Maddock 1988), can both be seen in terms of the symbolic
representation of ethnic boundaries. There are undoubtedly variations
between diverse contexts of ethnicity, in relations of power, modes of
representation and forms of social organization, which require historical
and contextual analysis. However, I suggest that there are certain basic
processes involved in the construction of ethnic identity across socio-
historical contexts which can be used as a framework for the analysis of
similarities and differences in the manifestation of ethnicity in radically
different situations.

Nevertheless, in adopting such a framework, it is necessary to examine
the ways in which specific discourses of identity in the present inform and
infiltrate such a comparative theory of ethnicity. The principles of self-
determination and cultural autonomy, which structure the political mobilization of ethnicity in many situations today, are embedded in a complex
of ideas about the nature of authentic cultural difference (Clifford 1988:
337–9; Handler 1988). As pointed out in Chapter 3, expectations of
boundedness, homogeneity and continuity have been built into 'western'
ideas concerning cultural authenticity since the nineteenth century, and
have since been reproduced in numerous variants throughout the world
(Clifford 1988: 232–3; Handler 1986: 2–4; Spencer 1990: 283; Williams
1989: 423–6). It is important to recognize that in the formulation of this
mode of cultural classification, our own societies 'did not *discover* the
general form of a universal difference, rather they invented this form of
difference' (Fardon 1987: 176, my emphasis). However, once objectified
and given autonomy, such modes of cultural classification have provided
the basis for practical relationships and strategies, and consequently structure the recognition and representation of cultural difference.[8] Studies of
Mashpee (Clifford 1988) and Chambra (Fardon 1987) ethnicity, and Quebecois (Handler 1988), Sinhala (Spencer 1990) and Palestinian (Bowman
1993) nationalism, all reveal that the construction of ethnic and national
identities involves an ongoing dialogue between the reproduction of
localized cultural practices and existing modes of cultural self-consciousness, and broader discourses which seek to produce images of 'authentic'
culture and identity (Norton 1993). The latter are located in the representations of various 'specialists', such as journalists, novelists, teachers,
ethnic and national organizations, and in the rationale of government
institutions.

Anthropologists and social scientists are themselves deeply implicated
in the construction of a vision of cultural authenticity in the form of
bounded, coherent cultural traditions, trained as they are 'to suppress the
signs of incoherence and multiculturalism . . . as inessential aspects of

modernization' (Barth 1989: 122).[9] In his analysis of the representation of 'pure' cultural products in ethnography, literature and art, Clifford (1988: 4, 14) argues that the association of cultural change and fragmentation with lost authenticity and cultural decay has been a powerful image in anthropology as in western thought generally. Within this framework anthropologists have often lamented the disintegration of 'authentic' cultures (e.g. Lévi-Strauss 1975 [1955]), and the revival of ethnic consciousness has been perceived as a retreat from the alienation and dislocation of modern society through the revival of primordial identities (e.g. Isaacs 1974; Novak 1974). Furthermore, whilst it is also argued that contemporary ethnic identities are constantly constructed, re-invented and contested, resulting in multiple configurations of cultural identity and invented tradition, these aspects of ethnicity have often been interpreted as a specific product of the increasing interconnectedness of social and cultural institutions in the context of modern world systems (e.g. Clifford 1988: 11, 13; Friedman 1992: 855).

To a greater or lesser degree these models contribute to the construction of an historical trajectory along which ethnic groups have developed from discrete, quasi-natural, primordial cultural entities into complex poly-ethnic, multidimensional interest groups in modern industrial societies. Such an evolutionary trajectory restores the 'cookie-cutter' view of ethnic groups as spatially and temporally discrete culture-bearing units, which has been a central theme in both nationalist discourses and academic theories about ethnicity, by imposing it on the past. A critical historicization of the very concepts of ethnic group and nation reveals that the idea of a bounded culture-bearing unit has impinged upon the articulation of ethnicity in some recent socio-historical contexts. However, viewed as a unitary principle of human differentiation, the idea of a bounded, monolithic cultural cum ethnic unit is also a modern classificatory myth projected onto all of human history (Handler 1988: 291). Ethnic groups are not neatly packaged territorially bounded culture-bearing units in the present, nor are they likely to have been in the past.

The formation and transformation of ethnicity is contingent on particular historical structures which impinge themselves on human experience and condition social action (Comaroff and Comaroff 1992: 54). In this manner processes such as the imposition of colonial regimes, the development of mass education and communication, and the emergence of ideologies of cultural relativism and self-determination all constitute new structures within which ethnicity is potentially reproduced and transformed. However, the imposition of a unitary evolutionary trajectory, as in many historical representations of the transformation of ethnicity, merely obscures the analysis of particular social and historical manifestations. Moreover, recent research has shown that ethnicity is not a unitary phenomenon either in contemporary societies or in the past, and that it is just as likely to have been a product of transient configurations of cultural difference reproduced and transformed in a variety of different social domains in the past as it is in the present (Fardon 1987: 182; Ranger 1983: 248; Sharp and McAllister 1993: 20).

Chapter 6

Ethnicity and material culture

Towards a theoretical basis for the interpretation of ethnicity in archaeology

PROBLEMS WITH THE IDEA OF ARCHAEOLOGICAL CULTURES AS ETHNIC ENTITIES

As we saw in Chapter 1, the identification of past cultures and peoples in archaeology has, for the most part, been dependent on the assumption that bounded, monolithic cultural entities ('archaeological cultures') correlate with past peoples, ethnic groups, tribes and/or races. This assumption has been subjected to a number of important critiques both within the framework of culture-historical archaeology, and subsequently within various processual and post-processual archaeologies. Taken collectively these critiques can be divided into three main categories. The first is concerned with the straightforward correlation of archaeological cultures with ethnic groups, the second with the nature of archaeological distributions and the status of archaeological cultures as classificatory entities, and the third with the nature of ethnicity and the very existence of bounded homogeneous ethnic and cultural entities.

(1) The question of the equivalence of archaeological cultures and past peoples was raised within the framework of culture-history. Doubts concerning the possibility of identifying prehistoric peoples on the basis of archaeological evidence alone were periodically expressed, for instance, by Tallgren (1937), and by Jacob-Friesen and Wahle in the 1920s and the 1940s (Veit 1989: 41). Moreover, a desire to distinguish between archaeological cultures and culture in the ethnological sense was frequently expressed, for instance by Braidwood and MacKern in the 1930s and 1940s, alongside a demand for the development of alternative archaeological terminology (Daniel 1978 [1950]: 319). However, critiques generally consisted of cautionary tales focusing on the apparent poverty of the archaeological record, rather than a questioning of the principal assumptions underlying culture-history (Tallgren 1937 was an exception). That is, it was argued that archaeological evidence might not provide access to the ideational norms of past cultures or to ethnic groups due to technical problems with the

data, rather than the interpretive principles themselves. The general response in the face of such problems, as in reaction against racist and nationalistic uses of ethnic reconstructions of the past, was a retreat into the study of chronology and typology as ends in themselves. Within this empiricist, typological framework, debates largely focused on the meaning of archaeological types, and in particular whether such types represent artificial (etic) categories imposed by the archaeologist, or whether they represent the mental (emic) categories of their makers (e.g. Ford 1954a, 1954b; Spaulding 1953, 1954).

A more fundamental critique of culture-historical epistemology rested on the recognition that archaeological distributions may reflect a diverse range of past activities and processes in addition to the ideational norms of past ethnic groups. Although this claim had been made by a number of archaeologists prior to the 1960s (e.g. Childe 1956; Daniel 1978 [1950]; Tallgren 1937; Taylor 1948), it was only with the emergence of the 'new archaeology' that it became widely accepted as a critique of culture-history, and provided the basis of a new framework for archaeological analysis. For instance, Binford claimed that, in contrast with the undifferentiated view of culture perpetuated by normative archaeology,

> culture is not necessarily shared; it is participated in. And it is participated in differentially. A basic characteristic of cultural systems is the integration of individuals and social units performing different tasks, frequently at different locations; these individuals and social units are articulated by means of various institutions into broader units that have different levels of corporate inclusiveness.
>
> (Binford 1965: 205)

On the basis of this argument it was suggested that the single explanatory frame of reference provided by culture-history is inadequate and that it is necessary to undertake an analysis of the structure of archaeological assemblages in terms of their function within a differentiated social system (e.g. Binford 1962: 219; Clarke 1978 [1968]; Renfrew 1972). Archaeological distributions, it was argued, could not be equated in a simplistic manner with ethnic groups, because within such a framework functional variations in archaeological assemblages could be mistakenly interpreted as ethnic differences. For instance, the question of whether variation in Mousterian assemblages was derived from the organization of different activities in space and time, or was a product of past ethnic differentiation, was central to the debate between the Binfords (1966; see also Binford 1973) and Bordes and de Sonneville-Bordes (1970; see also Bordes 1973).

Despite their critique of the idea that *all* variation in distributions of material culture can be understood in terms of the ideational norms of past ethnic groups, 'new archaeologists' continued to accept the idea that some bounded archaeological distributions, if only in the domain of stylistic variation, correlate with such groups (Conkey 1991: 10; Shennan 1989b: 18; and see below). However, more recently, the assumption that a one-to-one relationship exists between variation in *any* aspect of material culture, stylistic or otherwise, and the boundaries of ethnic groups has been questioned. Drawing on numerous anthropological and historical examples it has been shown that the relationship between variation in material culture and the expression of ethnic difference is complex (Hodder 1982a; Trigger 1978; Ucko 1969). Moreover, a number of archaeologists (e.g. Olsen and Kobylinski 1991; Renfrew 1987; Shennan 1989b, 1991) have followed recent anthropological and sociological theories of ethnicity in emphasizing that ethnic groups are rarely a reflection of the sum total of similarities and differences in 'objective' cultural traits. Rather, they are self-conscious/self-defining groups, which are based on the perception of real or assumed cultural difference.[1]

(2) Aside from problems concerning the relationship between archaeological cultures and ethnic entities, the actual existence of archaeological cultures has been questioned. Traditionally, higher level archaeological groupings, such as cultures or phases, were defined in monothetic terms on the basis of the presence or absence of a list of traits or types, which were often derived from the assemblages of a 'type site', or intuitively considered to be the most appropriate attributes in the definition of a particular culture. As Clarke observed,

> The intended nature of these groups was . . . transparently clear, they were solid and tangible defined entities like an artefact type or cultural assemblage, each possessed a necessary list of qualifying attributes and they could be handled like discrete and solid bricks.
>
> (Clarke 1978 [1968]: 35)

However, as he goes on to point out, in practice 'no group of cultural assemblages from a single culture ever contains, nor ever did contain, all of the cultural artefacts' as the ideal monothetic concept implies (ibid.: 36). This problem was recognized by Childe (1956: 33, 124), who emphasized that all the types assigned to a particular culture are unlikely to be present in every assemblage. Instead, he argued, it is the repeated association of a number of types which defines the group, and some of these types may be absent in some assemblages within the group, as well as present in assemblages belonging to other groups. However, Childe's (1956: 124) response was to discard the untidy information by demoting it from the rank of 'diagnostic' types, thus preserving the ideal of a univariate cultural block. The result in Childe's work, as in others, was the operation of a two-tier system: 'A theoretical level of interpretation in terms of rigid monothetic groupings and a practical level of groupings by broad affinity or similarity assessed on an intuitive basis' (Clarke 1978 [1968]: 37).

Other archaeologists in addition to Clarke have criticized the intuitive, arbitrary and constructed nature of archaeological classification in general, and cultural entities in particular (e.g. Binford 1965; Hodder 1978b; Renfrew 1977; Shennan 1978). It has been argued that culture-historical classification was based on the degree to which cultural traits are shared, and this had the effect of 'masking differences and . . . lumping together phenomena which would be discrete under another taxonomic method' (Binford 1965: 205). In a similar vein Hodder (1978b) and Shennan (1978) have shown that the traditional approach to the classification of cultural entities was too crude, and that a more sophisticated approach to the analysis of archaeological data reveals a much more complex structure. Moreover, it has been argued that archaeological cultures can be generated out of a continuum of change, and that in many instances such entities are purely constructs devised by archaeologists (Hodder 1982a: 6; McGuire 1992: 169; Renfrew 1977: 94).

The conceptualization of culture as a differentiated system stimulated the development of new approaches to the analysis of archaeological distributions. More sophisticated conceptual devices have been developed in an attempt to accommodate the nature of archaeological distributions, such as Clarke's polythetic approach to the definition of culture. However, the fact that Clarke (1978 [1968]: 368–9) still defined culture as an entity which could be equated with past ethnic groups served to obscure some of the problems involved. As Shennan points out, Clarke adopted a classificatory expedient:

> to remove the untidiness in the cross-cutting distributions, rather than taking the more radical step of recognizing that *this untidiness is, in fact, the essence of the situation*, arising from the fact that there are no such entities as 'cultures', simply the contingent interrelations of different distributions produced by different factors.
>
> (Shennan 1989b: 13; my emphasis)

Such an understanding of archaeological distributions represents a significant shift in archaeological classification, which has been stimulated by attempts to analyse different aspects of past cultural systems. The idea that culture is a multivariate rather than a univariate phenomenon resulting from many different factors has been accepted by many archaeologists, and sophisticated methods of data analysis appropriate to such a theoretical stance have been developed (e.g. Doran and Hodson 1975; Hodder and Orton 1976; Shennan 1988).

(3) Finally, a small minority of archaeologists have questioned the very existence of ethnic groups as fixed bounded entities. As discussed in

Chapters 4 and 5, the recognition that ethnic groups are a dynamic and situational phenomenon has dominated research into ethnicity in anthropology and sociology since the late 1960s. Studies have revealed that the boundaries of ethnic groups and the identification of individuals may change through time and from place to place, often as a result of the strategic manipulation of identity with relation to economic and political relations. In the archaeological literature it has also been suggested that ethnicity is a dynamic and instrumental phenomenon and that material culture is actively used in the justification and manipulation of inter-group relations (e.g. Hodder 1982a; Shennan 1989b). Furthermore, it has been argued that the intensity of ethnic consciousness, and consequently material culture differentiation, may increase in times of economic and political stress (e.g. Hodder 1979a, 1982a; Kimes *et al.* 1982).

However, whilst the dynamic and situational nature of ethnicity has been accommodated by such research, the existence of ethnic groups as bounded socio-cultural entities is still accepted (e.g. Hodder 1979a, 1982a; Kimes *et al.* 1982). Very few archaeologists have recognized the more radical conclusions of some recent anthropological research which questions the very existence of ethnic groups in the form of bounded, monolithic territorial entities (although see Shennan 1989b: 11–12), and suggests that such a conceptualization may itself be a legacy of nineteenth-century taxonomic systems (Renfrew 1987: 288; Shennan 1989b: 7–9).[2]

All of these critiques have fundamental implications for the analysis of ethnicity in archaeology. However, they have only been accommodated in a piecemeal fashion, and often as an unintended consequence of other developments in archaeological theory and practice. In what follows, the ways in which processual and post-processual archaeologies have approached ethnicity, whether explicitly or implicitly, will be explored, and a general theoretical approach for the analysis of ethnicity in archaeology will be developed.

THE DICHOTOMY BETWEEN STYLE AND FUNCTION: NEW ARCHAEOLOGY AND THE CONCEPTUALIZATION OF ETHNICITY

The conceptualization of culture as a system and the emphasis on functionalism in new archaeology led to the definition of different kinds of artefact and assemblage variation. For instance, Binford (1962: 219) specified three different classes, 'technomic', 'socio-technic' and 'ideo-technic', relating to the kind of social domain in which artefacts have their primary function. Cross-cutting these functional categories, he distinguished formal stylistic attributes which are not directly explicable in functional terms; rather, he argued that such attributes are determined by the enculturative milieu, and may play a secondary functional role in promoting group solidarity (ibid.: 220). In a later paper Binford (1965: 206–9) went on to outline three sources of assemblage variability: 'tradition', that is spatio-temporal continuity in stylistic variability derived from received knowledge about ways of doing things; 'interaction sphere', that is the distribution of a particular artefact or group of artefacts derived from regular and institutionally maintained inter-societal articulation; and 'adaptive area', that is a distribution of common artefacts arising from their use in coping directly with the physical environment.

Basically these different classes of artefact and sources of variation are founded on a distinction between the 'functional' characteristics of artefacts, whether these are utilitarian or non-utilitarian, and 'stylistic' characteristics which cross-cut functional categories and are regarded as residual formal variation, a frequently quoted example being decoration on pottery vessels. It is clear from Binford's (1962, 1965, 1972) discussion of these different classes of variation that he regarded stylistic variation in terms of normative variation and ultimately ethnic differences. For instance, he stated that 'stylistic variables are most fruitfully studied when questions of ethnic origin, migration, and interaction between groups are the subject of explication' (Binford 1962: 220). Although he attributed a functional role to such variation in terms of promoting group solidarity, stylistic variation is essentially regarded as a passive product of the enculturative milieu. Moreover, Binford (1965: 208) defined spatially and temporally discrete traditions on the basis of similarities and differences in stylistic attributes in much the same way as archaeologists working within a culture-historical framework.

Thus, with respect to stylistic variation, ethnic entities, although rarely an explicit focus of analysis in processual archaeology, are still equated with received normative tradition (Conkey 1991: 10; Shennan 1989b: 18). The main distinction being that, in contrast with most culture-historical archaeology, such normative tradition is assumed to be located in only certain dimensions of artefact variability.[3] On the basis of these assumptions research concerning the organization of past groups has focused on particular aspects of material culture, such as stylistic variation in pottery decoration (e.g. Whallon 1968). In short, such studies assume that ceramic form is determined by utilitarian function whereas decoration constitutes additional non-functional variation, and that it is in the domain of such variation that social information such as 'ethnic iconography' will be expressed (Sackett 1977: 377).

In a series of articles, Sackett (1977, 1982, 1985, 1986, 1991) has subjected the dichotomy between function and style to a cogent critique. He adopted a similar basic premise concerning normative processes and style to other processual archaeologists, and indeed proponents of traditional culture-history. That is, that stylistic variation, referred to by Sackett as 'isochrestic variation', is derived from variation in culturally prescribed ways of doing things. Similarity in the isochrestic dimensions of material culture is assumed to be a product of acculturation within a given social group, and therefore also an index of ethnic similarity and difference (Sackett 1977: 371).

However, in contrast to Binford, Sackett argued that style does not occupy a discrete realm of formal artefact variation distinct from function. On the contrary, he suggested that these two dimensions of artefact variability are embedded in one another (Sackett 1977: 371; 1986: 630). Whereas it has been assumed by some archaeologists that style is something that is additional to the basic functional form of the object it occupies (e.g. Binford 1962, 1965; Whallon 1968), Sackett (1982: 75; 1986: 630) sees style as inherent in the choices made by people from a broad spectrum of equally viable alternative means of achieving the same functional ends. Style, or isochrestic variation, therefore resides in all aspects of artefact variability, even those dimensions which appear to be explicitly functional, and it follows on the basis of Sackett's argument that 'in isochrestic perspective, a butchering technique may potentially convey as much ethnically stylistic variation as a pottery decoration' (Sackett 1986: 630).

The dichotomy between style and function in the new archaeology was created by a desire to identify the different processes involved in the creation of variation in the archaeological record. However, this led to an artificial distinction between style and function, as if such dimensions of material culture constitute discrete components which can be measured in some way, and contributed to ambiguity concerning the relationship between normative processes and variation in material culture. It has been stressed that there may be considerable variation in ideational norms within a given socio-cultural system (e.g. Binford 1965: 205), whilst at the same time spatial and temporal continuity in stylistic attributes has continued to be explained in terms of cultural tradition and regarded as a passive product of ethnicity. Some research has usefully indicated that normative traditions and associated stylistic patterns are more complex than assumed in traditional culture-historical archaeology, as learning patterns may vary at individual or household levels, and at community and regional levels, as a result of a range of variables (e.g. see contributions to Flannery 1976; Plog 1978, 1983). However, style was still predominantly regarded as an essentially passive reflection of normative rules, until the emergence of a different conceptualization of style in terms of active communication and information exchange.

STYLISTIC COMMUNICATION AND ETHNICITY

Despite the important realization that the manifestation of material culture in any particular context is a product of a variety of processes and not solely a reflection of ideational norms, new archaeology failed to address the relationship between normative variation in material culture and ethnicity. In effect, the problems engendered by equating ethnicity with culture were merely transposed to the peripheral domain of stylistic variation, where spatially and temporally discrete distributions were interpreted as a passive reflection of past ethnic groups. However, as we have seen, it has been widely recognized in anthropology and sociology that a one-to-one relationship between ethnic identity and cultural similarities and differences cannot be assumed, and ethnic groups have been conceptualized as self-defining entities. Moreover, a large body of recent research has suggested that the communication of ethnicity is an active process involved in the manipulation of economic and political resources.

Although only a few archaeologists have been directly influenced by recent anthropological and sociological theories of ethnicity, similar trends are evident in a particular archaeological approach to style as active communication which emerged in the late 1970s and early 1980s.[4] Style was re-defined as more than a passive product of the enculturative milieu, it came to be viewed as a form of communication and social marking in certain, usually highly visible, artefacts, and in certain social contexts (Conkey 1991: 10). In this respect, style was regarded as both functional and adaptive in that it facilitates the exchange of information concerning social and religious identification, group affiliation, status, and so on, in periods of environmental and social stress (e.g. Gamble 1982; Jochim 1983).

Wiessner (1983, 1984, 1985, 1989) has developed these ideas concerning style as active communication in her ethno-archaeological analysis of stylistic variation and the expression of social identity amongst the Kalahari San. Drawing on psychological theory concerning social identity (e.g. Tajfel 1982), she has suggested that both individual and group identity is ultimately based on a universal human cognitive process of comparison 'through which the self is differentiated from others and the ingroup from the outgroup' (Wiessner 1983: 191–2, 257). Style, she argued, is one of the many channels through which identity can be projected to others, and consequently it will be affected by the processes of social comparison, and determined by the outcome of that comparison in terms of the expression of similarity and difference. Moreover, with relation to social identity, style may be actively used in the disruption, alteration and creation of social relationships (Wiessner 1984: 194; 1985: 161).

Style then, in Wiessner's terms, refers to the active symbolic role of particular characteristics of material culture in mediating social relations and social strategies. She has argued that there are at least two distinct aspects of style, which have different referents, contain different kinds of information, are generated by different conditions and produce different kinds of variation:

emblemic style, that is, formal variation in material culture that has a distinct referent and transmits a clear message to a defined target population about conscious affiliation and identity... [and] ... *assertive style*, [that] is formal variation in material culture which is personally based and which carries information supporting individual identity.

(Wiessner 1983: 257–8)

Wiessner (ibid.) went on to argue that emblemic style usually refers to a social group and the norms and values associated with that group, whereas assertive style does not have a distinctive referent as it supports, but does not directly symbolize, individual identity. Moreover, unlike assertive style, emblemic style does not reflect degrees of interaction across group boundaries, because it carries information about such boundaries and as a result it is likely to have a distinct and discrete distribution, in contrast to the random or clinal distribution of assertive style (ibid.: 259).

Hodder (1979a, 1982a) has elaborated on this point, drawing on a number of ethno-archaeological studies conducted in Kenya, Zambia and Sudan. In his study of ethnic boundaries in the Baringo District of Kenya he showed that, despite interaction across tribal boundaries, clear material culture distinctions were being maintained in a wide range of artefact categories, whilst other material culture types crossed tribal boundaries (Hodder 1982a: 58). He argued that material culture distinctions are in part maintained in order to justify between-group competition and negative reciprocity, and that such patterning may increase in times of economic stress (see especially Hodder 1979a, but also 1982a: 55). However, he also stressed that different groups may adopt different adaptive strategies in the face of economic and political stress, and that 'the explanation of these strategies and the way in which material culture is involved in them depend on internally generated symbolic schemes' (Hodder 1982a: 186).

Such research has major implications for assumptions concerning the relationship between degrees of similarity in material culture and social difference. Archaeologists have tended to assume that the transmission of material culture is a function of social interaction and proximity. However, as Hodder has pointed out, there is no straightforward relationship between degrees of interaction or scales of production and material culture patterning:

the extent to which cultural similarity relates, for example to interaction depends on the strategies and intentions of the interacting groups and on how they use, manipulate and negotiate material symbols as part of these strategies.

(Ibid.: 185)

Like Wiessner, Hodder (ibid.: 186–7) suggested that the use of material culture in distinguishing between self-conscious ethnic groups will lead to

discontinuities in certain material culture distributions which may enable
the archaeologist to identify such groups (see also Haaland 1977). However,
he also emphasized that some groups may choose strategies of assimilation
in the context of regular interaction, and others may retain distinct identities without reference to material culture with the result that their boundaries will be invisible to archaeologists, as in the case of the Lozi in Zambia.

In contrast to some functionalist approaches to style (e.g. Wobst 1977;
Binford 1973), Hodder (1982a: 55) argued that ethnic identity may be
expressed in mundane utilitarian items as well as in decorative items, and
that such objects are not necessarily highly visible. Moreover, unlike Wiessner he illustrated that the form that between-group relations take is usually
related to the internal organization of social relations, and that the expression of ethnicity must be understood in terms of symbolic schemes of
meaning generated within the group (ibid.: 187–8). For instance, he argued
that in the Baringo District of Kenya, between-group differentiation and
hostility is linked to the internal differentiation of age sets and the domination of women and younger men by older men. Larick's (1986, 1991)
ethno-archaeological research amongst the Loikop in Kenya also supports
this argument, illustrating that items of material culture that are significant
in terms of ethnicity, such as spears, are constantly appropriated in the
signification of age differentiation amongst the male population. At the
most exclusive level owning a spear constitutes being Loikop, but in this
case the intensity of competition between age cohorts, and the expression
of differentiation between age grades in terms of stylistic variation in
spears, is greater than between ethnic groupings (Larick 1991: 317–18).

Such research is part of a significant trend in the analysis of style in
archaeology which emphasizes its active role in symbolizing identity and
negotiating social relations. In contrast to normative or isochrestic theories,
stylistic variation is not regarded as merely a passive reflection of enculturation within ethnically bounded contexts; rather it is actively produced,
maintained and manipulated in the process of communication, and the
mediation of social relationships. Such strategic manipulation of material
culture is likely to result in discontinuous non-random distributions of
material culture (see Hodder and Orton 1976), which are often the foci
of interaction rather than relative social isolation and distance. *Thus archaeologists cannot then assume that degrees of similarity and difference in material culture
provide a straightforward index of interaction.*

The research discussed here also represents a number of important
developments in the analysis of ethnic identity in archaeology (e.g. Hodder
1979a, 1982a; Larick 1986, 1991; Kimes *et al.* 1982; Wiessner 1983, 1984,
1985). Although the nature of ethnicity is not explicitly discussed in detail
in any of these studies, ethnic groups are conceptualized as self-conscious
identity groups constructed through the process of social and cultural
comparison *vis-à-vis* others, rather than as a passive reflection of cultural

tradition as in normative archaeology. It is also recognized that the expression of ethnicity may be confined to a limited range of stylistic attributes which have become associated with an ethnic referent, and these attributes may be actively maintained and manipulated in the negotiation of social relations; an observation that is backed up by a large body of anthropological literature.

However, none of these approaches provides an account of how ethnic identity is produced, reproduced and transformed. Why is there apparently a relationship between symbolic structures concerning intra-group relations and the form and expression of ethnic relations? How do particular stylistic attributes become attached to the active conscious expression of identity, ethnic or otherwise; that is, what are the processes involved in the objectification of ethnicity? What is missing from these studies is an 'adequate account of the social production of style' (Shanks and Tilley 1992 [1987]: 146). Hodder (1982a: 204–5) is, to some extent, an exception, in that he emphasizes the importance of the symbolic structures permeating *all* aspects of cultural practice and social relations in the differentiation of ethnic groups (and see pp. 120–2 below). However, functionalist explanations of style as communication, such as that of Wobst (1977), fall into the teleological trap of suggesting that distinctive styles come into existence in order to serve certain ends, such as the communication of ethnic difference in times of economic stress. Moreover, the relationship between such functional styles and other supposedly passive forms of stylistic variation remains unclear.

MATERIAL CULTURE, HUMAN AGENCY AND SOCIAL STRUCTURE

Proponents of the new archaeology reacted against traditional culture-history and the idea that material culture merely reflected social norms, but in doing so they imposed a functionalist conceptualization of culture, including material culture, as an epiphenomenal adaptive mechanism (Hodder 1982b: 4–5; Shanks and Tilley 1987: 94). Moreover, although the normative dimension of culture was not altogether dismissed, it was considered irrelevant in terms of the function of culture in most contexts of analysis, except in the case of style. The result is a pervasive dichotomy between functional utility and normative culture. However, there are problems with both a functionalist conceptualization of culture as an adaptive mechanism, and a normative or structuralist conceptualization of culture as a set of ideational rules determining behaviour.[5]

On the one hand, functionalist approaches fail to take into account the way in which cultural schemes structure social reality. As Hodder (1982b: 4) argues, 'all actions take place within cultural frameworks and their functional value is assessed in terms of the concepts and orientations which surround them'. Law-like models based on abstract notions of efficiency and adaptation (e.g. Torrence 1989) cannot account for the cultural diversity so clearly manifest in the varied responses of particular societies to similar environmental and social conditions (see McBryde 1984). Moreover, a functionalist approach is reductive in that human action is assumed to be primarily determined by specific environmental factors, with the exception of supposedly expedient stylistic peculiarities which are regarded as the product of normative processes.

On the other hand, normative and structuralist approaches fail to provide an adequate account of the generation of social structure in the course of social action, and as a result people are represented as culturally determined dupes mechanistically obeying normative rules or structures. As in functionalist approaches, where human agency is often subordinated to environmental determinism, the role of human agency is also curtailed in structuralist approaches, where it is determined by abstract structures that lie outside the domain of individual and group history (Bourdieu 1977: 72; Hodder 1982b: 8–9). Moreover, as normative and structuralist approaches tend to disregard adaptive processes, and fail to develop an account of the generation of norms or social structures with relation to human agency, they do not provide an adequate framework for the analysis of processes of social change (Hodder 1982b: 8).

All social practices and social relations are structured by cultural schemes of meaning which mediate social relations and social action. However, as discussed in Chapter 5, such structuring principles are not abstract mental rules, but rather durable dispositions towards certain perceptions and practices. Such dispositions become part of an individual's sense of self at an early age, and operate largely in the domain of practical consciousness – that is, these cultural dispositions structure people's decisions and actions, but often lie beyond their ability to describe, and thus formalize, their behaviour in the realm of discursive consciousness. The structural orientations making up the *habitus* are essentially dialectical in that they both structure, and are structured by, social practice – they are both the medium and the outcome of practice. Moreover, such structural orientations do not have an existence of their own outside of human action, but rather are only manifested in the context of social practice where they are reproduced and transformed. Such an approach provides a theoretical framework which resolves the dichotomy between functionalism and structuralism. Human behaviour can still be considered to achieve certain functional ends, to provide for basic needs, desires and goals; however, such needs and interests are defined and negotiated by people within a culturally structured situation, as are the functions that particular practices perform (Bourdieu 1977: 76).

Material culture is an active constitutive dimension of social practice in that it both structures human agency and is a product of that agency

(Hodder 1986: 74).[6] The social practices and social structures involved in the production, use and consumption of material culture become embodied by it, because such processes occur within meaningful cultural contexts (see MacKenzie 1991: 191–201; Miller 1985: 11–12). Yet material culture may operate simultaneously in a number of social fields and its meaning is not fixed, but subject to reproduction and transformation in terms of both material curation and interpretation throughout its social life (see Kopytoff 1986; MacKenzie 1991: 26–7; Thomas 1991: 28–9). Thus, material culture is polysemous, and its meanings may vary through time depending upon its particular social history, the position of particular social agents, and the immediate context of its use. Moreover, material culture is not merely a repository of accumulated meaning inscribed in it by its production and use in different social contexts and by differentially situated social agents. It plays an active role in the structuring of cultural practices, because the culturally specific meanings with which material culture is endowed as a result of former practices influence successive practices and interpretations.

For instance, MacKenzie's (1991) detailed analysis of the cultural construction of Telefol string bags illustrates the dialectical relationship between the meaning of a particular item of material culture and the reproduction and transformation of social relations in the spheres of gender, age differentiation, ethnic identities, exchange, kinship relations, ritual and myth. Mackenzie has convincingly demonstrated that, through their use in everyday practice and in ritual symbolism, the meanings attributed to string bags play an active role in the construction of an individual's social and cultural identity. Moreover, through their role in the mediation and justification of social relations, such as between men and women, they are involved in the structuring of social practices and social interaction. For instance, the bird-feather *bilum* (string bag) worn by men is an expression of sexual differentiation, which signifies both opposition/separation and dependency/integration between genders (MacKenzie 1991: 201). This particular *bilum* is introduced to boys at the beginning of male initiation and the ideas associated with it play a role in the internalization of notions of sexual differentiation and masculinity (ibid.: 204–5). The bird-feather *bilum* is polysemous, meaning different things to different people in different social contexts, and it is involved in the mediation and legitimation of social relations and the structuring of activities between genders, in different contexts, and at different stages in the life cycle of the Telefol (ibid.: 192–4, 204–5).

Miller's (1985) analysis of pottery from Dangwara village in the Malwa region of India, and Taylor's (1987) analysis of Kunwinjku bark paintings in western Arnhem Land, Australia, also provide compelling examples of the active, constitutive role of material culture in the mediation of social relations and the construction of identities. Such studies suggest that material culture cannot be regarded as a passive reflection of rule-governed activities as it has been within the so-called normative archaeology. More-over, any distinction between passive and active dimensions of material culture, such as between Sackett's isochrestic variation and Wiessner's communicative style, is undermined because *all* material culture is active in the processes of social production, reproduction and transformation (Conkey 1991: 13; Shanks and Tilley 1992 [1987]: 146). As Hodder (1982a: 213; see also Miller 1985: 205) has argued,

> Structures of meaning are present in all the daily trivia of life and in the major adaptive decisions of human groups. Material culture patterning is formed as part of these meaningful actions and it helps to constitute changing frameworks of action and belief.

Cultural change is generated by the intersection of the meanings embodied in the material and non-material worlds, and new contexts of interpretation and action in which agents act strategically on the basis of the structured dispositions of the *habitus*.

One of the main implications of this argument for archaeologists is that structure and function cannot be regarded as distinct domains – structure provides the framework through which function is defined. Moreover, the structured orientations of the *habitus* manifest themselves in different ways in different contexts with relation to various sets of social relations and cultural practices. It follows that it is necessary to adopt a contextual and historical approach to the analysis of archaeological remains in order to try to understand the social practices and social relations which extended beyond the structure and content of material culture distributions (Hodder 1982b; 1986).

ETHNICITY AND MATERIAL CULTURE

Having established a broad framework for the interpretation of material culture that avoids the problems associated with both functionalist and normative approaches, it is possible to reconsider the interpretation of ethnicity in archaeology. An overriding concern with the instrumental dynamics of ethnicity in anthropology and sociology since the late 1960s has resulted in a distinction between culture and ethnicity, the latter being framed in primarily socio-economic and political terms. The cultural dimensions of ethnicity, and to some extent the very existence of ethnic groups, have been taken for granted and research has tended to focus on the manipulation of cultural difference in the pursuit of individual and group interests. Culture, within this framework, is reduced to an epiphe-nomenal and arbitrary set of symbols randomly selected from existing practices and beliefs, or even brought into being in order to signify ethnicity and justify instrumental ends. A similar tendency can be identified in certain archaeological studies of the use of style in the communication of ethnicity and other forms of social identity (e.g. Hodder 1979a; Wiessner 1983; Wobst 1977). Such approaches are both functionalist and reductionist; stylistic patterns in material culture are assumed to exist in order to achieve certain ends, such as the communication of identity.

Theories that focus exclusively on instrumental aspects of ethnicity fail to address a number of key issues. How are the commonalities of identity and interest associated with ethnicity generated? What is the nature of the relationship between ethnic identities and the cultural practices, or symbols associated with them? In short, what is the relationship between culture and ethnicity?[7] It was argued in Chapter 5 that sensations of ethnic affinity are based on the recognition, at both a conscious and subconscious level, of similar habitual dispositions which are embodied in the cultural practices and social relations in which people are engaged. Such structural dispositions provide the basis for the perception of ethnic similarity and difference when people from diverse cultural traditions come into interaction with one another, leading to forms of self-reflexive cultural comparison. It is in such contexts that particular cultural practices and beliefs, which to some extent embody the underlying structures of the *habitus*, become objectified and rationalized in the representation of ethnic difference. Ethnicity is not a direct reflection of the *habitus*, or of culture. The construction of ethnicity, and the objectification of cultural difference that this entails, is a product of the intersection of people's habitual dispositions with the concrete social conditions characterizing any given historical situation. These conditions include the nature of social interaction, and the relative distribution of the material and symbolic means necessary for the imposition of dominant regimes of ethnic categorization.

Material culture is frequently implicated in both the recognition and expression of ethnicity; it both contributes to the formulation of ethnicity and is structured by it. Certain aspects of material culture may become involved in the self-conscious signification of identity, and the justification and negotiation of ethnic relations. As a result, distinctive forms and styles of material culture may be actively maintained and withheld in the process of signalling ethnicity, whilst other forms and styles may cross-cut ethnic boundaries (see Barth 1969a; Hodder 1982a). However, in contrast to instrumentalist theories, the approach developed here suggests that the 'choice' of distinctive cultural forms and styles used in signalling ethnic boundaries is not arbitrary. Rather, the self-conscious expression of ethnicity through material culture is linked to the structural dispositions of the *habitus*, which infuse all aspects of the cultural practices and social relations characterizing a particular way of life (see Burley *et al.* 1992: 6–7). This argument is supported by ethno-archaeological studies, such as those of Hodder (1982a) and Larick (1986; 1991), which have revealed that the manifestation of inter-ethnic relations, and the expression of ethnic difference, are linked to cultural practices and social differentiation within the group. Furthermore, Hodder's (1982a: 54–5) research indicated a correlation between dimensions of material culture that are not part of the overt signification of ethnicity, as in the case of the position of hearths within huts, and self-conscious ethnic signification in other dimensions of material culture, such as in items of dress. As Hodder (1982a: 56) has observed, 'tribal distinctions become acceptable and "naturalized" by their continued repetition in both public and private', and there is 'a continual interplay between different spheres and types of material culture'.

The practice theory of ethnicity advocated here provides the basis for a re-evaluation of the debate between Sackett (1985) and Wiessner (1983, 1984, 1985) about the nature of stylistic variation and the way in which ethnic markers are manifested in material culture. On the basis of her analysis of stylistic variation in San projectile points, and the ways in which such variation is articulated in terms of group differentiation by the San, Wiessner argued that emblemic style clearly marks differences between language groups and may function at the level of the dialect and/or band cluster:

> for the San, the emblemic style carries a clear message to members of a linguistic group as to whether arrows come from their own group or a foreign one. In the former case it signals that the maker also holds similar values. In the latter case, the stylistic difference may either signal another set of values or practices, if the two groups are known to one another, or if not, that its maker is foreign and his behaviour is unpredictable.
>
> (Wiessner 1983: 269)

In his critique, Sackett (1985: 156) disputed both Wiessner's theoretical approach and her interpretation of stylistic variation in San projectile points. He argued for a narrower view of active style, called iconological style, which he defined as conscious purposive signalling. According to Sackett, iconocism constitutes only a small dimension of ethnic style, most of which is inherent in isochrestic variation; that is passive variation which arises from enculturation within a bounded ethnic context. Moreover, he has argued that the formal variation that Wiessner has observed in San projectile points can be explained in terms of passive isochresticism rather than the active use of style to signal identity (Sackett 1985: 157–8).

Within the terms of their debate it appears that there is little evidence to suggest that the San projectile points are produced in a certain form *in order to* actively signal self-conscious identity to a specific target group such as a different language group. San who do not live in the vicinity of linguistic boundaries are only vaguely conscious of linguistic differentiation, so it is difficult to attribute the production and maintenance of stylistic difference in projectile points to an intentional desire to signal linguistic boundaries. However, the question of intentionality in the production of particular styles of projectile point is not a relevant issue; it is clear that in certain contexts, such as the ethnographic situation created by Wiessner's study, variation in projectile points underlies a consciousness of difference in a variety of spheres, and becomes implicated in the signification and structuring of social relations.

Thus, in many situations style in projectile points constitutes Sackett's so-called isochrestic variation, but in some contexts it becomes involved in the recognition of ethnic difference and may *become active* in signifying identity, a point that is recognized by Wiessner (1985: 162; 1989: 58) in her later work. The problem with Sackett's argument is that he assumes that his isochrestic variation can be correlated with ethnicity. On the contrary, isochrestic variation in material culture can be usefully compared with Bourdieu's concept of the *habitus*, although it constitutes a transformed and congealed representation of the generative structures of the *habitus*. As such, isochrestic variation 'provides the resources for ethnic identity, and indeed for emblemic and assertive uses of style in general' (Shennan 1989b: 20), but neither isochresticism nor the *habitus* is equivalent to ethnicity. In the case of the San projectile points, habitual modes of arrow-head production provide the basis for the generation of ethnicity, or at least a 'we'/'they' consciousness, in contexts where the arbitrary nature of particular modes of arrow-head production has been exposed through processes of cultural comparison.

If such contexts of interaction and comparison occur repeatedly and social action and interaction are expressed and mediated in terms of categories of cultural difference, then these categories are likely to become increasingly institutionalized. In some situations, such as inter-group conflict or competition over scarce resources, such categories may be more fixed, whereas in others they may be very fluid; yet in all instances they will vary in different spatial and temporal contexts. Moreover, ethnic categories may persist, whilst the material culture involved in the conscious signification of these categories changes, and likewise the ethnic referent of particular styles of material culture may change, whilst the styles themselves remain the same. Thus, the relationship between material culture styles and the expression of ethnicity may be constantly shifting according to time and place. Material styles which in some social and historical contexts are actively taken up in the signification and negotiation of ethnicity may, in other contexts, only form part of the meaningful environment in which ethnicity is generated (e.g. see MacKenzie 1991: 14; Praetzellis *et al.* 1987; Wiessner 1985: 162).

This approach has a number of important implications for the analysis of ethnicity in archaeology. In contrast to the traditional culture concept, it has been suggested that whether or not spatially and temporally bounded distributions of material culture are the product of a similar enculturative milieu, or a common *habitus*, they *do not necessarily 'map' the extent and boundaries of self-conscious ethnic groups in the past.* Ethnicity must be distinguished from mere spatial continuity and discontinuity in that it refers to self-conscious identification with a particular group of people (Shennan 1989b: 19). Although it has been argued that ethnic consciousness is, in part, based on the recognition of commonalities of practice and historical experience, it is also a product of the conditions prevailing in particular social and historical contexts. Thus, the extent to which ethnicity is embedded in pre-existing cultural realities, or a shared *habitus*, is highly variable and contingent upon the cultural transformations engendered by processes of interaction, and the nature of the power relations between the interacting 'groups'.[8] From an archaeological point of view these processes may lead to a variety of different scenarios. In some instances, there may be a high degree of homology between the structuring principles of the *habitus* and the signification of ethnicity in both material and non-material culture (as in Hodder's (1982a) study of the Baringo District). In other instances, there may be a dislocation of such homologous relationships between the structuring principles of the *habitus* and the generation and expression of a common ethnic identity, resulting in the incorporation of a *bricolage* of different cultural traditions (cf. Rowlands 1982: 164). The former situation will lead to a high degree of homology between so-called isochrestic style and the signification of ethnicity, and the latter to a much smaller degree of commensurability between the two.

Nevertheless, it is important to recognize that, even in situations characterized by a high degree of homology between the *habitus* and ethnicity, archaeologists may not be able to find 'ethnic entities' reflected in material culture distributions (cf. Miller 1985: 202 in relation to caste). It is possible to question the very existence of bounded, homogeneous ethnic entities except at a conceptual level in the abstract cultural categories employed in people's discursive articulation of ethnicity. Such conceptual categories are based on the reification or objectification of transient cultural practices taking place at different times and in different contexts, and the 'group' only exists in the context of interpretation where it justifies and explains past practices and modes of interaction, and structures future ones (cf. Bourdieu 1977: 20–2; Thomas 1996: 75). In contrast, the praxis of ethnicity, and this is what is most likely to be represented in the archaeological record, results in a set of transient, but often repeated, realizations of ethnic difference in particular contexts. These realizations of ethnicity are both structured and structuring, involving, in many instances, the production and consumption of distinctive styles of material culture. However, they are a product of the intersection of the perceptual and practical dispositions of social agents and the interests and oppositions engendered in particular social contexts rather than abstract categories of difference.

Thus, configurations of ethnicity, and consequently the styles of material culture involved in the signification and structuring of ethnic relations, may vary in different social contexts and with relation to different forms and scales of social interaction. The multidimensional nature of ethnicity may result in a complex pattern of overlapping material-culture distributions relating to the repeated realization and transformation of ethnicity in different social contexts, rather than a discrete monolithic cultural entity. Patterns in the production and consumption of material culture involved in the communication of the 'same' ethnic identity may vary qualitatively as well as quantitatively in different contexts. Furthermore, items of material culture that are widely distributed and used in a variety of social and historical contexts may be curated and consumed in different ways and become implicated in the generation and signification of a variety of expressions of ethnicity (see Thomas 1996: 78–82, for a similar argument).

The relationship between ethnicity and material culture thus appears to be intangible and fleeting, and particularly problematic for archaeologists. Not surprisingly, familiarity with recent anthropological theories of ethnicity has led some archaeologists to adopt an extremely sceptical stance and to suggest that ethnicity is not an appropriate or accessible phenomenon for archaeological enquiry (Trigger 1977: 22–3; 1996: 277; see also Buchignani 1987). This argument generally hinges on the time-worn issue of whether 'archaeologists can verifiably recover any ideas, as opposed to behaviour, of the groups they study' (Trigger 1977: 23); archaeologists do not have *direct* access to people's ideas and perceptions.

The inaccessibility of individual motivations and understandings is usually dealt with in social archaeology through the analysis of the 'deep' processes and structures that underpinned individual actions (cf. Barrett 1994: 2–3). Variations on such an approach tend to be adopted by the few archaeologists who have defined ethnicity as an aspect of social process involved in the organization of human behaviour, and acknowledged that the relationship between material culture and a consciousness of ethnicity is not a fixed or intrinsic one (e.g. Haaland 1977; Hodder 1979a; Kimes *et al.* 1982). Research from this position is based on the argument that the systematization and rationalization of distinctive cultural styles in the process of the recognition, expression, and negotiation of ethnic identity in the past may have produced discontinuous, non-random distributions of material culture accessible to the archaeologist. In addition, it is often proposed that, as ethnicity is involved in the organization of behaviour, it is possible to predict that under certain past conditions, such as economic stress, ethnic boundaries are likely to have been invoked, and to have been more marked than in other situations (e.g. Hodder 1979a; Blackmore *et al.* 1979). Yet such research has tended to be undermined by the fact that ethnic symbolism is culture-specific and there is little evidence for any cross-cultural universals (although see Washburn 1989). In response, the use of independent evidence has been advocated in an attempt to establish the kinds of identity and modes of behaviour that underlie particular distributions of material culture (e.g. Haaland 1977; Hodder 1979a; Wiessner 1989: 58). For instance, Hodder (1979a: 151–2) has argued that the localization of pottery styles evident in the French neolithic, was related to the symbolism of within-group solidarity and dependence, on the basis of positive evidence for environmental stress. He further strengthened his argument by arguing that localization of pottery styles cannot be otherwise explained in terms of a decrease in the scale of social interaction because there is also independent evidence for increased interaction and exchange between 'groups' at this time.

Despite the potential of such approaches, they have a tendency to fall into the functionalist mode of reasoning which has been criticized throughout this book. For instance, in her critique of the interpretation of Early Nubian tool types as ethnic idioms, Haaland (1977) argues that variation in these artefacts can be explained in terms of adaptive, socio-economic factors, thus ruling out an ethnic interpretation.[9] The problem with such an approach is that, as indicated in Wiessner's study of San projectile points, 'functional' or 'adaptive' variation may become involved in the recognition and articulation of ethnic difference. Furthermore, ethnicity may be actively involved in the mediation of social relations, including economic and political relationships. Thus, a functional or economic interpretation of a particular non-random distribution does not preclude an ethnic interpretation, because ethnicity may have been embedded in variation in subsistence and economy. In such circumstances it becomes very difficult to clearly 'rule out' ethnicity on the basis of other explanations for variation in material culture.

The theoretical approach developed here suggests an alternative to both an outright rejection of ethnicity as a valid subject of archaeological enquiry, and a functionalist approach to ethnicity in which culture is reduced to a seemingly arbitrary and secondary role. The analysis of contextual realizations of ethnicity is by no means entirely beyond the possibilities of archaeological interpretation if, as argued here, there is a relationship between the historically constituted dispositions and orientations that inform people's understandings and practices, and the recognition and expression of ethnicity. As such, the way in which particular styles of material culture are meaningfully involved in the articulation of ethnicity may be arbitrary across cultures, *but it is not random within particular socio-historical contexts*. Ethnic symbolism is generated, to varying degrees, from the existing cultural practices and modes of differentiation characterizing various social domains, such as gender and status differentiation, or the organization of space within households (see Eriksen 1991).[10]

Thus, a broad understanding of past cultural contexts derived from a variety of sources and classes of data is an essential part of any analysis of ethnicity in archaeology. In particular, it is necessary to examine modes of social interaction and the distribution of material and symbolic power between groups of people, because, as argued above, ethnicity is a product of the intersection of similarities and differences in people's *habitus* and the conditions characterizing any given historical situation. An adequate knowledge of past social organization is also important, as ethnicity is both a transient construct of repeated acts of interaction and communication, and an aspect of social organization which becomes institutionalized to different degrees, and in different forms, in different societies. Moreover, an historical approach is crucial, given the role of historical process in the generation and expression of ethnicity (cf. Olsen and Kobylinski 1991). Within a diachronic contextual framework it may be possible to pick up the transformation of habitual material variation into active self-conscious ethnic symbolism, and vice versa, on the basis of changes in the nature and distribution of the styles involved (Wiessner 1989: 58); to reveal something about the contexts in which ethnicity is generated, reproduced and transformed, and to examine 'the mobilization of group as process' (Conkey 1991: 13).

The approach developed here requires a reconsideration not only of the interpretation of ethnicity, but also of the assumptions that underlie the explanation of variation in material culture more generally in archaeology. The recognition that material culture plays an active role in the generation and signification of ethnicity undermines the common assumption that degrees of similarity and difference in material culture provide a straightforward indicator of the intensity of interaction between past groups (see Hodder 1982a). Furthermore, research into the role of material culture in the generation and expression of ethnicity has revealed that it is not a passive reflection of socialization within bounded ethnic units. Rather, material culture is actively structured and structuring throughout its social life, and consequently its meaning is not fixed but constantly subject to reproduction and transformation. As Shanks and Tilley (1987: 97) have indicated, a particular material form may remain the same, but its meaning will alter in different contexts; it will be 'consumed in different ways, appropriated and incorporated into various symbolic structures according to historical tradition and social context'. On this basis it cannot be assumed *a priori* that similarity in material culture reflects the presence of a particular group of people in the past, an index of social interaction, or a shared normative framework.

More fundamentally, the theoretical approach adopted here questions the very existence of ethnic groups as coherent, monolithic entities within which enculturation can be relied upon to have produced a uniform spread of culture which undergoes gradual change through time. As indicated in Chapter 2, such assumptions, although frequently challenged at an interpretive level, still underlie a great deal of archaeological classification. Thus, at a very fundamental level, questioning these taken-for-granted notions about the inherent boundedness of groups or the inevitable transformations of social units through time should lead to a radical change not just in the way we conceptualize culture but in how we conceptualize description or representation.

(Conkey 1991: 12)

Chapter 7

Conclusions
Constructing identities in the past and the present

A COMPARATIVE THEORY OF ETHNICITY

The theory of ethnicity put forward in this book addresses the relationship between ethnicity and culture. It has been shown that the construction of ethnicity is grounded in the shared subliminal dispositions of social agents which shape, and are shaped by, objective commonalities of practice, i.e. the *habitus*. Such subliminal dispositions provide the basis for the recognition of commonalities of sentiment and interest, and the perception and communication of cultural affinities and differences. Consequently, the dichotomy between primordial and instrumental approaches to ethnicity can be transcended. The cultural practices and representations that become objectified as symbols of ethnicity are derived from, and resonate with, the habitual practices and experiences of the people concerned, as well as reflecting the instrumental contingencies of a particular situation.

We have also seen that ethnicity is not directly congruent with either the *habitus*, or the cultural practices and representations that both structure, and are structured by, the *habitus*. Crucially, ethnic identification involves an objectification of cultural practices (which otherwise constitute subliminal modes of behaviour) in the recognition and signification of difference in opposition to others. The particular form that such objectifications of cultural difference take is constituted by the intersection of the *habitus* with the prevailing social conditions in any given moment. Hence, the extent to which ethnicity is embedded in pre-existing cultural realities represented by a shared *habitus* is highly variable and contingent upon the cultural transformations engendered by the nature of interaction and the power relations between groups of people.

As a result of such contingency, the cultural practices and representations involved in the signification of the 'same' identity may vary qualitatively as well as quantitatively in different social contexts characterized by different social conditions. Thus, there is rarely a one-to-one relationship between representations of ethnicity and the entire range of cultural practices and social conditions associated with a particular ethnic group. On the contrary, the resulting pattern will be one of overlapping ethnic boundaries produced by context-specific representations of cultural difference, which are at once transient, but also subject to reproduction and transformation in the ongoing processes of social life.

This theoretical framework is comparative and generalizing to the extent that it succeeds in identifying the basic processes involved in the reproduction and transformation of ethnicity across diverse social and historical contexts. Hence, used as an analytical framework, such a theory provides arguments about *similarities*, but, importantly, through the consideration of specific social and historical contexts, it also allows an understanding of *differences* in the manifestation of ethnicity (Eriksen 1992: 17).[1] As a result, it preserves the possibility of exploring difference in the past, rather than merely reproducing it in the image of the present.

ROMANIZATION RECONSIDERED

The implications and potential of this approach to ethnicity for archaeological interpretation in general can be exemplified with relation to the case of Romanization. Chapter 2 showed that, despite a recent concern with the particular socio-historical contexts in which 'Roman-style' material culture and ways of life were adopted in the negotiation of political power, such research is still largely framed in terms of bounded socio-cultural entities. Furthermore, the assumption that peoples and their cultures constitute bounded monolithic entities was also shown to be part of an implicit methodological framework which underlies much archaeological classification and methods of dating.

The theoretical approach developed in this book suggests that there are fundamental problems with such methodological and theoretical frameworks. In the last chapter we saw that material culture both structures and is structured by the expression and negotiation of ethnicity, undermining the common archaeological assumption that style is a passive reflection of isolation and interaction. Moreover, the recognition and articulation of ethnicity varies in different social domains, and with relation to different forms and scales of social interaction. The production and consumption of particular styles of material culture involved in the expression of the 'same' ethnic identity vary qualitatively as well as quantitatively in different social contexts. Hence, in many instances, ethnicity, amongst other factors, may disrupt regular spatio-temporal stylistic patterning, resulting in an untidy and overlapping web of stylistic boundaries (in different classes of material culture and in different contexts) which may be discontinuous in space and time.

Thus, it can be argued that the adoption of an analytical framework based on bounded socio-cultural units, whether these be 'Roman' and 'native' (or the 'Roman Empire' and 'Belgic Gaul', in contrast to 'central Gaul') leads to the reification of such groups and obscures the various heterogeneous processes involved in the negotiation of power and identity (cf. Barrett 1989: 235–6). For instance, the ethnic significations of various aspects of material culture, whether of Roman-style or otherwise, are unlikely to have been fixed; rather they will have actively constituted, and been constituted by, the negotiation of group identity by different people in different social contexts (for similar arguments see Hingley 1996: 43–4; Meadows 1994: 137; Willis 1994: 145). Thus, in order to explore the adoption and consumption of Roman-style material culture in the expression and negotiation of ethnicity it is necessary to adopt a contextual approach, leading to the dissolution of the social and cultural group as the primary unit of analysis. The definition of past contexts of interaction in archaeology is problematic in itself, as it is rarely possible to obtain fine details of particular moments of social interaction and identification, such as those which can be examined in anthropological fieldwork. Furthermore, the relationships between archaeological contexts and past activities and social interaction are not in themselves static. Nevertheless, in the case of late Iron Age and Roman Britain, particular 'locales' can be defined, such as rural settlements, nucleated settlements, military forts, extra-mural settlements, burial sites or cemeteries, and at a finer level 'private' versus 'public', and 'ritual' versus 'secular' domains. It is only through such an approach that variation in the use and distribution of material culture, 'Roman' or otherwise, can be identified, and the ways in which this material was involved in the construction of diverse identities explored.

Alongside this reformulation of the broader analytical framework, a critical evaluation of the assumptions underlying the classification and dating of the material evidence is also necessary. In the existing literature typological sequences of artefacts tend to be based on the assumption that stylistic groupings represent past historical entities, such as cultures or peoples, and that such entities tend towards homogeneity within a given spatial and temporal domain. On the basis of this assumption, similar styles of the same class of artefact have been attributed to the same date, whereas dissimilar styles have been attributed to different dates. Artefacts dated on these principles have then been used in the interpretation of site histories.[2]

This use of relative typology for dating and interpreting site histories serves to obscure the very kind of variation that is of interest for the analysis of ethnic identities and indeed of past cultural processes in general. As Spratling (1972: 280) has pointed out, 'one of the things which archaeologists should be trying to find out, namely what is the significance of variation in artefact design, is assumed at the outset in adopting the typological method'. Relative typologies and methods of seriation are ultimately dependent upon the truism that the way in which people do things varies in space and time, and the assumption that people closer together in space and time are more likely to do things in a similar manner than those who are more distant from one another. The typological method has been shown to achieve a rough approximation in the dating of sites and site contexts when used in conjunction either with radiocarbon dating, or dating through a chain of association on the basis of historically recorded events (see Millett 1983).[3] However, the use of such typological sequences in the analysis of fine variation in assemblages raises fundamental problems for the analysis of past socio-cultural processes, as it pre-supposes a normative view of culture (see Chapter 2). The use of such a concept of culture at a basic level of data analysis produces what is essentially an illusion of bounded uniform cultural entities, and obscures the heterogeneous and open nature of cultural and ethnic systems. Indeed, it can even be argued that the uncritical application of the typological method in the dating and interpretation of material assemblages leads to an artificial manipulation of the spatio-temporal distribution of particular styles of artefact.

The analysis of stylistic variation in material remains needs to be based on a chronological framework established through a critical examination of stratigraphic and contextual associations, in conjunction with historical dating. Such an approach to dating serves to undermine the circularity of relative typological dating on the basis of a single class of artefacts (see Millett 1983; Spratling 1972). Moreover, it is only by such an approach to the dating of sites and archaeological contexts that the kind of 'untidy' distributions of particular styles of material culture potentially associated with the construction of ethnicity may be identified. This is not to deny that regular temporal or spatial stylistic patterns may exist in the archaeological record, or that, in some instances, such stylistic structures may relate to, although not necessarily 'map', ethnic groups. However, such variation must be the subject of analysis rather than an *a priori* assumption in the construction of temporal sequences which are taken to constitute a neutral, descriptive basis for the study of socio-cultural processes. The theory of ethnicity put forward in this book suggests the need for a fundamental re-evaluation of the assumptions that underlie the interpretation of typological sequences, and further consideration of the cultural processes underlying stylistic variation over time (see also Hodder 1993).

The contextual approach to dating and analysis being proposed here is somewhat compromised by the nature of many existing excavations, and the subsequent processing and publication of the data, illustrating the inadequacy of existing methods of classification, publication and interpretation. Assemblages of material culture are rarely analysed and published in a holistic manner with relation to the stratified contexts in which they were found within a site (although see Partridge 1981). Instead, pottery and small finds are published as isolated artefact classes, and analysed and interpreted using the typological approach. Furthermore, certain classes and types of artefact are often implicitly prioritized at various stages in the processing and publication of data.[4] Nevertheless, although a certain amount of the information that is required for a quantitative analysis of assemblage variation across different contexts is irrevocably lost, it is possible to retrieve some of this information through a reconstruction of site contexts.

For the purposes of a preliminary exploration, a number of sites in Essex and Hertfordshire have been considered, and grouped into the kinds of broad context outlined above. Four specific sites, Kelvedon (Rodwell 1988), Skeleton Green (Partridge 1981), Gorhambury (Neal *et al.* 1990) and King Harry Lane (Stead and Rigby 1989), which have been the subject of recent large-scale excavations, have been examined in greater detail. These sites were all occupied during the late Iron Age and the Roman period and represent a number of different kinds of past activity. At Kelvedon there is evidence for a late Iron Age farmstead and subsequently a Roman nucleated settlement, at Gorhambury a late Iron Age farmstead followed by a Roman villa, at Skeleton Green a late Iron Age and Roman nucleated settlement, and finally at King Harry Lane a late Iron Age and early Roman cemetery followed by extra-mural settlement on the outskirts of Verulamium.

The material remains from these sites reveal considerable variation between different contexts which is currently ignored due to the constraints of the Romanization model with its emphasis on homogeneity and gradual uniform change (see Chapter 2; Hingley 1989, 1996: 43). A contextual examination of the structural remains, brooches and pottery reveals a complex and heterogeneous set of stylistic patterns, which have been masked by the conventional concern with a broad, uniform cultural shift during the first century AD (see Jones 1994). For instance, changes in architectural style occur at different times and take different forms. At Skeleton Green there is a break in the occupation of the site around AD 40–50, and an associated shift in the layout and style of the buildings, all of the buildings in the later phase being of sill-beam construction, and more uniform in plan and layout than the earlier buildings. In contrast, the structural remains at Gorhambury reveal different changes in architectural style taking place at different times, with the construction of masonry villa-style buildings and a bath house at about AD 100. Moreover, in comparison with Skeleton Green, Gorhambury shows considerable continuity in the layout of the buildings and in the overall occupation of the site over the conquest period. Although there is some evidence for increasing symmetry in the layout of the buildings within the enclosure during the second century AD, it is significant that many later buildings are constructed on the site of earlier buildings indicating a degree of continuity in the use of the site. Some of the other sites in Essex and Hertfordshire, such as Boxmoor, Park Street and Lockleys, show similar changes to those evident at Gorhambury, but, in marked contrast, other late Iron Age rural agricultural settlements do not show an equivalent transition to masonry construction and villa-style architecture. Other recent research has also demonstrated that the architectural changes that have been associated with the Roman conquest of Britain are highly variable (e.g. see Branigan 1981; Hingley 1989, forthcoming). Indeed, changes in the construction and layout of buildings take place in different ways at different times, in late Iron Age and Roman Britain.

There are also significant variations in the pottery assemblages from the Essex and Hertfordshire sites at any particular point in time and through time. In particular, changes in the form and fabric of first- and second-century AD locally produced pottery occur at different rates and in different ways in different contexts. Furthermore, there is considerable variation in the degree of imported pottery on the sites considered, and in the production and consumption of locally produced 'copies' of such imported pottery (see Jones 1994: 148–9; Willis 1994: 146). As in the case of architectural style, recent detailed studies of variation in the pottery assemblages dating to the late Iron Age and early Roman periods are beginning to reveal considerable heterogeneity (Hill 1995: 75; Willis 1993).

Such variation exposes the limitations of the idea of Romanization as an inevitable and uniform process of acculturation, and associated categories of culture and identity, such as 'Roman' and 'native'. The only way to sustain such categories when faced with this variation is to suggest that it is a product of other factors, such as trade and exchange, rather than the Romanization of the past population. However, this argument artificially divorces ethnicity from activities such as production and trade, when, as we have seen in Chapters 4 and 5, ethnic identity is often enmeshed in such areas of social life. Moreover, much of the variation that has been revealed directly undermines the traditional Romanization model, as it is found in precisely those styles of architecture, pottery and so on, which have been associated with supposed Romanized tastes and identity.

The heterogeneity which is manifested in the material culture from the sites considered here, and others in different regions of Britain, can be more convincingly explained in the context of the theory of ethnicity developed in this book, than through the traditional concept of Romanization. Any simplistic correlation of Roman-style material culture with Roman identity must be rejected, and the existence of cultural and ethnic entities such as 'Roman' and 'native' questioned. However, changes in the material culture of south-east England must, in part at least, reflect the articulation of cultural identities in the past: the expansion of the Roman Empire no doubt resulted in the creation of new forms of social interaction and social relationships, through which the basis of power, status and identity was reproduced and transformed (see also Willis 1994: 143–4). New manifestations of ethnicity almost inevitably must have been created, subsuming pre-existing configurations of culture and identity in some, although possibly not all, social domains. And variation in material culture may well be connected with such processes.

To give a concrete example, changes in settlement structure and architectural style at Skeleton Green and Gorhambury, and the absence of equivalent changes on other settlements, are likely to have constituted new contexts in which ethnicity was reproduced and transformed, whether or not they represented conscious expressions of ethnicity. As an important part of the *habitus*, domestic architecture, such as bath houses and villas, may have been involved in the recognition and signification of a broad Roman identity with relation to particular people in some social domains (cf. Meadows 1994). However, variation in other aspects of material culture, such as particular pottery styles or in burial rites, may cross-cut such a broad scale of identification and be part of the reproduction and transformation of regional ethnicities. Thus, different configurations of ethnicity and other forms of identity may have been expressed in different aspects of material culture in different social contexts, as in the case of the ubiquitous string bags (*bilums*) used in Telefol society today (see Chapter 6).[5]

Similarly, a particular style of artefact or structure may have been enmeshed in multiple expressions of identity. For instance, what have until now been regarded as essentially Roman styles of material culture, such as Gallo-Belgic pottery and locally produced 'copies', may have been used by certain sections of the population in the articulation of a broad pan-geographical identity, but they may also have been subverted and appropriated in more localized expressions of ethnicity. The relationship between a particular style of object and the articulation of different kinds or scales of identity may well have led to different configurations of such styles within the overall assemblages of the contexts concerned. Thus, it is important to consider the distribution of particular styles with relation to the entire assemblage of material culture derived from any particular context, rather than in isolation.

Whilst so-called 'Roman' and 'native'-style material culture may have been involved in the generation and expression of identity, it cannot be assumed that the meaning of such material styles was necessarily fixed – i.e. that it always conferred 'Roman' or 'native' identity. The heterogeneous way in which 'Roman' styles appear to have been appropriated on sites such as those discussed here is likely to be a product of the fact that the relationship between culture and ethnicity was often in flux, being reproduced and transformed in processes of social action. What archaeologists have regarded as 'native' and 'Roman' culture may have been appropriated, subverted and transformed in varying configurations of ethnicity.

In current research the adoption of 'Roman'-style material culture is largely considered in terms of its use in the negotiation and legitimation of status within indigenous systems of competitive emulation, rather than as past processes of ethnic identification (see Chapter 2). It is obviously difficult to establish the relationship between particular styles of material culture and particular kinds of past identity; whether a particular stylistic pattern represented the articulation of ethnicity, status or gender. Indeed, the actual role of particular types of material culture in terms of identity cannot be subordinated to universal laws. Thus, it is necessary to try to establish the relationship between particular stylistic patterns and past processes of identification on the basis of independent contextual evidence. However, we have also seen that ethnicity is often related to other dimensions of identity, such as gender and status, because the generation of ethnic identity is partly based upon the recognition of some level of commonality in the underlying cultural dispositions that structure social life. Consequently, there is no reason why the cultural expression of status and ethnicity may not have been embedded in one another during any period, and the kind of stylistic variation discussed above may well have been involved in the articulation of both ethnic identity and social status.

The heterogeneous nature of the material remains from the sites considered here suggests that the adoption of so-called 'Roman'-style material culture by the local population of south-east England, arguably in the expression and negotiation of identity, varied *within* socio-cultural groups as well as *between* them. Analysis of such variation constitutes the logical extension of recent studies of Romanization where it is argued that 'Roman'-style material culture was appropriated differentially by the people of western Europe in the reproduction and transformation of pre-existing hierarchical social relations. However, in contrast to such recent approaches to Romanization, the theoretical approach developed in this book suggests that in order to examine such complex processes of ethnic identification it is necessary to abandon a spatial and temporal framework based upon bounded coherent groups, in order to examine the contextual generation and expression of what can be recognized as ethnicity. Moreover, archaeologists should not merely be concerned with the identification of styles that were involved in the conscious expression of ethnicity, but with the makeup of entire assemblages of material culture in different spatial and temporal contexts, which may provide information about the social relations and cultural practices underlying the generation of transient, but repeated, expressions of ethnicity.

ARCHAEOLOGY AND THE POLITICS OF IDENTITY

There is always a tension in archaeology between past and present; between the desire to know what happened in the past, and to understand past societies, and the historically contingent concepts and meanings through which knowledge of the past is produced in the present (see McGuire 1992: 215–18, 247). This tension is nowhere greater than in the interpretation of ethnicity. Popular historical representations provide a touchstone for ethnicity and nationalism and vice versa; the end product being 'an historically validated continuity of identity' (Hall 1994: 167). The representation of national or ethnic traditions frequently involves the projection of an unchanging, essentialist culture and identity deep into the past in an attempt to establish the national community as 'so "natural" as to require no other definition than self-assertion' (Hobsbawm 1983: 14). The critical role that the past plays in the assertion and legitimation of modern ethnic and national identities ensures that archaeological knowledge is frequently used in the construction of such essentialist ethnic histories. Moreover, archaeology's relationship to ethnicity and nationalism is likely to continue and even expand due to the increasing political salience of diverse ethnicities with the concomitant representation of alternative cultures and pasts. In this context, archaeological knowledge is not only appropriated at an abstract level within nationalist and ethnic ideologies, but at a more pragmatic level it is being used in the determination of land claims and the ownership of cultural heritage.

As a result of the ways in which archaeological knowledge is implicated in the construction of ethnic and national traditions there is often a problematic slippage between contemporary concepts of group identity and the identification of past ethnic groups in archaeology. Culture-history has been the bastion of nationalist (and colonialist) representations of the past (Ucko 1995b: 11), and it continues to be successfully used for such purposes in many countries today. Ethnic and national groups in direct competition over land frequently utilize the same basic culture-historical framework, as in the use of archaeology in support of competing German and Polish territorial claims (see Chapter 1). Furthermore, a culture-historical approach is often maintained even when those in power change, for instance from colonial regime to independent nation-state.

One of the main reasons for this close association between culture-history and nationalist claims lies in the similitude of the concepts of culture which are central to both. It has been argued in this book that the identification of past cultures in archaeology has been based on historically contingent assumptions about the nature of cultural diversity (see also Jones 1996: 64–6). Expectations of boundedness, homogeneity and continuity, which have been built into ideas concerning culture since the nineteenth century, are related to nationalism and the emergence of the nation-state (Handler 1988: 7–8; Spencer 1990: 283; Wolf 1982: 387). Nations are considered, in the words of Handler, to be 'individuated beings'; endowed with the reality of natural things, they are assumed to be bounded, continuous and precisely distinguishable from other analogous entities (Handler 1988: 6, 15). The idea of culture is intricately enmeshed with nationalist discourse; it is culture that distinguishes between nations and that constitutes the content of national identity (Díaz-Andreu 1996: 53–4). Moreover, 'culture symbolises individuated existence: the assertion of cultural particularity is another way of proclaiming the existence of a unique collectivity' (Handler 1988: 39).

There are striking similarities between the representation of culture in nationalist discourses and the conceptualization of 'culture' and 'society' in academic theory and practice, where they have been regarded as well-integrated, bounded, continuous entities, occupying exclusive spatio-temporal positions (see Chapter 3). The concept of an archaeological culture represents a particular variant of the culture concept. Bounded material-culture complexes are assumed to be the manifestation of particular past peoples, who shared a set of prescriptive, learned, norms of behaviour. Archaeological cultures came to be regarded as organic, individuated entities, the prehistorian's substitute for the individual agents that have traditionally made up the historian's repertoire. As in the case of contemporary claims concerning the relationship between nations and cultures, the relationship between archaeological cultures and past peoples is based on teleological reasoning in that culture is both representative of, and constitutive of, the nation or 'people' concerned. Thus,

> the almost a priori belief in the existence of the culture follows inevitably from the belief that a particular human group . . . exists. The existence of the group is in turn predicated on the existence of a particular culture.
> (Handler 1988: 39)

Furthermore, whilst the concept of an 'archaeological culture' was the product of cultural-historical archaeology, many of the assumptions concerning culture and identity which it embodies continue to underpin processual and, to some extent, post-processual archaeologies (see Chapters 2 and 6). Indeed, most archaeological research still takes place within an already established framework of bounded, socio-cultural entities, which are assumed to correlate with past social or ethnic entities, whether or not this correlation is explicitly acknowledged.

In both archaeology and anthropology the definition of ethnic or 'tribal' groups on the basis of the culture concept has traditionally invoked an inventory of cultural, linguistic and material traits. As Devalle (1992: 234) indicates, 'the resulting picture has been one of people with a "museum culture", uprooted from the *deep historical field*, devoid of dynamism and meaning' (see also Morris 1988). The consequences of such an approach are not restricted to academic studies and reports, but are also manifest in areas such as political policy, administrative practice, legislation and heritage management. For instance, the preservation of Quebec's *Patrimoine* provides a typical example of such an objectification of culture whereby a body of static cultural characteristics becomes reified as an object possessed by the nation (see Handler 1988: 140–58). Handler demonstrates that the definition, inventory, acquisition and enclosure of what is regarded as 'authentic' Quebecois culture is embedded in a nationalist worldview. Having classified

Quebecois culture through the production of inventories, the nation (or an official collective body representative of the nation) seeks to acquire cultural objects and historic buildings, and then to enclose them by protection through law, and/or containment in museums. As in the case of the *Place Royale*, an area of Quebec City where seventeenth- and eighteenth-century architecture has been preserved and reconstructed, such processes have the effect of appropriating places and objects, arresting ongoing social and cultural processes and alienating the people who have engaged with them for generations. *Place Royale*, Handler (ibid.: 151) laments, has been turned 'into a museum frozen in time', providing a static set of reference points, in the form of stylistic traits, for Quebec's architectural tradition.

Similar processes can be seen in the treatment of archaeological remains and their objectification as the static property of national and ethnic groups. For instance, in Zimbabwe a static, reconstructionist approach to the past has been adopted in some areas, such as at the site of Great Zimbabwe (see Ucko 1994). At this site, a particular architectural phase in the highly complex past of the monument is being preserved and reconstructed. Such an approach leads to the reification of the monument as part of the heritage of the nation, and the alienation and the denial of contemporary, heterogeneous, beliefs and practices associated with the monument (Ucko 1994: 271).[6] Many other examples abound, ranging from Stonehenge (see Bender 1993: 269–70) to Australian Aboriginal rock art (see Ucko 1983a: 33–6), where a static, reconstructionist approach has resulted in the reification of particular, supposedly 'authentic', moments in the history of particular sites or material remains, and their extrapolation from ongoing social life.

It seems that archaeology is often used to provide a fixed set of reference points where previously there was negotiation and dynamism (Ucko 1995b: 20). Culture-historical frameworks contribute to such an objectification of culture, enabling a reconstruction of the past in terms of the distribution of homogeneous cultures whose history unfolds in a coherent linear narrative; a narrative that is measured in terms of objectified events, such as contacts, migrations and conquests, with intervals of homogeneous, empty time in between them. Thus, attempts to identify past cultural entities in archaeology have been particularly suited to the construction of national traditions, which as Devalle (1992: 21) points out, 'are concerned with establishing a legitimating continuity with the past, not with understanding historical discontinuities and the evolution of social contradictions'.

What this analysis of the relationship between nationalist ideologies and archaeology suggests is that the identification of past ethnic groups has taken place within a closed system of thought, constraining the dialectical interaction between past and present. That is, there has been a high degree of correspondence between the concepts about culture and identity that form part of a powerful internationally recognized discourse of collective identity in the present, and those that inform our understanding of the past, moulding the description and classification of archaeological evidence as well as its interpretation. The unfortunate implication of such a situation is that archaeologists, and other social scientists, may have developed paradigms 'to explain that which they have themselves created' (Bond and Gilliam 1994b: 13).

Of course, this argument entails acceptance of the idea that the production of archaeological knowledge is contingent not only on the political interests and background of individual practitioners, but also on the socio-historical origins of the very paradigms that are used in the description and interpretation of the past. The theories, concepts and questions that we adopt influence the selection, description and interpretation of particular 'facts' (i.e., data are theory-laden), and these theories, concepts and questions are to some extent a product our own socio-historical context (Gathercole 1990: 1–4; Shanks and Tilley 1992 [1987]: 247–8; Shennan 1989b: 1–5). However, regardless of what some might suggest (e.g. Anthony 1995: 83), this observation does not require descent into a nihilistic relativism which states that evidence is entirely determined by theory, and therefore there can be no basis for arbitrating between competing theories. On the contrary, whilst evidence is not free from theoretical and interpretive influences, it also imposes constraints on the kinds of interpretations and theories that can be built up, and at times forces us to reconsider interpretive possibilities and even deep-seated assumptions about the nature of social phenomena (Fricker 1994; McGuire 1992: 248; Wylie 1989: 105–7; 1993: 25). In the case of theories of ethnicity, traditional assumptions about ethnic groups as culture-bearing entities have, in part, been challenged on the basis of ethnographic *evidence* that there is no one-to-one correlation between culture and ethnicity, and as a result there has been a significant shift in the understanding of group identity in anthropology. Yet there is not a straightforward relationship between the continual accumulation of evidence and the development of more adequate theoretical and interpretive frameworks as some have implied (e.g. Díaz-Andreu and Champion 1996a: 19; Trigger 1995: 275). Instead, as we saw in Chapters 3 and 5, the shift in our understanding of ethnicity during the 1960s and 1970s involved a complex interplay between new evidence concerning ethnicity and broader social and political changes, including processes of decolonization and the political mobilization of ethnic groups. Theories concerning particular social phenomena and evidence about such phenomena exist in dialectical relationship to one another; the two are always in flux and are never completely determined by one another.

In the case of archaeology, a high degree of closure between the reconstruction of past ethnic groups and specifically nationalist discourses of identity in the present has been perpetuated partly as a result of the empiricist framework that has dominated the discipline until recently.

The description and classification of data has been assumed to be in some way pre-theoretical and therefore concepts and assumptions concerning culture and identity have remained largely unquestioned by many in the archaeological community. Ironically, it is just such a denial of the theory-laden nature of archaeological evidence which allows a particular set of ideas to be imposed upon the past, and precludes debate about the concepts and interpretive frameworks which are used in the description and interpretation of archaeological evidence. Thus, the acknowledgement that there are no neutral, factual 'givens' does not weaken the validity of archaeological enquiry. Rather, such a realization constitutes a primary condition for strengthening our interpretations through debate concerning the socio-historical contexts in which particular concepts and theories were produced, and the extent to which they are supported by ethnographic and archaeological evidence.

One of the most important arguments in this book has been that traditional definitions of ethnic groups involve the extraction of cultural 'types' from ongoing social practice in different contexts and at different times, and their location on a single plane for the purposes of analysis. This process of 'methodological objectification' substitutes a coherent, seamless whole in place of the often patchy, discontinuous, overlapping and con-textualized praxis of ethnicity (cf. Bourdieu 1990: 84, on mapping and genealogy). Such an approach denies the existence of any active engage-ment with ethnic consciousness in social practice, and serves to obscure the processes involved in the reproduction and transformation of ethnic iden-tities. In effect, ethnicity becomes conceptualized as the historical legacy of a primordial, essentialist identity.

In contrast, the approach developed here focuses on people's conscious-ness of ethnicity and the reproduction and transformation of transient expressions of cultural difference in the context of particular historical structures which impinge on human experience and condition social action (see Devalle 1992: 18–19). Within such a framework, a static one-to-one correlation between particular monuments or items of material culture and a particular ethnic group is untenable, because the significance of such material culture is continuously reproduced and transformed in changing social and historical contexts by different people occupying varying posi-tions within society. Instead, monuments and assemblages of material culture have to be understood in the context of heterogeneous and often conflicting constructions of cultural identity. There is no single, unambig-uous ethnic association, because no such single social reality has ever existed (cf. Barrett 1994: 73, 171 and Thomas 1996: 62–3, on interpretation generally). Even within a self-identifying ethnic group, such an identity and the material forms that come to symbolize it are differently lived and articulated by different people. As Ohnuki-Tierney (1995: 245) concludes from an exploration of the role of rice as a metaphor in the representation of Japanese identities,

> The [Japanese] self has changed time and again at every historical encounter with the other. The Japanese identity in relation to the Chinese is certainly different from the Japanese identity when contrasted with Westerners. Rice thus has represented the different selves of the Japanese. Moreover the meaning of rice in other respects has dramatically altered through time.

If archaeologists persist in assuming that there is only one ethnic meaning or association to be 'extracted' from a particular monument or a particular style of material culture then they will never be able to understand the multiple strands of practice involved in the reproduction and maintenance of ethnicity in the past. Furthermore, within archaeology, the past will continue to be represented as a fixed and distant monolithic reality, either encouraging simplistic and exclusive associations with particular ethnic and national groups, or alienating present-day communities altogether (see Ucko 1994). The acceptance that the past is never dead, and that archaeological remains are likely to be involved in the ongoing construction of potentially diverse and fluid identities, will facilitate the development of dynamic and engaged relationships between archaeology and living communities. In practice, in the context of heritage management and museum presentations, this kind of approach may highlight contestation and negotiation between different identity groups in the present (see Ucko 1994: 249, 255). However, it is as well that archaeology as a discipline is actively engaged with these processes, rather than unwittingly providing an inevitable source of information for the construction and legitimation of contemporary identities (Mackie 1994: 186).

As with any research into the relationship between culture, identity and the past, the political implications of the theoretical approach laid out in this book are manifold. The approach serves to undermine the monolithic and essentialist accounts of the past that have so often been used to support the political goals of certain nationalists. Nationalist groups, such as those in the Caucasus, who attempt to use archaeological reconstructions to make exclusive and often expansionist claims to territory do so on the assumption that archaeological remains provide evidence for a single, homogeneous ethnos at some point in the past to which they can trace their origins. Thus, contrary to what some archaeologists have argued (e.g. Kohl and Tsetskhladze 1995: 169), the suggestion that multiple and diverse identities and associated histories can co-exist does not mean that 'anything goes', because it has the potential to invalidate exclusive nationalist claims within their own terms of reference. If particular archaeological sites and other material remains have been involved in the construction of multiple, fluid and diverse identities in different contexts then the historical justification for any nationalist claim to exclusive rights over a given territory is negated (see Barth 1994: 30; Bernbeck and Pollock 1996: 141 for similar arguments). Although nationalists may disregard the caveats voiced by archaeologists in their representations of the past (Dietler 1994: 597–8), we can still strive to change primordial and essentialist understandings of ethnicity through what we write, and in our presentation of the past in museums and at archaeological sites.

At the same time, however, it has to be acknowledged that recent work emphasizing the discontinuity, transformation and fluidity of identities has the potential to undermine the basis of minority ethnic claims for land and cultural self-determination (see Mascia-Lees et al. 1989: 24–5).[7] 'Western' academic theory has often provided a conceptual framework for modes of domination, as in the case of the tribal and ethnic classifications used by colonial regimes. Yet more recently, such concepts of culture and identity have also become embedded in national and international law concerning rights to land and cultural heritage (see Mackie 1994: 189–90). For instance, in Australia the success of Aboriginal land claims in the Northern Territory was, and to some extent still is, dependent upon establishing continuity in the use of a particular area of land, and the ownership of cultural heritage can also centre around issues of continuity and identity (Murray 1993: 109–12; Ucko 1983a, 1983b). Thus, it can be argued that recent theories lead to the deconstruction of monolithic and essentialist concepts of culture and identity just as these concepts are becoming a means of political mobilization and the basis for minority claims to land (and, in some instances, cultural property). However, this situation is more complex, because in land-rights cases indigenous populations often have to choose between an outright rejection of a culture-historical representation of their past, or a renegotiation of the ways in which their particular culture-historical trajectory has been interpreted by others (Ucko 1995b: 10). The former option would in most instances require a change in the legal definition of indigenous land ownership, whereas in many cases the latter option will not satisfy a court of law which gives precedence to historical documents and archaeological facts, as in the case of the Mashpee land claim (see Campisi 1991; Clifford 1988: 277–346). Moreover, such cases almost always involve the critical scrutiny of a minority group's identity and history by the dominant society rather than vice versa, ultimately perpetuating the relations of power between groups (see Chapman et al. 1989: 17–18). Minority groups are subjected to a relentless discourse which requires them, in one form or another, to possess a traditional, homogeneous culture and identity stretching in a continuous and unilinear fashion into the past. Many will inevitably fail such a requirement given that this discourse incorporates rigid expectations about the continuous and bounded nature of culture and identity, and fails to accommodate the social and historical processes involved in the construction of ethnicity (see Campisi 1991; Jacobs 1988).

One of the most common responses in the human sciences to such morally and politically laden situations is to argue that a distinction must be maintained between 'scientific' and 'moral' models (e.g. D'Andrade 1995). For instance, it has been suggested that archaeologists should keep ethically based and factually based critiques of a particular nationalistic or racist interpretation distinct from one another (e.g. Anthony 1995: 88), and consequently, in

> good conscience, one can admit a potentially damaging archaeological reconstruction as the most plausible and objective interpretation of the evidence, and then condemn the state policy that bends and distorts that reconstruction for its own questionable political purposes.
>
> (Kohl and Fawcett 1995a: 9)

However, such a neat distinction between archaeological knowledge and political or moral judgement is impossible to maintain. On the one hand, the very methodological and interpretive frameworks used by archaeologists are based on assumptions about culture and identity that are already inscribed with particular political positions within a given historical context. On the other hand, 'political beliefs are unintelligible in isolation from relevant empirical claims about real states of affairs in the world' (Fricker 1994: 99) and theories that have been derived from such evidence. Political and moral engagement must be grounded in an understanding of the way the world works (Barth 1994: 31; Friedman 1995: 422), just as critical perspectives on the political and moral assumptions underlying the production of knowledge must be maintained.

One of the motives for writing this book has been to provide a reassessment of the relationship between material-culture objects and ethnicity which should provide a stronger basis for political and moral engagement in particular concrete situations. It has been suggested that ethnicity involves the subjective and situational construction of identity in opposition to particular 'others' in the context of social interaction (see also Megaw and Megaw 1996). However, ethnic identities are not free-floating constructions whereby individuals and groups choose to identify themselves and others in any way that suits them. Instead, particular ethnic identities, and the representations of the past associated with them, are produced in specific socio-historical contexts characterized by relations of power. For instance, in Australia the power of the state has been used to bring Australian Aboriginal identity into varying degrees of conformity with its own constructions of their identity (see Jacobs 1988, Morris 1988, Beckett 1988a), with the result that 'Compared with, and at times comparing themselves with, the "real Aborigines", Aboriginal people are caught between the attribution of unchanging essences (with the implication of an inability to change) and the reproach of inauthenticity' (Beckett 1988a:

194). Furthermore, anthropological and archaeological research has been actively involved in the construction of an image of traditional Aboriginal culture which informs perceptions of the 'real Aborigines'.

Archaeologists need to address the ways in which specific representations of the past have contributed to the construction of particular identities, and how the domination of certain representations over others is embedded in power relations both within and between groups (e.g. see Dietler 1994). At the same time, it cannot be assumed that archaeologists (or other social scientists) hold some privileged perspective outside of society and its ideological constructs. Consequently, we also need to examine, and take responsibility for, the way in which the modes of classification and interpretation used in archaeology have been involved in the constitution of power relations between groups, providing the basis for practical relationships and strategies, as well as the attribution of political legitimacy in the contemporary world. As Bernbeck and Pollock (1996: 141) argue, archaeologists can work to 'expose the interests of all parties concerned (including archaeologists) in defining and shaping identities in the way that they do'. However, such a project should not be a purely critical one; it should also involve dialogue and negotiation between archaeologists and other groups in order to build common areas of understanding and to strengthen our interpretations of the past. Ultimately, it is such modes of interaction and analysis that will provide the way towards a fuller understanding of the construction of identities in the past and the present.

Notes

1 INTRODUCTION

1 'New archaeology' refers to the initial period of processual archaeology connected in particular with Lewis Binford (1962, 1965, 1972), although others include Clarke (1978 [1968]), Renfrew (1972), and contributors to Binford and Binford (1968). For critical perspectives of the new archaeology see, amongst others, Hodder (1982b, 1986) and Shanks and Tilley (1992 [1987]).

2 A considerable body of literature focusing on archaeology as a contemporary practice and its social and political contexts has been produced in the 1980s and 1990s; see, amongst others, Kristiansen (1992), Shanks and Tilley (1992 [1987]), Trigger (1984, 1989), Ucko (1983b; 1987), and contributions to Gathercole and Lowenthal (1990), Pinsky and Wylie (1989), Stone and MacKenzie (1990), Ucko (1995a).

3 For general discussions of the role of archaeology in the construction of communities of shared memory see, amongst others, Jones and Graves-Brown (1996), Kristiansen (1992), Layton (1989b), Rowlands (1994), Trigger (1984), Ucko (1995b). For detailed case studies, see Arnold (1990), Dietler (1994); Fleury-Ilett (1996), Kohl (1993b), Murray (1993), Olsen (1986), and contributions to Bond and Gilliam (1994a), Díaz-Andreu and Champion (1996b); Graves-Brown et al. (1996), Kohl and Fawcett (1995b), Layton (1989a), Ucko (1995a).

4 Even in recent books, the complexity of the relationship between archaeological enquiry and the construction of diverse forms of identity has been ignored or acknowledged only in passing. This tendency can facilitate the detailed analysis of particular areas such as the influence of the structures of the nation-state on the institutionalization of archaeology (e.g. see contributions to Díaz-Andreu and Champion 1996b). But it can also lead to an oversimplification of the issues and a preoccupation with the ills of extreme nationalism at the expense of a consideration of other forms of group identity, such as minority and indigenous identities (e.g. see contributions to Kohl and Fawcett 1995b).

5 It should be noted that the works of many so-called 'post-processual' archaeologists do not fit Kohl's (1993a) caricature. Post-processualists are often explicitly concerned with the political realities which Kohl refers to while at the same time engaging in abstract theoretical debates. Indeed, in later work, Kohl himself refers to some of the work of these post-processual archaeologists in a discussion of studies concerning the relationship between archaeological enquiry and its socio-political contexts (Kohl and Fawcett 1995a: 15).

2 THE ARCHAEOLOGICAL IDENTIFICATION OF PEOPLES AND CULTURES

1 This approach to ethnicity is drawn from social anthropology and in particular the work of the Norwegian anthropologist, Fredrik Barth, which will be discussed in detail in Chapter 4. Not surprisingly, Scandinavian archaeologists (e.g. Haaland 1977; Odner 1985; Olsen 1985; Olsen and Kobylinski 1991) have been particularly influential in applying such an approach to the analysis of ethnicity in archaeology (although see also Hodder 1979a, 1982a; Larick 1986; Renfrew 1987, 1996; Shennan 1989b).

2 Late Iron Age/late pre-Roman Iron Age is used here to refer to the period between the early first century BC and the Roman occupation of much of Britain during the mid/later first century AD. It has traditionally been associated with the presence of wheel-made pottery in south-eastern England and metal-work with continental late La Tène affinities (Haselgrove 1982: 87)

3 Prehistoric and Roman archaeology have been characterized by differences in theory, methodology and research strategy, which have restricted communication and comparison (as indicated by Burnham and Johnson 1979; Cunliffe 1988; Hingley 1989), and undermined the holistic study of past social and cultural processes transcending the actual Roman conquest (Barrett and Fitzpatrick 1989: 9; Haselgrove 1989: 2).

4 Although this framework was based on the classification of cultural entities, they have often been taken to represent chronological divisions (Champion 1984 [1979]: 348), despite Hawkes's (1959) insistence to the contrary.

5 See also, amongst others, Blackmore et al. (1979), Millet (1990a, ch. 2) and Rodwell (1976).

6 For later discussions of the problem of the Belgae, see Hachmann (1976), Hawkes (1968) and Rodwell (1976).

7 In particular, see the Social Science Research Council *Memorandum for the Study of Acculturation* (Redfield et al. 1936) for a programmatic statement on the methodology of acculturation studies, which illustrates the essentially descriptive and trait-oriented nature of this field of research. However, there have been exceptions such as Beals (1953), Dohrenwend and Smith (1962) and Thurnwald (1932).

3 TAXONOMIES OF DIFFERENCE: THE CLASSIFICATION OF PEOPLES IN THE HUMAN SCIENCES

1 The term 'race' was used prior to the nineteenth century, as were 'nation', 'tribe' and 'ethnic', although the latter was probably used specifically in relation to 'heathen' or 'gentile' peoples (see Hodgen 1964: 214; Stocking 1988: 4). Nevertheless, prior to the early nineteenth century all these terms were largely used to refer to groups whose perceived distinctiveness was explained in terms of shared lineal descent.

2 Within this Christian chronological tradition, understandings of human diversity were determined by the problem of how to explain present diversity in the light of the unity of blood and culture which resulted from the Creation (Hodgen 1964: 222–3). Explanations of human diversity generally conformed to the Mosaic account of human history, focusing on the sequence of major demographic events outlined in Genesis, coupled with theories of isolation and

environmental determinism. For more detailed analyses of such national gen-
ealogies see Hodgen (1964) and Poliakov (1974 [1971]).

3 The anatomical and physiological criteria used in the classification of racial
types became increasingly elaborate during the nineteenth century, leading to
skeletal and cranial classificatory systems, such as the 'cephalic index', and
systems of classification based on physiological characteristics, such as the
'index of nigrescence' (see Biddiss 1979: 15–16; Gossett 1975 [1963]: 69–83;
Stocking 1987: 65–6).

4 For further discussion, see Banton (1977), Biddiss (1979), Odum (1967) and
Stocking (1987).

5 Evolutionary ideas were formulated in the mid-nineteenth century, for instance
in the work of Henry Maine and Herbert Spencer, who were both concerned to
develop general rules about the evolution of human societies and employed a
form of the comparative method (see Bowler 1989: 37).

6 In this respect, socio-cultural evolutionism represented a re-emergence of the
universalizing framework which had been central to Enlightenment philosophy
in the late eighteenth century. Indeed, the socio-cultural evolutionist view of
culture as a universal process of development was closely related to the
concept of 'civilization' which can be traced back to the eighteenth century
(Stocking 1987: 11; Williams 1983 [1976]: 88–9).

7 The development of a unilinear evolutionary framework did not result in a
complete disjunction with the particularist historical approach of the earlier
ethnological tradition. A complex interplay between these two approaches
is evident in the work of both John Lubbock and E. B. Tylor, two
prominent socio-cultural evolutionists (for further discussion see Stocking
1987: 152–62).

8 See Stocking's (1968: 58–9) discussion of the work of Paul Topinard who
became increasingly sceptical about the idea of 'pure' homogeneous races, but
still could not reject the notion of an ideal racial 'type', which he argued had
been submerged by the present level of racial mixing.

9 The concept of 'tribal society' has a long history in the development of
anthropological ideas about 'primitive culture' as opposed to 'modern culture'.
This is discussed in detail by Kuper (1988).

10 There was, however, considerable disagreement about the definition of tribal
society and numerous more technical definitions were devised. For instance, in
the work of some British anthropologists the tribe was often taken to be 'the
widest territorially defined, politically independent unit' (Lewis 1968: 149), or,
as in Evans-Pritchard's (1940: 5) analysis of the Nuer, a group who come
together in warfare against outsiders. For further discussion of the variety of
different ways in which the concept of tribe has been used in anthropology, see
Fried (1975) and Gulliver (1969).

11 For further discussion, see Barkan (1988), Kuper (1975a), Leiris (1975 [1956]),
Lévi-Strauss (1975 [1955]), Stepan (1982), Wade (1992). The way in which the
issue of racial determinism dominated debate is epitomized in a series of
UNESCO statements on race issued in the 1950s and 1960s which are
reprinted in Kuper (1975b).

12 For a bibliographic guide to some of the vast literature on ethnicity, see Bentley
(1981).

13 It is worth noting that the ethnic concept has the potential to encompass the
same problems and ideological connotations of marginal and backward status
as the term tribe (Gulliver 1969: 8; Williams 1989: 439). For instance, in a
number of post-colonial African nation-states, both tribalism and ethnicity

have been perceived as destructive influences running counter to modernization, development and the emergence of a cohesive national identity (see Vail
1988: 2).

14 For further discussion of these assumptions concerning assimilation, see Bash
(1979: 78–9), Glazer and Moynihan (1975: 6–7), Roosens (1989: 9), Scott
(1990: 147–8) and Vail (1989: 1–2).

4 ETHNICITY: THE CONCEPTUAL AND THEORETICAL TERRAIN

1 The term 'emic' refers to the perspective of a society produced by the
explication of indigenous models of reality, whereas 'etic' refers to a view
generated by the description and analysis of social systems on the basis of
the observer's perception and models.

2 For further discussion of the notion of 'objectivity' in the social sciences, see
Harding (1986), Maquet (1964), Rosaldo (1993 [1989]).

3 As Mitchell (1974: 25) points out, Moerman's (1965) initial analysis conflates
the anthropological category of Lue ethnicity and Lue perceptions of their
identity. The local construct of the category 'Lue' is reified as an analytical
category, rather than taking perceptions of Lueness as a starting point for the
analysis of the role of ethnic categorizations in the mediation of social relations
and social practices. However, in a subsequent paper, Moerman (1968) does
pay explicit attention to the relationship between anthropological categories
and those of the people who are the focus of the enquiry.

4 Moreover, Narroll's (1968) emphasis on characteristics such as statehood,
leadership and ability to participate in warfare is reminiscent of western ideas
about the cultural and political body embedded in discourses of nationalism.

5 Others who adopted a subjectivist approach to the definition of ethnic groups
prior to Barth (1969a) include Moerman (1965, 1968), Shibutani and Kwan
(1965: 40) and Wallerstein (1960: 131). However, Dorman's (1980: 26) claim
that such a definition represented the consensus of opinion prior to Barth's
work can hardly be substantiated.

6 For other definitions that take political mobilization to be a fundamental aspect
of ethnicity see Bell (1975) and Ross (1980).

7 For a critique of the idea that kinship groups are based on selection in favour
of individuals who are genetically related to one another see Sahlins (1977).

8 This point is made by Hechter (1986) with reference to Jewish assimilation and
separatist behaviour and there are many other glaring examples of the fluid
nature of individual and group identity (e.g. see Barth 1969a; Haaland 1969).

9 Kellas (1991) does pay considerable attention to the historical development of
the idea of the nation. However, his acceptance of socio-biological theories
inevitably results in a reification and naturalization of the ethnic unit which, he
suggests, underlies modern national formations.

10 There are numerous studies that focus on the historical emergence of the
concepts of ethnic group and nation. In particular they illustrate that the nation
and nationalism are relatively recent phenomena emerging in the late eighteenth century in Europe. For further discussion see Chapter 5, and Gellner
(1983), Handler (1988), Hobsbawm (1990), Sharp and McAllister (1993),
Spencer (1990).

11 This perspective has also been called the 'circumstantialist' perspective (Glazer
and Moynihan 1975: 19; Scott 1990: 147), in that ethnicity is seen as very much

context-dependent, and the 'rational' perspective (Burgess 1978: 266), in that many such explanations are based, to a greater or lesser extent, on the idea of rational self-interested human action inherent in the notion, 'economic man'.

12 For further discussion of the polarization of the primordial–instrumental debate, and the problems it raises, see Bentley (1987), Burgess (1978), de Vos and Romanucci-Ross (1982a [1975]), Douglass (1988), Keyes (1981), McKay (1982), Meadwell (1989), Scott (1990), Smith (1984) and van den Berghe (1978).

5 MULTIDIMENSIONAL ETHNICITY: TOWARDS A CONTEXTUAL ANALYTICAL FRAMEWORK

1 The concept of the *habitus* was explicitly formulated by Bourdieu with the aim of breaking with 'objectivist' intellectual traditions such as structuralism, and 'subjectivist' intellectual traditions such as phenomenology (Bourdieu and Wacquant 1992: 120–1; see also Bourdieu 1990).

2 Bourdieu uses the notion of 'objective social conditions' to refer to the conditions of existence encountered by any particular actor or group of actors, such as the distribution of economic and cultural resources, which characterize a particular social domain. However, he has been criticized in this respect for failing to operationalize his own argument that 'objective conditions' are only objective in as much as they are perceived as such and confirmed through the practices of social actors (e.g. Jenkins 1982: 272; but see Bourdieu 1990).

3 An emphasis on changing, and sometimes novel, contexts of social practice is more prominent in the work of Sahlins (1981) than Bourdieu (1977). Bourdieu tends to place greater importance on the emergence of a consciousness of alternative ways of viewing the world, and the possibility of critique and direct political action which such a consciousness enables (see Ortner 1984: 155–6).

4 If this argument is extended to national identity it directly contradicts Foster's (1991: 240) claim that national culture and identity are *doxic* in nature. However, Foster's own discussion of the contested and negotiated nature of many national identities and culture suggests that his use of Bourdieu's concept of *doxa* is inappropriate.

5 Although ethnic categories become part of the *habitus*, the dispositions and symbols which are objectified in the reproduction and transformation of ethnic consciousness at any particular time will belong to the sphere of opinion, not to that of *doxa*.

6 In order to distinguish qualitative variation in the kind of cultural difference involved in the signification of identity Eriksen employs Wittgenstein's concept of language games, which has some similarities with the concept of the *habitus* in that both involve the production and reproduction of shared meaning structures. He uses the concept of language games as an analytical tool to differentiate between the kinds of cultural difference involved in the communication of ethnicity in different contexts, and produces a classification of three basic kinds of context characterized by: (1) one language game (or shared meaning system); (2) overlapping language games; and (3) incommensurable language games.

7 The phrase 'the pure products go crazy' is derived from Clifford (1988: 1) who uses it to characterize the fragmentation and hybridization of culture and identity which he claims to be characteristic of modern life.

8 This point has been made by a number of people in analyses of ethnicity in the contemporary world, for example, Benthall and Knight (1993: 2), Danforth

(1993: 7), Fardon (1987: 177), Foster (1991: 239), Handler and Linnekin (1984: 288), Ranger (1983: 252–9), Spencer (1990: 288) and Williams (1989: 423–6).

9 The ways in which 'anthropological' and 'native' concepts of ethnicity intersect with one another have been discussed by Clifford (1988: 232–3), Fardon (1987: 182), Foster (1991: 236), Handler (1986: 2; 1988: 6–9), Spencer (1990: 288) and Turner (1991: 300–3).

6 ETHNICITY AND MATERIAL CULTURE: TOWARDS A THEORETICAL BASIS FOR THE INTERPRETATION OF ETHNICITY IN ARCHAEOLOGY

1 Although Hodder (1982a) and Wiessner (1983, 1984) do not explicitly define ethnic groups as self-defining systems, their ethno-archaeological studies suggest that they are also concerned with the role of material culture in expressing the boundaries of self-conscious groups.

2 Shanks and Tilley (1992 [1987]: 120) question the notion of 'society' as a bounded, monolithic unit, and Rowlands (1982: 163–4) argues that such a view of society is the product of nineteenth-century nationalism. Others such as Binford (1972) and Renfrew (1977: 95–6; 1995: 157) have questioned the existence of widespread, homogeneous ethnic groups or 'peoples' in early prehistory from an evolutionary perspective. However, they are concerned to define such groups as characteristic of particular stages of evolutionary development, and they do not question the existence of such groups in certain historical periods or in the present.

3 The distinction between function and style which is characteristic of new archaeology can also be identified in culture-historical archaeology. For instance, such a distinction underlies Childe's (1956: 37–8) assertion that arbitrary stylistic and behavioural details were the most useful attributes for the purpose of defining cultures, and were of limited importance with relation to the analysis of culture as a functioning system. Nevertheless, these ideas were not central to culture-historical epistemology.

4 Some of the main proponents of such an approach, which was particularly prevalent in the analysis of palaeolithic art, as well as the signalling of ethnic and social identities generally, include Conkey (1978), Gamble (1982), Jochim (1983), Wiessner (1983) and Wobst (1977).

5 For a more general discussion of the problems associated with this dichotomy, see Hodder (1982b; 1986), Shanks and Tilley (1987, 1992 [1987]) and Tilley (1982).

6 A number of archaeologists and anthropologists have argued that the relationship between material culture and human agency is a recursive one, for example, see Barrett (1994: 36–7), Conkey (1991: 13), Hodder (1982a, 1982b: 10), MacKenzie (1991), Miller (1985) and Shanks and Tilley (1987, 1992 [1987]).

7 In a review of anthropological and archaeological approaches to ethnicity Olsen and Kobylinski (1991: 23; my emphasis) have also argued that the question of the relationship between culture and ethnicity represents one of the key issues for archaeologists: 'Before we start sticking ethnic labels to archaeologically distinguishable complexes of finds we have to understand the phenomenon of ethnicity itself *and particularly we have to develop a theory of relationships between ethnic consciousness and material culture.*'

8 It is this critical break between ethnicity and the *habitus* (see also Chapter 5) which distinguishes the theory adopted here from that of Burley *et al.* (1992)

who argue for a much more direct relationship between ethnicity and the *habitus* following on from Bentley's (1987) work.

9 A similar argument is adopted by the Binfords (1966; see also Binford 1973) in their criticism of ethnic interpretations of Mousterian lithic assemblages, and by Peacock (1969, 1979) in his critique of ethnic interpretations of regional pottery styles in Iron Age Britain.

10 Olsen and Kobylinski (1991: 16) have adopted a similar position, arguing that archaeologists should attempt to investigate the ways in which basic value orientations and their behavioural effects underlie the maintenance of ethnic boundaries. However, they do not provide a theoretical framework for exploring the relationship between such 'basic value orientations' and overt ethnic symbolism.

7 CONCLUSIONS: CONSTRUCTING IDENTITIES IN THE PAST AND THE PRESENT

1 See Webster (1996: 8) for a similar argument in defence of comparative research based on the concept of colonialism in opposition to the recent trend towards historical particularism.

2 To give an example, even the absence of Rosette brooches from phase III assemblages at Skeleton Green has been interpreted as indicating a change in the character of the settlement (possibly a decline in occupation) between AD 25–40, because such brooches are present at the nearby sites of King Harry Lane and Camulodunum (Mackreth 1981: 139). Such an interpretation makes direct use of the 'homogeneity principle', assuming that Skeleten Green *should* follow the same patterns of development, as represented by artefact types, as adjacent sites. No allowance is made for the possibility that such brooches may themselves have been actively used in the articulation of identities, therefore indicating heterogeneity within a given region.

3 Without historical or radiocarbon 'controls' at various points the typological method can lead to serious distortions largely produced by a priori assumptions about the nature and direction of change (see Renfrew 1972).

4 It is accepted that a certain selectivity is an inevitable product of the pragmatic limitations placed upon excavation; limitations of finance, storage, time and so on. However, problems are raised by the reasoning employed in the prioritization of certain classes of artefact, the methods used, and the implicit nature of the assumptions involved.

5 Similar arguments have been made in the recent literature emphasizing what Woolf (1992) has referred to as the 'unity and diversity of Romanization' (e.g. Haselgrove 1990; Hingley 1996; Meadows 1994; Willis 1994), and in recent publications on the late pre-Roman Iron Age (e.g. Hill 1995).

6 Furthermore, problems have arisen concerning attempts to set up 'culture houses', which are intended to form the locus of a local, dynamic ongoing involvement with the past, and active centres for community cultural activities in the present. Despite these initial aims, such cultural centres have been subject to control and intervention by national authorities which effectively alienates the local populations. For instance, at Murewa Culture House the traditional spirit mediums, *n'angas*, have been banned, because they are seen as a source of tension by the national authorities. Ironically, such tensions, and their resolution, could have been seen as an indication of the success of the culture house as a focus of ongoing social life in the community (Ucko 1994: 255).

7 Somewhat surprisingly, minority and 'Fourth' World indigenous groups are often ignored in books concerning nationalism and archaeology (e.g. see contributions to Kohl and Fawcett 1995), despite the fact that their claims to land and heritage are increasingly expressed within a nationalist framework (see Mackie 1994).

References

Anthony, D.W. (1995) 'Nazi and eco-feminist prehistories: ideology and empiricism in Indo-European archaeology.' In P.L. Kohl and C. Fawcett (eds) *Nationalism, Politics and the Practice of Archaeology*, pp. 82–96. London: Routledge.

Appadurai, A. (1986) 'Introduction: commodities and the politics of value.' In A. Appadurai (ed.) *The Social Life of Things*, pp. 3–63. Cambridge: Cambridge University Press.

Arens, W. (1976) 'Changing patterns of ethnic identity and prestige in East Africa.' In W. Arens (ed.) *A Century of Change in Eastern Africa*, pp. 65–75. Paris: Mouton.

Arnold, B. (1990) 'The past as propaganda: totalitarian archaeology in Nazi Germany.' *Antiquity* 64: 464–78.

Asad, T. (1980) 'Comment: indigenous anthropology in non-Western countries.' *Current Anthropology* 21(5): 661–2.

Babington, W.D. (1895) *Fallacies of Race Theories as Applied to National Characteristics*. London: Longmans, Green & Co.

Banton, M.(1977) *The Idea of Race*. London: Tavistock.

Barkan, E. (1988) 'Mobilizing scientists against Nazi racism.' In G.W. Stocking (ed.) *Bones, Bodies, Behaviour: essays in biological anthropology*, pp. 180–205. Madison: University of Wisconsin Press.

Barrett, J.C. (1989) 'Afterword: render unto Caesar. . . .' In J.C. Barrett and A.P. Fitzpatrick (eds) *Barbarians and Romans in North-West Europe*, pp. 235–41. Oxford: British Archaeological Research.

Barrett, J.C. (1994) *Fragments from Antiquity: an archaeology of social life in Britain, 2900–1200 BC*. Oxford: Blackwell.

Barrett, J.C. and A.P. Fitzpatrick (1989) 'Introduction.' In J.C. Barrett and A.P. Fitzpatrick (eds) *Barbarians and Romans in North-West Europe*, pp. 9–13. Oxford: British Archaeological Research.

Barth, F. (1969a) 'Introduction.' In F. Barth (ed.) *Ethnic Groups and Boundaries*, pp. 9–38. Boston: Little Brown.

Barth, F. (1969b) 'Pathan identity and its maintenance.' In F. Barth (ed.) *Ethnic Groups and Boundaries*, pp. 117–34. Boston: Little Brown.

Barth, F. (ed.) (1969c) *Ethnic Groups and Boundaries*. Boston: Little Brown.

Barth, F. (1989) 'The analysis of complex societies.' *Ethnos* 54(3–4): 120–42.

Barth, F. (1994) 'Enduring and emerging issues in the analysis of ethnicity.' In H. Vermeulen and C. Govers (eds) *The Anthropology of Ethnicity: beyond 'Ethnic Groups and Boundaries'*, pp. 11–32. Amsterdam: Het Spinhuis.

Bash, H.H. (1979) *Sociology, Race and Ethnicity: a critique of American ideological intrusions upon sociological theory*. London: Gordon & Breach.

Beals, R.A. (1932) 'Aboriginal survivals in Mayo culture.' *American Anthropologist* 34: 28–39.

Beals, R.A. (1953) 'Acculturation.' In S. Tax (ed.) *Anthropology Today: selections*, pp. 375–95. Chicago: University of Chicago Press.

Beckett, J.R. (1988a) 'The past in the present; the present in the past: constructing a national Aboriginality.' In J.R. Beckett (ed.) *Past and Present: the construction of Aboriginality*, pp. 191–217. Canberra: Aboriginal Studies Press.

Beckett, J.R. (ed.) (1988b) *Past and Present: the construction of Aboriginality.* Canberra: Aboriginal Studies Press.

Beddoe, J.W. (1885) *The Races of Britain.* Bristol: J.W. Arrowsmith.

Bell, D. (1975) 'Ethnicity and social change.' In N. Glazer and D.P. Moynihan (eds) *Ethnicity: theory and experience*, pp. 141–74. Cambridge, Mass.: Harvard University Press.

Bender, B. (1993) 'Stonehenge – contested landscapes (medieval to present-day).' In B. Bender (ed.) *Landscape, Politics and Perspectives*, pp. 245–79. Oxford: Berg.

Benthall, J. and J. Knight (1993) 'Ethnic alleys and avenues.' *Anthropology Today* 9(5): 1–2.

Bentley, G.C. (1981) *Ethnicity and Nationality: a bibliographic guide.* Seattle: University of Washington Press.

Bentley, G.C. (1983) 'Theoretical perspectives on ethnicity and nationality.' *Sage Race Relations Abstracts* 8(2): 1–53 and 8(3): 1–26.

Bentley, G.C. (1987) 'Ethnicity and practice.' *Comparative Studies in Society and History* 29: 24–55.

Bentley, G.C. (1991) 'Response to Yelvington.' *Comparative Studies in Society and History* 33: 169–75.

Bernbeck, R. and S. Pollock (1996) 'Ayodha, archaeology, and identity.' *Current Anthropology* 37: 138–42.

Biddiss, M.D. (1979) 'Introduction.' In M.D. Biddiss (ed.) *Images of Race*, pp. 11–35. New York: Holmes & Meier.

Binford, L.R. (1962) 'Archaeology as anthropology.' *American Antiquity* 28: 217–25.

Binford, L.R. (1965) 'Archaeological systematics and the study of culture process.' *American Antiquity* 31: 203–10.

Binford, L.R. (1972) *An Archaeological Perspective.* New York: Seminar Press.

Binford, L.R. (1973) 'Interassemblage variability – the mousterian and the "functional" argument.' In C. Renfrew (ed.) *The Explanation of Culture Change: models in prehistory*, pp. 227–54. London: Duckworth.

Binford, L.R. (1983) *In Pursuit of the Past.* London: Thames & Hudson.

Binford, L.R. and S.R. Binford (1966) 'A preliminary analysis of functional variability in the mousterian levallois facies.' *American Anthropologist* 68(2): 238–95.

Binford, S.R. and L.R. Binford (1968) *New Perspectives in Archaeology.* New York: Aldine.

Birchall, A. (1965) 'The Aylesford-Swarling culture: the problem of the Belgae reconsidered.' *Proceedings of the Prehistoric Society* 31: 241–367.

Blackmore, C., M. Braithwaite and I. Hodder (1979) 'Social and cultural patterning in the late Iron Age in southern Britain.' In B.C. Burnham and J. Kingsbury (eds) *Space, Hierarchy and Society: interdisciplinary studies in social area analysis*, pp. 93–112. Oxford: British Archaeological Research.

Blagg, T. and M. Millett (1990) 'Introduction.' In T. Blagg and M. Millett (eds) *The Early Roman Empire in the West*, pp. 1–4. Oxford: Oxbow Books.

Blu, K.I. (1980) *The Lumbee Problem: the making of an American Indian people.* Cambridge: Cambridge University Press.

Boas, F. (1974 [1887]) 'The occurrence of similar inventions in areas widely apart' and 'Museums of ethnology and their classification' *Science* 9: 485–6, 587–9. (Reprinted as 'The principles of ethnological science.' In G.W. Stocking (ed.) (1974) *The Shaping of American Anthropology 1883–1911. A Franz Boas reader*, pp. 61–7. New York: Basic Books.)

Boas, F. (1974 [1905]) 'The mythologies of the Indians.' *International Quarterly* 12: 157–73. (Reprinted in G.W. Stocking (ed.) (1974) *The Shaping of American Anthropology 1883–1911. A Franz Boas reader*, pp. 135–48. New York: Basic Books.)

Bond, G.C. and A. Gilliam (eds) (1994a) *Social Construction of the Past: representation as power*. London: Routledge.

Bond, G.C. and A. Gilliam (1994b) 'Introduction.' In G.C. Bond and A. Gilliam (eds) *Social Construction of the Past: representation as power*, pp. 1–22. London: Routledge.

Bordes, F. (1968) *The Old Stone Age*. London: Weidenfeld & Nicolson.

Bordes, F. (1973) 'On the chronology and contemporeneity of different palaeolithic cultures in France.' In C. Renfrew (ed.) *The Explanation of Culture Change: models in prehistory*, pp. 217–26. London: Duckworth.

Bordes, F. and D. de Sonneville-Bordes (1970) 'The significance of variability in palaeolithic assemblages.' *World Archaeology* 2: 61–73.

Bosanquet, R.C. (1921) 'Discussion of "The Dorian invasion reviewed in the light of new evidence".' *Antiquaries Journal* 1: 219.

Bourdieu, P. (1977) *Outline of a Theory of Practice*. Cambridge: Cambridge University Press.

Bourdieu, P. (1990) *The Logic of Practice*. Cambridge: Polity Press.

Bourdieu, P. and L.J.D. Wacquant (1992) *An Invitation to Reflexive Sociology*. Cambridge: Polity Press.

Bowler, P.J. (1989) *The Invention of Progress: the Victorians and the past*. Oxford: Basil Blackwell.

Bowman, G. (1993) 'Nationalizing the sacred: shrines and shifting identities in the Isreali-Occupied Territories.' *Man* 28(3): 431–60.

Bradley, R. (1984) *The Social Foundations of Prehistoric Britain: themes and variations in the archaeology of power*. London: Longman.

Branigan, K. (1981) 'Celtic farm to Roman villa.' In D. Miles (ed.) *The Romano-British countryside*, pp. 81–96. Oxford: British Archaeological Research.

Bromley, Y. (1980) 'The object and subject matter of ethnography.' In E. Gellner (ed.) *Soviet and Western Anthropology*, pp. 151–60. London: Duckworth.

Brook, S. (1983) 'Principles of identification and classification of peoples.' In A. Kochin (ed.) *Ethnic Geography and Cartography*, pp. 39–64. Moscow: Social Sciences Today.

Brumfiel, E. (1994) 'Ethnic groups and political development in ancient Mexico.' In E.M. Brumfiel and J.W. Fox (eds) *Factional Competition and Political Development in the New World*, pp. 89–102. Cambridge: Cambridge University Press.

Buchignani, N. (1982) *Anthropological Approaches to the Study of Ethnicity: occasional papers in ethnic and immigration studies*. Toronto: The Multicultural Society of Ontario.

Buchignani, N. (1987) 'Ethnic phenomena and contemporary social theory: their implications for archaeology.' In R. Auger, M.F. Glass, S. MacEachern and P.H. McCartney (eds) *Ethnicity and Culture: proceedings of the eighteenth annual conference of the Archaeological Association of the University of Calgary*, pp. 15–24. Calgary: University of Calgary.

Burgess, M.E. (1978) 'The resurgence of ethnicity: myth or reality?' *Ethnic and Racial Studies* 1(3): 265–85.

Burkitt, M.C. (1933) *The Old Stone Age: a study of palaeolithic times.* Cambridge: Cambridge University Press.

Burley, D.V., G.A. Horsfall and J.D. Brandon (1992) *Structural Considerations of Métis Ethnicity. An archaeological, architectural and historical study.* Vermillion: The University of South Dakota Press.

Burnham, B.C. and H.B. Johnson (1979) 'Introduction.' In B.C. Burnham and H.B. Johnson (eds) *Invasion and Response: the case of Roman Britain*, pp. 1–8. Oxford: British Archaeological Research.

Butcher, S. (1990) 'The brooches.' In D.S. Neal, A. Wardle and J. Hunn *Excavation of the Iron Age, Roman and Medieval Settlement at Gorhambury, St Albans*, pp. 115–20. London: Historic Buildings and Monuments Commission for England.

Cairnes, J.E. (1865) 'The negro suffrage.' *Macmillan's Magazine* 12: 334–43. (Reprinted in M.D. Biddiss (ed.) (1979) *Images of Race*, pp. 73–88. New York: Holmes & Meier.)

Calhoun, C. (1993) 'Habitus, field and capital: the question of historical specificity.' In C. Calhoun, E. LiPuma and M. Postone (eds) *Bourdieu: critical perspectives*, pp. 61–88. Cambridge: Polity Press.

Calhoun, C. (1994) 'Social theory and the politics of identity.' In C. Calhoun (ed.) *Social Theory and the Politics of Identity*, pp. 9–36. Oxford: Blackwell.

Campisi, J. (1991) *The Mashpee Indians: tribe on trial.* New York: Syracuse University Press.

Casson, S. (1921) 'The Dorian invasion reviewed in the light of some new evidence.' *The Antiquaries Journal* 1: 198–221.

Champion, T.C. (1975) 'Britain in the European Iron Age.' *Archaeologia Atlantica* 1: 127–45.

Champion, T.C. (1984 [1979]) 'The Iron Age (c. 600 B.C.–A.D. 200).' In J.V.S. Megaw and D.A. Simpson (eds) *Introduction to British Prehistory*, pp. 344–432. Leicester: Leicester University Press.

Chapman, M., M. McDonald and E. Tonkin (1989) 'Introduction.' In E. Tonkin, M. McDonald and M. Chapman (eds) *History and Ethnicity*, pp. 1–33. London: Routledge.

Childe, V.G. (1927 [1925]) *The Dawn of European Civilization.* London: Kegan Paul, Trubner & Co.

Childe, V.G. (1929) *The Danube in Prehistory.* Oxford: Clarendon.

Childe, V.G. (1933a) 'Is prehistory practical?' *Antiquity* 7: 410–18.

Childe, V.G. (1933b) 'Races, peoples and cultures in prehistoric Europe.' *History* 18: 193–203.

Childe, V.G. (1935) 'Changing methods and aims in prehistory, Presidential Address for 1935.' *Proceedings of the Prehistoric Society* 1: 1–15.

Childe, V.G. (1940) *Prehistoric Communities of the British Isles.* London: W. & R. Chambers.

Childe, V.G. (1956) *Piecing Together the Past: the interpretation of archaeological data.* London: Routledge & Kegan Paul.

Childe, V.G. (1969 [1950]) *Prehistoric Migrations in Europe.* Oosterhout: Anthropological Publications.

Clarke, D. (1978 [1968]) *Analytical Archaeology.* London: Methuen.

Clifford, J. (1988) *The Predicament of Culture.* Cambridge, Mass.: Harvard University Press.

Clifford, J. (1992) 'Travelling cultures.' In L. Grossberg, C. Nelson and P.A. Treichler (eds) *Cultural Studies*, pp. 96–116. London: Routledge.

Cohen, A. (1969) *Custom and Politics in Urban Africa.* London: Routledge & Kegan Paul.

Cohen, A. (1974) 'Introduction: the lesson of ethnicity.' In A. Cohen (ed.) *Urban Ethnicity*, pp. ix–xxiv. London: Tavistock Publications.

Cohen, R. (1978) 'Ethnicity: problem and focus in anthropology.' *Annual Review of Anthropology* 7: 379–403.

Colson, E. (1968) 'Contemporary tribes and the development of nationalism.' In J. Helm (ed.) *Essays on the Problem of Tribe*, pp. 201–6. Seattle: University of Washington Press.

Comaroff, J. and J. Comaroff (1992) *Ethnography and the Historical Imagination*. Boulder: Westview Press.

Conkey, M.W. (1978) 'Style and information in cultural evolution: toward a predictive model for the Palaeolithic.' In C.L. Redman, J. Berman, E. Curtin, W. Langhorne, N. Versaggi and J. Wanser (eds) *Social Archaeology: beyond dating and subsistence*, pp. 61–85. New York: Academic Press.

Conkey, M.W. (1991) 'Experimenting with style in archaeology: some historical and theoretical issues.' In M.W. Conkey and C.A. Hastorf (eds) *The Uses of Style in Archaeology*, pp. 5–17. Cambridge: Cambridge University Press.

Connor, W. (1978) 'A nation is a nation, is a state, is an ethnic group, is a. . . .' *Ethnic and Racial Studies* 1: 377–400.

Crawford, O.G.S. (1921) *Man and his Past*. London: Oxford University Press.

Crawford, O.G.S. and R.E.M. Wheeler (1921) 'The Llynfawr and other hoards of the Bronze Age.' *Archaeologia* 71: 133–40.

Cunliffe, B.W. (1978 [1974]) *The Iron Age Communities of the British Isles*. London: Routledge & Kegan Paul.

Cunliffe, B.W. (1988) *Greeks, Romans and Barbarians: spheres of interaction*. London: B.T. Batsford.

Cunliffe, B.W. (1990) *Iron Age Communities in Britain*. London: Routledge

D'Andrade, R. (1995) 'Moral models in anthropology.' *Current Anthropology* 36(3): 399–408.

Danforth, L. (1993) 'Competing claims to Macedonian identity: the Macedonian question and the breakup of Yugoslavia.' *Anthropology Today* 9(4): 3–10.

Daniel, G. (1978 [1950]) *One Hundred and Fifty Years of Archaeology*. London: Duckworth.

Davis, W. (1990) 'Style and history in art history.' In M.W. Conkey and C.A. Hastorf (eds) *The Uses of Style in Archaeology*, pp. 18–31. Cambridge: Cambridge University Press.

Deshen, S. (1974) 'Political ethnicity and cultural ethnicity in Israel during the 1960s.' In A. Cohen (ed.) *Urban Ethnicity*, pp. 281–309. London: Tavistock Publications.

Despres, L.A. (1975) 'Ethnicity and resource competition in Gutanese society.' In L.A. Despres (ed.) *Ethnicity and Resource Competition in Plural Societies*, pp. 87–117. Paris: Mouton Publishers.

Devalle, S.B.C. (1992) *Discourses of Ethnicity: culture and protest in Jharkhand*. London: Sage Publications.

de Vos, G. (1982 [1975]) 'Ethnic pluralism: conflict and accommodation.' In G. de Vos and L. Romanucci-Ross (eds) *Ethnic Identity: cultural continuities and change*, pp. 5–41. Chicago: University of Chicago Press.

de Vos, G. and L. Romanucci-Ross (1982a [1975]) 'Introduction 1982.' In G. de Vos and L. Romanucci-Ross (eds) *Ethnic Identity: cultural continuities and change*, pp. ix–xvii. Chicago: University of Chicago Press.

de Vos, G. and L. Romanucci-Ross (1982b [1975]) 'Ethnicity: vessel of meaning and emblem of contrast.' In G. de Vos and L. Romanucci-Ross (eds) *Ethnic*

Identity: cultural continuities and change, pp. 363–91. Chicago: University of Chicago Press.

Díaz-Andreu, M. (1996) 'Constructing identities through culture: the past in the forging of Europe.' In P. Graves-Brown, S. Jones and C. Gamble (eds) *Cultural Identity and Archaeology: the construction of European communities*, pp. 48–61. London: Routledge.

Díaz-Andreu, M. and T.C. Champion (1996a) 'Nationalism and archaeology in Europe: an introduction.' In M. Díaz-Andreu and T.C. Champion (eds) *Nationalism and Archaeology in Europe*, pp. 1–23. London: University College London Press.

Díaz-Andreu, M. and T.C. Champion (eds) (1996b) *Nationalism and Archaeology in Europe*. London: University College London Press.

Diaz-Polanco, H. (1987) '*Neoindigenismo* and the ethnic question in Central America.' *Latin American Perspectives* 14: 87–99.

Dietler, M. (1994) '"Our ancestors the Gauls": archaeology, ethnic nationalism, and the manipulation of Celtic identity in modern Europe.' *American Anthropologist* 96: 584–605.

DiMaggio, P. (1979) 'Review essay: on Pierre Bourdieu.' *American Journal of Sociology* 84(6): 1460–74.

Dohrenwend, B.P. and R.J. Smith (1962) 'Toward a theory of acculturation.' *Southwestern Journal of Anthropology* 18: 30–9.

Dolukhanov, P. (1994) *Environment and Ethnicity in the Ancient Middle East*. Aldershot: Avebury Press.

Doornbos, M. (1972) 'Some conceptual problems concerning ethnicity in integration analysis.' *Civilisations* 22: 263–83.

Doran, J. and F. Hodson (1975) *Mathematics and Computers in Archaeology*. Edinburgh: Edinburgh University Press.

Dorman, J.H. (1980) 'Ethnic groups and ethnicity: some theoretical considerations.' *Journal of Ethnic Studies* 7(4): 23–36.

Douglass, W.A. (1988) 'A critique of recent trends in the analysis of ethnonationalism.' *Ethnic and Racial Studies* 11(2): 192–206.

Eidheim, H. (1969) 'When ethnic identity is a social stigma.' In F. Barth (ed.) *Ethnic Groups and Boundaries*, pp. 39–57. Boston: Little Brown.

Elliot Smith, G. (1928) *In the Beginning: the origin of civilization*. London: Gerald Howe.

Elston, R.G., D. Hardesty and C. Zeier (1982) *Archaeological Investigations on the Hopkins Land Exchange, Volume II: an analysis of archaeological and historical data collected from selected sites*. Nevada City: Tahoe National Forest.

Erich, R.W. (1954) *Relative Chronologies in Old World Archaeology*. Chicago: University of Chicago Press.

Erich, R.W. (1965) *Chronologies in Old World Archaeology*. Chicago: University of Chicago Press.

Eriksen, T.H. (1991) 'The cultural contexts of ethnic differences.' *Man* 26: 127–44.

Eriksen, T.H. (1992) *Us and Them in Modern Societies: ethnicity and nationalism in Mauritius, Trinidad and beyond*. London: Scandinavian University Press.

Eriksen, T.H. (1993a) *Ethnicity and Nationalism. Anthropological perspectives*. London: Pluto Press.

Eriksen, T.H. (1993b) 'Formal and informal nationalism.' *Ethnic and Racial Studies* 16(1): 1–25.

Etter, P.A. (1980) 'The west coast Chinese and opium smoking.' In R. Schuyler (ed.) *Archaeological Perspectives on Ethnicity in America*, pp. 97–101. Farmingdale: Baywood Press.

Evans-Pritchard, E.E. (1940) *The Nuer*. Oxford: Clarendon Press.

Fabian, J. (1983) *Time and the Other: how anthropology makes its object*. New York: Colombia University Press.

Fardon, R. (1987) '"African ethnogenesis": limits to the comparability of ethnic phenomena.' In L. Holy (ed.) *Comparative Anthropology*, pp. 168–87. Oxford: Basil Blackwell.

Farrar, F.W. (1867) 'Aptitudes of races.' *Transactions of the Ethnological Society* 5: 115–26. (Reprinted in M.D. Biddiss (ed.) (1979) *Images of Race*, pp. 141–56. New York: Holmes & Meier.)

Flannery, K. (ed.) (1976) *The Early Mesoamerican Village*. London: Academic Press.

Fleure, H.J. (1922) *The Peoples of Europe*. Oxford: Oxford University Press.

Fleury-Ilett, B. (1996) 'The identity of France: archetypes in Iron Age studies.' In P. Graves-Brown, S. Jones and C. Gamble (eds) *Cultural Identity and Archaeology: the construction of European communities*, pp. 196–208. London: Routledge.

Ford, J. (1954a) 'The type concept revisited.' *American Anthropologist* 56: 42–54.

Ford, J. (1954b) 'Comment on A.C Spaulding, "Statistical techniques for the study of artefact types".' *American Antiquity* 19: 390–1.

Fortes, M. (1969 [1945]) *The Dynamics of Clanship Among the Tallensi: being the first part of an analysis of the social structure of a trans-Volta tribe*. London: Oxford University Press.

Fortes, M. (1980) 'Introduction.' In E. Gellner (ed.) *Soviet and Western Anthropology*, pp. xix–xxv. London: Duckworth.

Foster, R.J. (1991) 'Making national cultures in the global ecumene.' *Annual Review of Anthropology* 20: 235–60.

Fox, C. (1923) *The Archaeology of the Cambridge Region*. Cambridge: Cambridge University Press.

Francis, E.K. (1947) 'The nature of the ethnic group.' *American Journal of Sociology* 52: 393–400.

Freeman, T.A. (1877) 'Race and language.' *Contemporary Review* 29: 711–41. (Reprinted in M.D. Biddiss (ed.) (1979) *Images of Race*, pp. 205–36. New York: Holmes & Meier.)

Fricker, M. (1994) 'Knowledge as construct: theorizing the role of gender in knowledge.' In K. Lennon and M. Whitford (eds) *Knowing the Difference: feminist perspectives in epistemology*, pp. 95–109. London: Routledge.

Fried, M.H. (1968) 'On the concepts of "tribe" and "tribal society".' In J. Helm (ed.) *Essays on the Problem of Tribe*, pp. 3–20. Seattle: University of Washington Press.

Fried, M.H. (1975) *The Notion of Tribe*. Menlo Park: Cummings.

Friedman, J. (1989) 'Culture, identity and world process.' In D. Miller, M. Rowlands and C. Tilley (eds) *Domination and Resistance*, pp. 246–60. London: Unwin Hyman; Routledge, pbk 1995.

Friedman, J. (1992) 'The past in the future: history and the politics of identity.' *American Anthropologist* 94(4): 837–59.

Friedman, J. (1995) 'Comment on "Objectivity and militancy: a debate".' *Current Anthropology* 56(3): 421–3.

Galton, F. (1865) 'Hereditary talent and character.' *Macmillan's Magazine* 12: 318–27. (Reprinted in M.D. Biddiss (ed.) (1979) *Images of Race*, pp. 55–71. New York: Holmes & Meier.)

Gamble, C.S. (1982) 'Interaction and alliance in palaeolithic society.' *Man* 17: 92–107.

Garlake, P. (1982) 'Prehistory and ideology in Zimbabwe.' *Africa* 52: 1–19.

Gathercole, P. (1990) 'Introduction.' In P. Gathercole and D. Lowenthal (eds) *The Politics of the Past*, pp. 1–4. London: Unwin & Hyman; Routledge, pbk 1994.

Gathercole, P. and D. Lowenthal (eds) (1990) *The Politics of the Past*. London: Unwin & Hyman; Routledge, pbk 1994.

Geertz, C. (1963) 'The integrative revolution: primordial sentiments and civil politics in the new states.' In C. Geertz (ed.) *Old Societies and New States*, pp. 105–57. New York: The Free Press.

Gellner, E. (1983) *Nations and Nationalism*. Oxford: Basil Blackwell.

Giddens, A. (1984) *The Constitution of Society: outline of the theory of structuration*. Cambridge: Polity Press.

Gifford, J.C. (1960) 'The type variety method of ceramic classification as an indicator of cultural phenomena.' *American Antiquity* 25: 341–7.

Gilroy, P. (1992) 'Cultural studies and ethnic absolutism.' In L. Grossberg, C. Nelson and P.A. Treichler (eds) *Cultural Studies*, pp. 187–98. London: Routledge.

Glazer, N. and D.P. Moynihan (1975) 'Introduction.' In N. Glazer and D.P. Moynihan (eds) *Ethnicity: theory and experience*, pp. 1–26. Cambridge, Mass.: Harvard University Press.

Glock, A. (1994) 'Archaeology as cultural survival: the future of the Palestinian past.' *Journal of Palestine Studies* 23: 70–84.

Gluckman, M. (1971) 'Tribalism, ruralism and urbanism in south and central Africa.' In V. Turner (ed.) *Colonialism in Africa 1870–1960*, pp. 127–66. Cambridge: Cambridge University Press.

Going, C.J. (1992) 'Economic "long waves" in the Roman period? A reconnaissance of the Romano-British ceramic evidence.' *Oxford Archaeological Journal* 11: 93–118.

Gordon, M.M. (1964) *The Assimilation of American Life*. Oxford: Oxford University Press.

Gordon, M.M. (1975) 'Toward a general theory of racial and ethnic group relations.' In N. Glazer and D.P. Moynihan (eds) *Ethnicity: theory and experience*, pp. 84–110. Cambridge, Mass.: Harvard University Press.

Gossett, T.F. (1975 [1963]) *Race: the history of an idea in America*. Dallas: Southern Methodist University Press.

Graves-Brown, P., S. Jones and C. Gamble (eds) (1996) *Cultural Identity and Archaeology: the construction of European communities*. London: Routledge.

Greenwell, W. (1905) 'Early Iron Age burials in Yorkshire.' *Archaeologia* 60: 251–324.

Gruber, J. (1973) 'Forerunners.' In R. Narroll and F. Narroll (eds) *Main Currents in Cultural Anthropology*, pp. 25–56. New York: Meredith Corporation.

Gruber, J. (1986) 'Archaeology, history and culture.' In D.J. Meltzer, D.D. Fowler and J.A. Sabloff (eds) *American Archaeology Past and Future: a celebration of the Society for American Archaeology*, pp. 163–86. Washington: Smithsonian Press.

Gulliver, P.H. (1969) 'Introduction.' In P.H. Gulliver (ed.) *Tradition and Transition in East Africa: studies of the tribal element in the modern era*, pp. 5–38. London: Routledge & Kegan Paul.

Haaland, G. (1969) 'Economic determinants in ethnic processes.' In F. Barth (ed.) *Ethnic Groups and Boundaries*, pp. 58–73. London: George Allen & Unwin.

Haaland, R. (1977) 'Archaeological classification and ethnic groups: a case study from Sudanese Nubia.' *Norwegian Archaeological Review* 10: 1–31.

Hachmann, R. (1976) 'The problem of the Belgae seen from the continent.' *Bulletin of the Institute of Archaeology* 13: 117–37.

Hall, H.R. (1921) 'Discussion of "The Dorian invasion reviewed in the light of new evidence".' *Antiquaries Journal* 1: 219–20.

Hall, M. (1994) 'Lifting the veil of popular history: archaeology and politics in urban Cape Town.' In G.C. Bond and A. Gilliam (eds) *Social Construction of the Past: representation as power*, pp. 167–82. London: Routledge.

Hall, M. (1995) 'Great Zimbabwe and the lost city.' In P.J. Ucko (ed.) *Theory in Archaeology: a world perspective*, pp. 28–45. London: Routledge.

Haller, J.S. Jr (1971) 'Race and the concept of progress in nineteenth century American ethnology.' *American Anthropologist* 73: 710–24.

Handelman, D. (1977) 'The organization of ethnicity.' *Ethnic Groups* 1: 187–200.

Handler, R. (1986) 'Authenticity.' *Anthropology Today* 2(1): 2–4.

Handler, R. (1988) *Nationalism and the Politics of Culture in Quebec*. Madison: University of Wisconsin Press.

Handler, R. and J. Linnekin (1984) 'Tradition, genuine or spurious.' *Journal of American Folklore* 97: 273–90.

Hannerz, U. (1974) 'Ethnicity and opportunity in urban America.' In A. Cohen (ed.) *Urban Ethnicity*, pp. 37–76. London: Tavistock Publications.

Hannerz, U. (1989) 'Culture between center and periphery: toward a macroanthropology.' *Ethnos* 54: 200–16.

Harding, S. (1986) 'Introduction: is there a feminist methodology?' In S. Harding (ed.) *Feminism and Methodology: issues in the social sciences*, pp. 1–14. Milton Keynes: Open University Press.

Härke, H. (1991) 'All quiet on the Western Front? Paradigms, methods and approaches in West German archaeology.' In I. Hodder (ed.) *Archaeological Theory in Europe*, pp. 187–222. London: Routledge.

Härke, H. (1995) '"The Hun is a methodical chap." Reflections on the German tradition of pre- and proto-history.' In P.J. Ucko (ed.) *Theory in Archaeology: a world perspective*, pp. 46–60. London: Routledge.

Harries, P. (1989) 'Exclusion, classification and internal colonialism: the emergence of ethnicity among the Tsonga-speakers of South Africa.' In L. Vail (ed.) *The Creation of Tribalism in Southern Africa*, pp. 82–117. London: James Curry.

Harris, M. (1968) *The Rise of Anthropological Theory*. London: Routledge & Kegan Paul.

Haselgrove, C. (1982) 'Wealth, prestige and power: the dynamics of late Iron Age political centralisation in south-east England.' In S.J. Shennan and C. Renfrew (eds) *Ranking, Resource and Exchange*, pp. 79–88. Cambridge: Cambridge University Press.

Haselgrove, C. (1984) 'Romanization before the conquest: Gaulish precedents and British consequences.' In T.F.C. Blagg and A.C. King (eds) *Military and Civilian in Roman Britain*, pp. 1–64. Oxford: British Archaeological Research.

Haselgrove, C. (1987) 'Culture process on the periphery: Belgic Gaul and Rome during the late Republic and early Empire.' In M. Rowlands, M. Larsen and K. Kristiansen (eds) *Centre and Periphery in the Ancient World*, pp. 104–24. Cambridge: Cambridge University Press.

Haselgrove, C. (1989) 'The late Iron Age in southern Britain and beyond.' In M. Todd (ed.) *Research in Roman Britain*, pp. 1–18. London: Britannia Monograph Series, no. 11.

Haselgrove, C. (1990) 'The Romanization of Belgic Gaul: some archaeological perspectives.' In T. Blagg and M. Millett (eds) *The Early Roman Empire in the West*, pp. 45–71. Oxford: Oxbow Books.

Haverfield, F. (1911) 'An inaugural address delivered before the first annual general meeting of the Society.' *Journal of Roman Studies* 1: xi–xx.

Haverfield, F. (1923 [1912]) *Romanization of Roman Britain*. Oxford: Clarendon Press.

Hawkes, C.F.C. (1931) 'Hillforts.' *Antiquity* 5: 60–97.

Hawkes, C.F.C. (1940) *The Prehistoric Foundations of Europe: to the Mycean age.* London: Methuen.

Hawkes, C.F.C. (1959) 'The ABC of the British Iron Age.' *Antiquity* 33: 170–82.

Hawkes, C.F.C. (1968) 'New thoughts on the Belgae.' *Antiquity* 42: 6–16.

Hawkes, C.F.C. and G.C. Dunning (1930) 'The Belgae of Britain and Gaul.' *Archaeological Journal* 87: 150–335.

Hawkes, C.F.C. and M.R. Hull (1947) *Camulodunum: first report on the excavations at Colchester 1930–1939.* Oxford: The Society of Antiquaries.

Hechter, M. (1976) *Internal Colonialism. The Celtic fringe in British national development 1536–1966.* London: Routledge & Kegan Paul.

Hechter, M. (1986) 'Theories of ethnic relations.' In J.F. Stack (ed.) *The Primordial Challenge: ethnicity in the contemporary world,* pp. 13–24. London: Greenwood Press.

Heine-Geldern, R. (1964) 'One hundred years of ethnological theory in German speaking countries: some milestones.' *Current Anthropology* 5: 407–18.

Hides, S. (1996) 'The genealogy of material culture and cultural identity.' In P. Graves-Brown, S. Jones and C. Gamble (eds) *Cultural Identity and Archaeology: the construction of European communities,* pp. 25–47 London: Routledge.

Hill, J.D. (1995) 'The pre-Roman Iron Age in Britain and Ireland (ca. 800 B.C. to A.D. 100): an overview.' *Journal of World Prehistory* 9(1): 47–98.

Hingley, R. (1984) 'Towards a social analysis in archaeology: Celtic society in the Iron Age of the Upper Thames Valley.' In B. Cunliffe and D. Miles (eds) *Aspects of the Iron Age in Central Southern Britain,* pp. 72–88. Oxford: Oxford University Committee for Archaeology.

Hingley, R. (1988) 'The influence of Rome on indigenous social groups in the Upper Thames Valley.' In R.F. Jones, J.H.F. Bloemers and S.L. Dyson (eds) *First Millenium Papers: Western Europe in the first millenium AD,* pp. 73–98. Oxford: British Archaeological Research.

Hingley, R. (1989) *Rural Settlement in Roman Britain.* London: Seaby.

Hingley, R. (1991) 'Past, present and future – the study of Roman Britain.' *Scottish Archaeological Review* 8: 90–101.

Hingley, R. (1996) 'The "legacy" of Rome: the rise, decline, and fall of the theory of Romanization.' In J. Webster and N. Cooper (eds) *Roman Imperialism: post-colonial perspectives,* pp. 35–48. Leicester: School of Archaeological Studies, University of Leicester.

Hingley, R. (forthcoming) 'The imperial context of Romano-British studies and proposals for a new understanding of social change.' In P. Funari, M. Hall and S. Jones (eds) *Back from the Edge: Archaeology in History.* London: Routledge.

Hinton, P. (1981) 'Where have all the new ethnicists gone wrong?' *Australian and New Zealand Journal of Sociology* 17(3): 14–19.

Hobsbawm, E.J. (1983) 'Introduction: inventing traditions.' In E. Hobsbawm and T. Ranger (eds) *The Invention of Tradition,* pp. 1–14. Cambridge: Cambridge University Press.

Hobsbawm, E.J. (1990) *Nations and Nationalism since 1780: programme, myth, reality.* Cambridge: Cambridge University Press.

Hobsbawm, E.J. and T. Ranger (eds) (1983) *The Invention of Tradition.* Cambridge: Cambridge University Press.

Hodder, I. (1977a) 'How are we to study distributions of Iron Age material?' In J.R. Collis (ed.) *The Iron Age in Britain: a review,* pp. 8–16. Sheffield: J.R. Collis.

Hodder, I. (1977b) 'Some new directions in the spatial analysis of archaeological data.' In D.L. Clarke (ed.) *Spatial Archaeology,* pp. 223–351. London: Academic Press.

Hodder, I. (1978a) 'Simple correlations between material culture and society: a review.' In I. Hodder (ed.) *The Spatial Organisation of Culture*, pp. 3–24. London: Duckworth.

Hodder, I. (1978b) 'The spatial structure of material "cultures": a review of some of the evidence.' In I. Hodder (ed.) *The Spatial Organisation of Culture*, pp. 93–111. London: Duckworth.

Hodder, I. (1979a) 'Economic and social stress and material culture patterning.' *American Antiquity* 44(3): 446–54.

Hodder, I. (1979b) 'Pre-Roman and Romano-British tribal economies.' In B.C. Burham and H.B. Johnson (eds) *Invasion and Response: the case of Roman Britain*, pp. 189–96. Oxford: British Archaeological Research.

Hodder, I. (1982a) *Symbols in Action*. Cambridge: Cambridge University Press.

Hodder, I. (1982b) 'Theoretical archaeology: a reactionary view.' In I. Hodder (ed.) *Symbolic and Structural Archaeology*, pp. 1–16. Cambridge: Cambridge University Press.

Hodder, I. (1986) *Reading the Past: current approaches to interpretation in archaeology*. Cambridge: Cambridge University Press.

Hodder, I. (1991a) 'Preface.' In I. Hodder (ed.) *Archaeological Theory in Europe*, pp. vii–xi. London: Routledge.

Hodder, I. (1991b) 'Archaeological theory in contemporary European societies: the emergence of competing traditions.' In I. Hodder (ed.) *Archaeological Theory in Europe*, pp. 1–24. London: Routledge.

Hodder, I. (ed.) (1991c) *Archaeological Theory in Europe: the last three decades*. London: Routledge.

Hodder, I. (1993) 'The narrative and rhetoric of material culture sequences.' *World Archaeology* 25(2): 268–81.

Hodder, I. and C. Orten (1976) *Spatial Analysis in Archaeology*. Cambridge: Cambridge University Press.

Hodgen, M.T. (1964) *Early Anthropology in the Sixteenth and Seventeenth Centuries*. Philadelphia: University of Pennsylvania Press.

Hodson, F.R. (1960) 'Reflections on the "ABC of the British Iron Age".' *Antiquity* 34: 318–19.

Hodson, F.R. (1962) 'Some pottery from Eastbourne, the "Marnians" and the pre-Roman Iron Age in southern England.' *Proceedings of the Prehistoric Society* 28: 140–55.

Hodson, F.R. (1964) 'Cultural grouping within the British pre-Roman Iron Age.' *Proceedings of the Prehistoric Society* 30: 99–110.

Hodson, F.R. (1980) 'Cultures as types? Some elements of classificatory theory.' *Bulletin of the Institute of Archaeology* 17: 1–10.

Honigmann, J.J. (1976) *The Development of Anthropological Ideas*. Illinois: The Dorsey Press.

Horowitz, D.L. (1975) 'Ethnic identity.' In N. Glazer and D.P. Moynihan (eds) *Ethnicity: theory and experience*, pp. 111–40. Cambridge, Mass.: Harvard University Press.

Horvath, S.M. Jr (1983) 'Ethnic groups as subjects of archaeological enquiry.' In A.E. Ward (ed.) *Forgotten Places and Things*, pp. 23–5. Albuquerque: Center for Anthropological Studies.

Hunt, C.H. and L. Walker (1974) *Ethnic Dynamics: patterns of intergroup relations in various societies*. Illinois: Dorsey Press.

Hunt, J. (1863) 'Introductory address in the study of anthropology.' *The Anthropological Review* 1: 1–20.

Hurst, P.Q. (1976) *Social Evolution and Social Categories*. London: George Allen & Unwin.

Hutchinsen, J. and A.D. Smith (eds) (1994) *Nationalism*. Oxford: Oxford University Press.

Huxley, J.S. and A.C. Haddon (1935) *We Europeans: a survey of 'racial' problems*. London: Jonathan Cape.

Huxley, T. (1870) 'The forefathers and forerunners of the English people.' *Pall Mall Gazette*, 10 January, 8–9. (Reprinted in M.D. Biddiss (ed.) (1979) *Images of Race*, pp. 157–70. New York: Holmes & Meier.)

Isaacs, H. (1974) 'Basic group identity: idols of the tribe.' *Ethnicity* 1: 15–41.

Isajiw, W.W. (1974) 'Definitions of ethnicity.' *Ethnicity* 1: 111–24.

Jackson, J.W. (1866) 'Race in legislation and political economy.' *Anthropological Review* 4: 113–35. (Reprinted in M.D. Biddiss (ed.) (1979) *Images of Race*, pp. 133–40. New York: Holmes & Meier.)

Jacobs, J. (1988) 'The construction of identity.' In J. Beckett (ed.) *Past and Present: the construction of Aboriginality*, pp. 31–43. Canberra: Aboriginal Studies Press.

Jaspan, M. (1964) 'Comment on R. Narroll, "On ethnic unit classification".' *Current Anthropology* 5(4): 298.

Jenkins, R. (1982) 'Pierre Bourdieu and the reproduction of determinism.' [Critical Note] *Sociology* 16(4): 270–81.

Jochim, M.A. (1983) 'Palaeolithic cave art in ecological perspective.' In G.N. Bailey (ed.) *Hunter-Gatherer Economy in Prehistoric Europe*, pp. 212–19. Cambridge: Cambridge University Press.

Jones, D. and J. Hill-Burnett (1982) 'The political context of ethnogenesis: an Australian example.' In M.C. Howard (ed.) *Aboriginal Power in Australian Society*, pp. 214–46. St Lucia: University of Queensland Press.

Jones, S. (1994) 'Archaeology and ethnicity: constructing identities in the past and the present.' Unpublished Ph.D. thesis, University of Southampton.

Jones, S. (1996) 'Discourses of identity in the interpretation of the past.' In P. Graves-Brown, S. Jones and C. Gamble (eds) *Cultural Identity and Archaeology: the construction of European communities*, pp. 62–80. London: Routledge.

Jones, S. and P. Graves-Brown (1996) 'Introduction: archaeology and cultural identity in Europe.' In P. Graves-Brown, S. Jones and C. Gamble (eds) *Cultural Identity and Archaeology: the construction of European communities*, pp. 1–24. London: Routledge.

Just, R. (1989) 'Triumph of the ethnos.' In E. Tonkin, M. McDonald and M. Chapman (eds) *History and Ethnicity*, pp. 71–88. London: Routledge.

Kapferer, B. (1989) 'Nationalist ideology and a comparative anthropology.' *Ethnos* 54: 161–99.

Keen, I. (1988) *Being Black: Aboriginal cultures in settled Australia*. Canberra: Aboriginal Studies Press.

Kellas, J.G. (1991) *The Politics of Nationalism and Ethnicity*. London: Macmillan.

Kennedy, K.A.R. (1973) 'Race and culture.' In R. Narroll and F. Narroll (eds) *Main Currents in Cultural Anthropology*, pp. 25–56. New York: Meredith Corporation.

Keyes, C.F. (1976) 'Towards a new formulation of the concept of ethnic group.' *Ethnicity* 3: 202–13.

Keyes, C.F. (1981) 'The dialectics of ethnic change.' In C.F. Keyes (ed.) *Ethnic Change*, pp. 3–31. Seattle: University of Washington Press.

Khan, A. (1992) 'Ethnicity, culture and context.' *Man* 27(4): 873–7.

Kidder, A.V. (1962 [1924]) *An Introduction to the Study of Southwestern Archaeology with a Preliminary Account of the Excavations at Pecos* (revised edition with an introduction by I. Rouse). London: Yale University Press.

Kim, Y.Y. (1986) 'Introduction: a communication approach to interethnic relations.' In Y.Y. Kim (ed.) *Interethnic Communication: current research*, pp. 9–18. London: Sage.

Kimes, T., C. Haselgrove and I. Hodder (1982) 'A method for the identification of the location of regional cultural boundaries.' *Journal of Anthropological Archaeology* 1: 113–31.

Kinahan, J. (1995) 'Theory, practice and criticism in the history of Namibian archaeology.' In P.J. Ucko (ed.) *Theory in Archaeology: a world perspective*, pp. 76–95. London: Routledge.

Kochin, A. (ed.) (1983) *Ethnic Geography and Cartography*. Moscow: Social Sciences Today.

Kohl, P.L. (1993a) 'Limits to a post-processual archaeology.' In N. Yoffee and A. Sherratt (eds) *Archaeological Theory: who sets the agenda?*, pp. 13–19. Cambridge: Cambridge University Press.

Kohl, P.L. (1993b) 'Nationalism, politics, and the practice of archaeology in Soviet Transcaucasia.' *Journal of European Archaeology* 1(2): 181–8.

Kohl, P.L. and C. Fawcett (1995a) 'Introduction. Archaeology in the service of the state: theoretical considerations.' In P.L. Kohl and C. Fawcett (eds) *Nationalism, Politics and the Practice of Archaeology*, pp. 3–18. London: Routledge.

Kohl, P.L. and C. Fawcett (eds) (1995b) *Nationalism, Politics and the Practice of Archaeology*. London: Routledge

Kohl, P.L. and G.R. Tsetskhladze (1995) 'Nationalism, politics and the practice of archaeology in the Caucasus.' In P.L. Kohl and C. Fawcett (eds) *Nationalism, Politics and the Practice of Archaeology*, pp. 149–74. London: Routledge.

Kopytoff, I. (1986) 'The cultural biography of things: commoditization as process.' In A. Appadurai (ed.) *The Social Life of Things: commodities in perspective*, pp. 64–91. Cambridge: Cambridge University Press.

Kossack, G. (1992) 'Prehistoric archaeology in Germany: its history and current situation.' *Norwegian Archaeological Review* 25: 73–109.

Kossinna, G. (1911) *Die Herkunft der Germanen*. Leipzig: Kabitzsch.

Kossinna, G. (1921 [1914]) *Die Deutsche Vorgeschichte: eine Hervorragend Nationale Wissenschaft*. Mannus-Bibliothek 9.

Kristiansen, K. (1992) 'The strength of the past and its great might: an essay on the use of the past.' *Journal of European Archaeology* 1: 3–33.

Kroeber, A.L. and C. Kluckhohn (1952) *Culture: a critical review of concepts and definitions*. New York: Vintage.

Kuper, A. (1988) *The Invention of Primitive Society: transformations of an illusion*. London: Routledge.

Kuper, L. (1975a) 'Introduction.' In L. Kuper (ed.) *Race, Science and Society*, pp. 13–28. Paris: UNESCO Press.

Kuper, L. (1975b) (ed.) *Race, Science and Society*. Paris: UNESCO Press.

Larick, R. (1986) 'Age grading and ethnicity in the style of Loikop (Sanbura) spears.' *World Archaeology* 18: 269–83.

Larick, R. (1991) 'Warriors and blacksmiths: mediating ethnicity in East African spears.' *Journal of Anthropological Archaeology* 10: 299–331.

Layton, R. (ed.) (1989a) *Conflict in the Archaeology of Living Traditions*. London: Unwin Hyman; Routledge, pbk 1994.

Layton, R. (1989b) 'Introduction: conflict in the archaeology of living traditions.' In R. Layton (ed.) *Conflict in the Archaeology of Living Traditions*, pp. 1–31. London: Unwin Hyman; Routledge, pbk 1994.

Leach, E. (1964 [1954]) *Political Systems of Highland Burma: a study in Kachin social structure*. London: G. Bell & Sons.

Leiris, M. (1975 [1956]) 'Race and culture.' In L. Kuper (ed.) *Race, Science and Society*, pp. 135–72. Paris: UNESCO Press.

Lévi-Strauss, C. (1975 [1955]) *Tristes Tropiques*. New York: Athenaeum.

Lévi-Strauss, C. (1975 [1956]) 'Race and history.' In L. Kuper (ed.) *Race, Science and Society*, pp. 95–134. Paris: UNESCO Press.

Lewis, I.M. (1968) 'Tribal society.' In D.L. Sills (ed.) *International Encyclopedia of the Social Sciences*, pp. 135–72. London: Macmillan Company and Free Press.

LiPuma, E. (1993) 'Culture and the concept of culture in a theory of practice.' In C. Calhoun, E. LiPuma and M. Postone (eds) *Bourdieu: critical perspectives*, pp. 14–34. Cambridge: Polity Press.

Lloyd, P.C. (1974) 'Ethnicity and the structure of inequality in a Nigerian town in the mid-1950s.' In A. Cohen (ed.) *Urban Ethnicity*, pp. 223–50. London: Tavistock Publications.

Lockwood, D. (1970) 'Race and conflict in plural society.' In S. Zaida (ed.) *Race and Racialism*, pp. 57–72. London: Tavistock.

Lowenthal, D. (1985) *The Past is a Foreign Country*. Cambridge: Cambridge University Press.

Lowie, R.H. (1937) *The History of Ethnological Theory*. New York: Holt, Rinehart & Winston.

McBryde, I. (1984) 'Kulin greenstone quarries: the social contexts of production and distribution for the Mt. William site.' *World Archaeology* 16(2): 267–85.

McCann, W.J. (1990) '"Volk and Germanentum": the presentation of the past in Nazi Germany.' In P. Gathercole and D. Lowenthal (eds) *The Politics of the Past*, pp. 74–88. London: Unwin Hyman; Routledge, pbk 1994.

McGuire, R.H. (1982) 'The study of ethnicity in historical archaeology.' *Journal of Anthropological Archaeology* 1: 159–78.

McGuire, R.H. (1983) 'Ethnic group, status and material culture at the Rancho Punta de Agua.' In A.E. Ward (ed.) *Forgotten Places and Things: archaeological perspectives on American history*, pp. 193–203. Albuquerque: Center for Anthropological Studies.

McGuire, R.H. (1992) *A Marxist Archaeology*. London: Academic Press.

Mackay, C. (1866) 'The negro and the negrophilists.' *Blackwood's Edinburgh Magazine* 99: 581–97. (Reprinted in M.D. Biddis (ed.) (1979) *Images of Race*, pp. 89–112. New York: Holmes & Meier.)

McKay, J. (1982) 'An exploratory synthesis of primordial and mobilizationist approaches to ethnic phenomena.' *Ethnic and Racial Studies* 5(4): 395–420.

MacKenzie, M.A. (1991) *Androgynous Objects: string bags and gender in central New Guinea*. Reading: Harwood Academic Publishers.

McKern, W.C. (1939) 'The midwestern taxanomic method as an aid to archaeological culture study.' *American Antiquity* 4: 301–13.

Mackreth, D. (1981) 'The brooches.' In C. Partridge, *Skeleton Green: a Late Iron Age and Romano-British site*, pp. 130–52. London: Society for the Promotion of Roman Studies.

Mackie, Q. (1994) 'Prehistory in a multicultural state: a commentary on the development of Canadian archaeology.' In P.J. Ucko (ed.) *Theory in Archaeology: a world perspective*, pp. 178–96. London: Routledge.

Maddock, K. (1988) 'Myth, history and a sense of oneself.' In J. Beckett (ed.) *Past and Present: the construction of Aboriginality*, pp. 11–30. Canberra: Aboriginal Studies Press.

Malina, J. and Z. Vašíček (1990) *Archaeology Yesterday and Today: the development of archaeology in the sciences and humanities*. Cambridge: Cambridge University Press.

Malinowski, B. (1944) *A Scientific Theory of Culture and Other Essays*. Chapel Hill: University of North Carolina.

Mangi, J. (1989) 'The role of archaeology in nation building.' In R. Layton (ed.) *Conflict in the Archaeology of Living Traditions*, pp. 217–27. London: Unwin Hyman; Routledge, pbk 1994.

Maquet, C. (1964) 'Objectivity and anthropology.' *Current Anthropology* 5: 47–55.

Marcus, C. (1989) 'A prolegomena to contemporary cosmopolitan conversations on conference occasions such as the present one, entitled representations of otherness: cultural hermeneutics, east and west.' *Criticism, Heresy and Interpretation* 2: 23–35.

Mascia-Lees, F.E., P. Sharpe and C. Ballerino Cohen (1989) 'The postmodernist turn in anthropology: cautions from a feminist perspective.' *Signs* 15(1): 7–33.

Mattingly, D.J. (1996) 'From one colonialism to another: imperialism and the Magreb.' In J. Webster and N. Cooper (eds) *Roman Imperialism: post-colonial perspectives*, pp. 49–69. Leicester: School of Archaeological Studies, University of Leicester.

Meadows, K.I. (1994) 'You are what you eat: diet, identity and Romanisation.' In S. Cottam, D. Dungworth, S. Scott and J. Taylor (eds) *Proceedings of the Fourth Annual Theoretical Roman Archaeology Conference*, pp. 133–40. Oxford: Oxford Books.

Meadwell, H. (1989) 'Cultural and instrumental approaches to ethnic nationalism.' *Ethnic and Racial Studies* 12(3): 309–27.

Megaw, J.V.S. and M.R. Megaw (1996) 'Ancient Celts and modern ethnicity.' *Antiquity* 70: 175–81.

Messing, S.D. (1964) 'Comment on R. Narroll "On ethnic unit classification".' *Current Anthropology* 5(4): 300.

Michalska, A. (1991) 'Rights of peoples to self-determination in international law.' In N.W. Twining (ed.) *Issues of Self-Determination*, pp. 71–90. Aberdeen: Aberdeen University Press.

Miller, D. (1985) *Artefacts as Categories: a study in ceramic variability in central India*. Cambridge: Cambridge University Press.

Millett, M. (1983) 'A comparative study of some contemporaneous pottery assemblages.' Unpublished D.Phil. thesis, University of Oxford.

Millett, M. (1990a) *The Romanization of Britain: an essay in archaeological interpretation*. Cambridge: Cambridge University Press.

Millett, M. (1990b) 'Romanization: historical issues and archaeological interpretaion.' In T.F.C. Blagg and M. Millett (eds) *The Early Roman Empire in the West*, pp. 35–41. Oxford: Oxbow Books.

Mitchell, J.C. (1974) 'Perceptions of ethnicity and ethnic behaviour: an empirical exploration.' In A. Cohen (ed.) *Urban Ethnicity*, pp. 1–35. London: Tavistock Publications.

Moberg, C.-A. (1985) 'Comments on Saamis, Finns and Scandinavians in history and prehistory.' *Norwegian Archaeological Review* 18: 1–28.

Moerman, M. (1965) 'Who are the Lue?' *American Anthropologist* 67: 1215–30.

Moerman, M. (1968) 'Uses and abuses of ethnic identity.' In J. Helm (ed.) *Essays on the Problem of Tribe*, pp. 153–69. Seattle: University of Washington Press.

Montagu, Ashley M.F. (1945) *Man's Most Dangerous Myth*. New York: Colombia University Press.

Moody, R. (ed.) (1984) *The Indigenous Voice: visions and realities*, vol. 1. London: Zed Books.

Moore, H.L. (1988) *Feminism and Anthropology*. Cambridge: Polity Press.

Morgan, L.H. (1974 [1877]) *Ancient Society, or Researches in the Lines of Human Progress from Savagery through Barbarism to Civilization*. Gloucester, Mass.: Peter Smith.

Morris, B. (1988) 'The politics of identity: from Aborigines to the first Australian.' In J. Beckett (ed.) *Past and Present: the construction of Aboriginality*, pp. 63–85. Canberra: Aboriginal Studies Press.

Moser, S. (1995) 'The "Aboriginalization" of Australian archaeology: the contribution of the Australian Institute of Aboriginal Studies to the indigenous transformation of the discipline.' In P.J. Ucko (ed.) *Theory in Archaeology: a world perspective*, pp. 150–77. London: Routledge.

Muga, D. (1984) 'Academic sub-cultural theory and the problematic of ethnicity: a tentative critique.' *Journal of Ethnic Studies* 12: 1–51.

Müller, M. (1877) *Lectures on the Science of Language*. London: Longman, Green & Co.

Murray, T. (1993) 'Communication and the importance of disciplinary communities: who owns the past?' In N. Yoffee and A. Sherratt (eds) *Archaeological Theory: who sets the Agenda?* pp. 105–16. Cambridge: Cambridge University Press.

Narroll, R. (1964) 'On ethnic unit classification.' *Current Anthropology* 5: 283–91 and 306–12.

Narroll, R. (1968) 'Who the Lue are.' In J. Helm (ed.) *Essays on the Problem of Tribe*, pp. 72–9. Seattle: University of Washington Press.

Neal, D.S., A. Wardle and J. Hunn (1990) *Excavation of the Iron Age, Roman and Medieval Settlement at Gorhambury, St Albans*. London: Historic Buildings and Monuments Commission.

Nettheim, G. (1992) 'International law and indigenous political rights.' In H. Reynolds and R. Nile (eds) *Indigenous Rights in the Pacific and North America: race and nation in the late twentieth century*, pp. 13–27. London: Sir Robert Menzies Centre for Australian Studies, University of London.

Norton, R. (1993) 'Culture and identity in the South Pacific: a comparative analysis.' *Man* 28(4): 741–59.

Novak, M. (1974) 'The new ethnicity.' *Center Magazine* 7: 18–25.

O'Meara, J.T. (1995) 'Comment on "Objectivity and Militancy: a Debate".' *Current Anthropology* 36(3): 427–8.

Odner, K. (1985) 'Saamis (Lapps), Finns and Scandinavians in history and prehistory.' *Norwegian Archaeological Review* 18: 1–12.

Odum, H.H. (1967) 'Generalizations on race in nineteenth-century physical anthropology.' *I.S.I.S.* 58: 5–18.

Ohnuki-Tierney, E. (1995) 'Structure, event and historical metaphor: rice and identities in Japanese history.' *Journal of the Royal Anthropological Institute* 1(2): 227–53.

Olivier, L. and A. Coudart (1995) 'French tradition and the central place of history in the human sciences: preamble to a dialogue between Robinson Crusoe and his Man Friday.' In P.J. Ucko (ed.) *Theory in Archaeology: a world perspective*, pp. 363–81. London: Routledge.

Olsen, B. (1985) 'Comments on Saamis, Finns and Scandinavians in history and prehistory.' *Norwegian Archaeological Review* 18: 13–18.

Olsen, B. (1986) 'Norwegian archaeology and the people without (pre-)history: or how to create a myth of a uniform past.' *Archaeological Review from Cambridge* 5: 25–42.

Olsen, B. and Z. Kobylinski (1991) 'Ethnicity in anthropological and archaeological research: a Norwegian–Polish perspective.' *Archaeologia Polona* 29: 5–27.

Ortner, S.B. (1984) 'Theory in anthropology since the sixties.' *Comparative Studies in Society and History* 26: 126–66.

Otite, O. (1975) 'Resource competition and inter-ethnic relations in Nigeria.' In L.A. Despres (ed.) *Ethnicity and Resource Competition in Plural Societies*, pp. 119–30. Paris: Mouton Publishers.

Paddayya, K. (1995) 'Theoretical perspectives in Indian archaeology: an historical overview.' In P.J. Ucko (ed.) *Theory in Archaeology: a world perspective*, pp. 110–49. London: Routledge.

Parkin, F. (1978) 'Social stratification.' In T. Borrowmore and R. Nisket (eds) *A History of Sociological Thought*, pp. 599–632. London: Heinemann.

Parminter, Y. (1990) 'The pottery.' In D.S. Neal, A. Wardle and J. Hunn, *Excavation of the Iron Age, Roman and Medieval Settlement at Gorhambury, St Albans*, pp. 175–85. London: Historic Buildings and Monuments Commission for England.

Partridge, C. (1981) *Skeleton Green: a late Iron Age and Romano-British site*. London: Society for the Promotion of Roman Studies.

Patterson, O. (1975) 'Context and choice in ethnic allegiance: a theoretical framework and Caribbean case study.' In N. Glazer and D.P. Moynihan (eds) *Ethnicity: theory and experience*, pp. 305–49. Cambridge, Mass.: Harvard University Press.

Peacock, D.P.S. (1969) 'A contribution to the study of Glastonbury ware from southwestern England.' *Antiquaries Journal* 49: 41–61.

Peacock, D.P.S. (1979) 'Glastonbury ware: an alternative view (being a reply to Blackmore et al.).' In B.C. Burnham and J. Kingsbury (eds) *Space, Hierarchy and Society: interdisciplinary studies in social area analysis*, pp. 113–15. Oxford: British Archaeological Research.

Perlstein Pollard, H. (1994) 'Ethnicity and political control in a complex society: the Tarascan state of prehispanic Mexico.' In E.M. Brumfiel and J.W. Fox (eds) *Factional Competition and Political Development in the New World*, pp. 79–88. Cambridge: Cambridge University Press.

Perry, W.J. (1924) *The Growth of Civilization*. London: Methuen & Co.

Piggott, S. (1965) *Ancient Europe: from the beginnings of agriculture to Classical antiquity*. Edinburgh: Edinburgh University Press.

Pinsky, V. and A. Wylie (eds) (1989) *Critical Traditions in Contemporary Archaeology: essays in the philosophy, history and socio-politics of archaeology*. Cambridge: Cambridge University Press.

Plog, S. (1978) 'Social interaction and stylistic similarity: a re-analysis.' In M.B. Schiffer (ed.) *Advances in Archaeological Method and Theory*, vol. 1, pp. 143–82. New York: Academic Press.

Plog, S. (1983) 'Analysis of style in artefacts.' *Annual Review of Anthropology* 12: 125–42.

Poliakov, L. (1974 [1971]) *The Aryan Myth: a history of racist and nationalist ideas in Europe*. London: Sussex University Press.

Politis, G. (1995) 'The socio-politics of the development of archaeology in Hispanic Latin America.' In P.J. Ucko (ed.) *Theory in Archaeology: a world perspective*, pp. 197–235. London: Routledge.

Postone, M., E. LiPuma and C. Calhoun (1993) 'Introduction: Bourdieu and social theory.' In C. Calhoun, E. LiPuma and M. Postone (eds) *Bourdieu: Critical Perspectives*, pp. 1–13. Cambridge: Polity Press.

Praetzellis, A., M. Praetzellis and M. Brown III (1987) 'Artefacts as symbols of identity: an example from Sacramento's Gold Rush Era Chinese community.' In A. Saski (ed.) *Living in Cities: current research in historical archaeology*, pp. 38–47. Pleasant Hill: Society for Historical Archaeology.

Prichard, J.C. (1973 [1813]) *Researches into the Physical History of Man*. Chicago: University of Chicago Press.

Radcliffe-Brown, A.R. (1952) *Structure and Function in Primitive Society: essays and addresses*. London: Cohen & West.

Ranger, T. (1983) 'The invention of tradition in colonial Africa.' In E. Hobsbawm and T. Ranger (eds) *The Invention of Tradition*, pp. 211–62. Cambridge: Cambridge University Press.

Rao, N. (1994) 'Interpreting silences: symbol and history in the case of Ram Janmabhoomi/Babri Masjid.' In G.C. Bond and A. Gilliam (eds) *Social Construction of the Past: representation as power*, pp. 154–64. London: Routledge.

Redfield, R., L. Linton and M.J. Herskovits (1936) 'Memorandum for the study of acculturation.' *American Anthropologist* 38: 149–52.

Renfrew, C. (1972) *The Emergence of Civilisation: the Cyclades and the Aegean in the third millenium B.C.* London: Methuen and Co.

Renfrew, C. (1973) *Before Civilization: the radiocarbon revolution and prehistoric Europe.* London: Jonathan Cape.

Renfrew, C. (1977) 'Space, time and polity.' In J. Friedman and M.J. Rowlands (eds) *The Evolution of Social Systems*, pp. 89–112. London: Duckworth.

Renfrew, C. (1979) *Problems in European Prehistory.* Edinburgh: Edinburgh University Press.

Renfrew, C. (1987) *Archaeology and Language: the puzzle of Indo-European origins.* London: Penguin Books.

Renfrew, C. (1995) 'The identity of Europe in prehistoric archaeology.' *Journal of European Archaeology* 2: 153–73.

Renfrew, C. (1996) 'Prehistory and the identity of Europe, or don't lets be beastly to the Hungarians.' In P. Graves-Brown, S. Jones and C. Gamble (eds) *Cultural Identity and Archaeology: the construction of European communities*, pp. 125–37. London: Routledge.

Renfrew, C. and P. Bahn (1991) *Archaeology: theories, methods and practice.* London: Thames & Hudson.

Reynolds, V. (1980) 'Sociobiology and the idea of primordial discrimination.' *Ethnic and Racial Studies* 3(3): 303–15.

Reynolds, V., V.S.E. Falger and I. Vine (eds) (1987) *The Sociobiology of Ethnocentrism: evolutionary dimensions of xenophobia, discrimination, racism and nationalism.* London: Croom Helm.

Rodwell, K.A. (1988) *The Prehistoric and Roman Settlement at Kelvedon, Essex.* London: Chelmsford Archaeological Trust and the Council for British Archaeology.

Rodwell, R. (1976) 'Coinage, oppida and the rise of Belgic power in south-eastern Britain.' In B.W. Cunliffe and T. Rowley (eds) *The Beginnings of Urbanisation in Barbarian Europe*, pp. 181–367. Oxford: British Archaeological Research.

Roe, D. (1970) *Prehistory: an introduction.* London: Macmillan.

Roosens, E.E. (1989) *Creating Ethnicity: the process of ethnogenesis.* London: Sage.

Rosaldo, R. (1993 [1989]) *Culture and Truth: the remaking of social analysis.* London: Routledge.

Ross, J.A. (1980) 'The mobilization of collective identity: an analytical overview.' In A.B. Cottrel and J.A. Ross (eds) *The Mobilization of Collective Identity*, pp. 1–30. Lanham: University Press of America.

Rowlands, M.J. (1982) 'Processual archaeology as historical social science.' In C. Renfrew, M.J. Rowlands and B.A. Seagraves (eds) *Theory and Explanation in Archaeology*, pp. 155–74. London: Academic Press.

Rowlands, M.J. (1994) 'The politics of identity in archaeology.' In G.C. Bond and A. Gilliam (eds) *Social Construction of the Past: representation as power*, pp. 129–43. London: Routledge.

Sackett, J.R. (1977) 'The meaning of style in archaeology: a general model.' *American Antiquity* 42(3): 369–80.

Sackett, J.R. (1982) 'Approaches to style in lithic archaeology.' *Journal of Anthropological Archaeology* 1: 59–112.

Sackett, J.R. (1985) 'Style and ethnicity in the Kalahari: a reply to Weissner.' *American Antiquity* 50: 154–60.

Sackett, J.R. (1986) 'Style, function, and assemblage variability: a reply to Binford.' *American Antiquity* 51(3): 628–34.

Sackett, J.R. (1991) 'Style and ethnicity in archaeology: the case for isochresticism.' In M.W. Conkey and C.A. Hastorf (eds) *The Uses of Style in Archaeology*, pp. 32–43. Cambridge: Cambridge University Press.

Sahlins, M. (1977) *The Use and Abuse of Biology.* London: Tavistock Publications.

Sahlins, M. (1981) *Historical Metaphors and Mythical Realities: structure in the early history of the Sandwich Islands Kingdom.* Ann Arbor: University of Michigan Press.

Salamone, F.A. and C.H. Swanson (1979) 'Identity and ethnicity: ethnic groups and interactions in a multi-ethnic society.' *Ethnic Groups* 2: 167–83.

Sawday, J. (1995) 'Site of debate.' *The Times Higher Education Supplement*, 13 January, 16–17.

Schildkrout, E. (1974) 'Ethnicity and generational differences among immigrants in Ghana.' In A. Cohen (ed.) *Urban Ethnicity*, pp. 187–222. London: Tavistock Publications.

Scott, G.M. (1990) 'A resynthesis of the primordial and circumstantial approaches to ethnic group solidarity: towards an explanatory model.' *Ethnic and Racial Studies* 13: 147–71.

Seymour-Smith, C. (1986) *Macmillan Dictionary of Anthropology.* London: Macmillan.

Shanks, M. and C. Tilley (1987) *Social Theory and Archaeology.* Oxford: Polity Press.

Shanks, M. and C. Tilley (1992 [1987]) *Re-constructing Archaeology: theory and practice.* London: Routledge.

Sharp, J. and P. McAllister (1993) 'Ethnicity, identity and nationalism: international insights and the South African debate.' *Anthropology Today* 9: 18–20.

Shennan, S.J. (1978) 'Archaeological cultures: an empirical investigation.' In I. Hodder (ed.) *The Spatial Organisation of Culture*, pp. 113–39. London: Duckworth.

Shennan, S.J. (1988) *Quantifying Archaeology.* Edinburgh: Edinburgh University Press.

Shennan, S.J. (ed.) (1989a) *Archaeological Approaches to Cultural Identity.* London: Unwin & Hyman; Routledge, pbk 1994.

Shennan, S.J. (1989b) 'Introduction.' In S.J. Shennan (ed.) *Archaeological Approaches to Cultural Identity*, pp. 1–32. London: Unwin & Hyman; Routledge, pbk 1994.

Shennan, S.J. (1991) 'Some current issues in the archaeological identification of past peoples.' *Archaeologia Polona* 29: 29–37.

Sherratt, A. (1982) 'Mobile resources: settlement and exchange in early agricultural Europe.' In C. Renfrew and S.J. Shennan (eds) *Ranking, Resource and Exchange: aspects of the archaeology of early European society*, pp. 13–26. Cambridge: Cambridge University Press.

Shibutani, T. and K.M. Kwan (1965) *Ethnic Stratification: a comparative approach.* New York: Macmillan.

Shils, E.A. (1957) *Center and Periphery: essays in macrosociology. Selected papers of Edward Shils*, vol. II, 111–26. Chicago: Chicago University Press.

Singer, M. (1968) 'The concept of culture.' In D.L. Sills (ed.) *International Encyclopedia of the Social Sciences*, pp. 527–43. London: Macmillan and Free Press.

Sklenár, K. (1983) *Archaeology in Central Europe: the first five hundred years.* Leicester: Leicester University Press.

Slofstra, J. (1983) 'An anthropological approach to the study of Romanization processes.' In R. Brandt and J. Slofstra (eds) *Roman and Native in the Low Countries*, pp. 71–103. Oxford: British Archaeological Research.

Smith, A.D. (1981) *The Ethnic Revival.* Cambridge: Cambridge University Press.

Smith, A.D. (1984) 'Ethnic myths and ethnic revivals.' *Archives Européenes de Sociologie*, 24(3): 283–303.

Southall, A. (1976) 'Nuer and Dinka are people: ecology, economy and logical possibility.' *Man* 11: 463–91.

Spaulding, A. (1953) 'Statistical techniques for the discovery of artefact types.' *American Antiquity* 18: 305–13.

Spaulding, A. (1954) 'Reply to Ford.' *American Antiquity* 19: 391–3.

Spencer, J. (1990) 'Writing within: anthropology, nationalism, and culture in Sri Lanka.' *Current Anthropology* 31: 283–300.

Spratling, M.G. (1972) 'Southern British decorated bronzes of the late pre-Roman Iron Age.' Unpublished Ph.D. thesis, University of London.

Stack, J.F. (1986) 'Ethnic mobilization in world politics: the primordial perspective.' In J.F. Stack (ed.) *The Primordial Challenge: ethnicity in the contemporary world*, pp. 1–11. London: Greenwood Press.

Staski, E. (1987) 'Border city, border culture: assimilation and change in late 19th century El Paso.' In A. Saski (ed.) *Living in Cities: current research in historical archaeology*, pp. 48–55. Pleasant Hill: Society for Historical Archaeology.

Stead, I.M. and V. Rigby (1989) *Verulamium: the King Harry Lane site*. London: Historic Buildings and Monuments Commission.

Stepan, N. (1982) *The Idea of Race in Science: Great Britain 1800–1960*. London: Macmillan.

Stocking, G.W. (1968) *Race, Culture and Evolution: essays in the history of anthropology*. London: Collier-Macmillan.

Stocking, G.W. (1973) 'From chronology to ethnology: James Cowles Prichard and British Anthropology 1800–1850.' In J.C. Prichard ((1973)[1813]) *Researches into the Physical History of Man*, ix–cx. Chicago: University of Chicago Press.

Stocking, G.W. (1974) 'Introduction: the basic assumptions of Boasian anthropology.' In G.W. Stocking (ed.) *The Shaping of American Anthropology 1883–1911: a Franz Boas reader*, pp. 1–20. New York: Basic Books.

Stocking, G.W. (1987) *Victorian Anthropology*. New York: The Free Press.

Stocking, G.W. (1988) 'Bones, bodies, behaviour.' In G.W. Stocking (ed.) *Bones, Bodies, Behaviour: essays on biological anthropology*, pp. 3–17. Madison: University of Wisconsin Press.

Stone, P.G. and R. MacKenzie (eds) (1990) *The Excluded Past: archaeology in education*. London: Unwin Hyman; Routledge, pbk 1994.

Tajfel, H. (1982) 'Introduction.' In H. Tajfel (ed.) *Social Identity and Intergroup Relations*, pp. 1–11. New York: Academic Press.

Tallgren, A.M. (1937) 'The method of prehistoric archaeology.' *Antiquity* 11: 152–64.

Targett, S. (1995) 'Nationalism's healthy state.' *Times Higher Education Supplement*, 27 March, 9.

Taylor, L. (1987) 'The same but different: social reproduction and innovation in the art of the Kunwinjku of western Arnhem Land.' Unpublished Ph.D. thesis, Australian National University.

Taylor, W.W. Jr (1948) *A Study of Archaeology*. Menasha: American Anthropological Association.

Thomas, N. (1991) *Entangled Objects: exchange, material culture, and colonialism in the Pacific*. Cambridge, Mass.: Harvard University Press.

Thomas, J. (1996) *Time, Culture and Identity: an interpretive archaeology*. London: Routledge.

Thurnwald, R. (1932) 'The psychology of acculturation.' *American Anthropologist* 34: 557–69.

Tilley, C. (1982) 'Social formation, social structures and social change.' In I.

Hodder (ed.) *Symbolic and Structural Archaeology*, pp. 26–38. Cambridge: Cambridge University Press.

Tilley, C. (1991) *Material Culture and Text: the art of ambiguity*. London: Routledge.

Tonkin, E., M. McDonald and M. Chapman (eds) (1989) *History and Ethnicity*. London: Routledge.

Tonkinson, M.E. (1990) 'Is it in the blood? Australian Aboriginal identity.' In J. Linnekin and L. Poyer (eds) *Cultural Identity and Ethnicity in the Pacific*, pp. 191–309. Honolulu: University of Hawaii Press.

Torrence, R. (1989) 'Tools as optimal solutions.' In R. Torrence (ed.) *Time, Energy and Stone Tools*, pp. 1–6. Cambridge: Cambridge University Press.

Trigger, B.G. (1977) 'Comments on archaeological classification and ethnic groups.' *Norwegian Archaeological Review* 10: 20–3.

Trigger, B.G. (1978) *Time and Traditions: essays in archaeological interpretation*. Edinburgh: Edinburgh University Press.

Trigger, B.G. (1980) *Gordon Childe: revolutions in archaeology*. London: Thames & Hudson.

Trigger, B.G. (1984) 'Alternative archaeologies: nationalist, colonialist, imperialist.' *Man* 19: 355–70.

Trigger, B.G. (1989) *A History of Archaeological Thought*. Cambridge: Cambridge University Press.

Trigger, B.G. (1995) 'Romanticism, nationalism and archaeology.' In P.L Kohl and C. Fawcett (eds) *Nationalism, Politics and the Practice of Archaeology*, pp. 263–79. London: Routledge.

Turner, T. (1991) 'Representing, resisting, rethinking: historical transformations of Kayapo culture and anthropological consciousness.' In G.W. Stocking (ed.) *Colonial Situations: essays on the contextualization of ethnographic knowledge*, pp. 285–313. Madison: University of Wisconsin Press.

Tylor, E.B. (1873 [1871]) *Primitive Culture*, vols 1 and 2. London: John Murray.

Ucko, P.J. (1969) 'Ethnography and archaeological interpretation of funerary remains.' *World Archaeology* 1(2): 262–80.

Ucko, P.J. (1983a) 'The politics of the indigenous minority.' *Journal of Biosocial Science Supplement* 8: 25–40.

Ucko, P.J. (1983b) 'Australian academic archaeology. Aboriginal transformations of its aims and practices.' *Australian Archaeology* 16: 11–26.

Ucko, P.J. (1987) *Academic Freedom and Apartheid: the story of the World Archaeological Congress*. London: Duckworth.

Ucko, P.J. (1989) 'Foreword.' In S.J. Shennan (ed.) *Archaeological Approaches to Cultural Identity*, pp. ix–xx. London: Unwin & Hyman; Routledge, pbk 1994.

Ucko, P.J. (1994) 'Museums and sites: cultures of the past within education – Zimbabwe some ten years on.' In P.G. Stone and B.L. Molyneux (eds) *The Presented Past: heritage, museums, education*, pp. 237–82. London: Routledge.

Ucko, P.J. (ed.) (1995a) *Theory in Archaeology: a world perspective*. London: Routledge.

Ucko, P.J. (1995b) 'Introduction: archaeological interpretation in a world context.' In P.J. Ucko (ed.) *Theory in Archaeology: a world perspective*, pp. 1–27. London: Routledge.

UNESCO (1950) 'Statement on race.' Reprinted in L. Kuper (ed.) (1975) *Race, Science and Society*, pp. 343–7. Paris: UNESCO Press.

Vail, L. (1988) 'Introduction: ethnicity in southern African prehistory.' In L. Vail (ed.) *The Creation of Tribalism in Southern Africa*, pp. 1–19. London: James Curry.

van den Berghe, P.L. (1978) 'Race and ethnicity: a sociobiological perspective.' *Ethnic and Racial Studies* 1: 401–11.

Veit, U. (1989) 'Ethnic concepts in German prehistory: a case study on the relationship between cultural identity and objectivity.' In S.J. Shennan (ed.) *Archaeological Approaches to Cultural Identity*, pp. 35–56. London: Unwin & Hyman; Routledge, pbk 1994.

Vermeulen, H. and C. Govers (1994) 'Introduction.' In H. Vermeulen and C. Govers (eds) *The Anthropology of Ethnicity: beyond 'Ethnic Groups and Boundaries'*, pp. 1–9. Amsterdam: Het Spinhuis.

Vincent, J. (1974) 'The structuring of ethnicity.' *Human Organisation* 33(4): 375–9.

Wade, P. (1992) '"Race", nature and culture.' *Man* 28: 17–34.

Wallerstein, I. (1960) 'Ethnicity and national integration in West Africa.' *Cahiers d'Etudes Africaines* 1(3): 129–39.

Wallman, S. (1977) 'Ethnicity research in Britain.' *Current Anthropology* 18(3): 531–2.

Washburn, D.K. (1989) 'The property of symmetry and the concept of ethnic style.' In S.J. Shennan (ed.) *Archaeological Approaches to Cultural Identity*, pp. 157–73. London: Unwin & Hyman; Routledge, pbk 1994.

Webster, J. (1996) 'Roman imperialism and the "post-imperial age".' In J. Webster and N. Cooper (eds) *Roman Imperialism: post-colonial perspectives*, pp. 1–17. Leicester: School of Archaeological Studies, University of Leicester.

Whallon, J. Jr (1968) 'Investigations of late prehistoric social organization in New York State.' In S.R. Binford and L.R. Binford (eds) *New Perspectives in Archeology*, pp. 223–44. Chicago: Aldine.

Whitehouse, R. and J.B. Wilkins (1989) 'Greeks and natives in south-east Italy: approaches to the archaeological evidence.' In T.C. Champion (ed.) *Centre and Periphery: comparative studies in archaeology*, pp. 102–26. London: Unwin & Hyman.

Wiessner, P. (1983) 'Style and ethnicity in the Kalahari San projectile point.' *American Antiquity* 48: 253–76.

Wiessner, P. (1984) 'Reconsidering the behavioural basis for style: a case study among the Kalahari San.' *Journal of Anthropological Archaeology* 3: 190–234.

Wiessner, P. (1985) 'Style or isochrestic variation? A reply to Sackett.' *American Antiquity* 50: 160–5.

Wiessner, P. (1989) 'Style and changing relations between the individual and society.' In I. Hodder (ed.) *The Meanings of Things*, pp. 56–63. London: Unwin & Hyman.

Willey, G.R. and P. Phillips (1958) *Method and Theory in American Archaeology*. Chicago: University of Chicago Press.

Willey, G.R. and J.A. Sabloff (1974) *A History of American Archaeology*. London: Thames & Hudson.

Williams, B. (1989) 'A class act: anthropology and the race to nation across ethnic terrain.' *Annual Review of Anthropology* 18: 401–44.

Williams, R. (1983 [1976]) *Keywords: a vocabulary of culture and society*. London: Fontana.

Willis, S. (1993) 'Aspects of pottery assemblages of the late Iron Age/first century A.D. in the east and north-east of England.' Unpublished Ph.D. thesis, University of Durham.

Willis, S. (1994) 'Roman imports into late Iron Age British societies: towards a critique of existing models.' In S. Cottam, D. Dungworth, S. Scott and J. Taylor (eds) *Proceedings of the Fourth Annual Theoretical Roman Archaeology Conference*, pp. 141–50. Oxford: Oxford Books.

Wilson, R. (ed.) (1970) *Rationality*. Oxford: Basil Blackwell.

Wiwjorra, I. (1996) 'German archaeology and its relation to nationalism and racism.' In M. Díaz-Andreu and T.C. Champion (eds) *Nationalism and Archaeology in Europe*, pp. 164–88. London: University College London Press.

Wobst, M. (1977) 'Stylistic behaviour and information exchange.' In C.E. Cleland (ed.) *For the Director: research essays in honour of the late James B. Griffin*, pp. 317–42. Ann Arbor: University of Michigan.

Wobst, M. (1989) 'Commentary: a socio-politics of socio-politics in archaeology.' In V. Pinsky and A. Wylie (eds) *Critical Traditions in Contemporary Archaeology: essays in the philosophy, history and socio-politics of archaeology*, pp. 136–40. Cambridge: Cambridge University Press.

Wolf, E.R. (1982) *Europe and the People Without History*. Berkeley: University of California Press.

Woodman, P. (1995) 'Who possesses Tara? Politics in archaeology in Ireland.' In P.J. Ucko (ed.) *Theory in Archaeology: a world perspective*, pp. 278–97. London: Routledge.

Woolf, G. (1992) 'The unity and diversity of Romanization.' *Journal of Roman Archaeology* 5: 349–52.

Wylie, A. (1989) 'Matters of fact and matters of interest.' In S.J. Shennan (ed.) *Archaeological Approaches to Cultural Identity*, pp. 94–109. London: Unwin & Hyman; Routledge, pbk 1994.

Wylie, A. (1993) 'A proliferation of new archaeologies: "beyond objectivism and relativism".' In N. Yoffee and A. Sherratt (eds) *Archaeological Theory: who sets the agenda?*, pp. 20–6. Cambridge: Cambridge University Press.

Yelvington, K.A. (1991) 'Ethnicity as practice? A comment on Bentley.' *Comparative Studies in Society and History* 33: 158–68.

Yinger, M.J. (1983) 'Ethnicity and social change: the interaction of structural, cultural and personality factors.' *Ethnic and Racial Studies* 6(4): 395–409.

Yoffee, N. and A. Sherratt (1993) 'Introduction: the sources of archaeological theory.' In N. Yoffee and A. Sherratt (eds) *Archaeological Theory: who sets the agenda?*, pp. 1–9. Cambridge: Cambridge University Press.

Young, R.J.C. (1995) *Colonial Desire: hybridity in theory, culture and race*. London: Routledge.

Zerubavel, Y. (1994) 'The death of memory and the memory of death: Masada and the Holocaust as historical metaphors.' *Representations* 45: 72–100.

Zwernemann, J. (1983) *Culture History and African Anthropology: a century of research in Germany and Austria*. Uppsala: Acta University Uppsala.

Index

acculturation: conceptualization of society as holistic and static 50–1, 63; process of 53–4; theorization of 50; *see also* Romanization

America: culture-history, discussion of its characteristics in 18–21; cultural anthropology, characteristics of 46–7

anthropology: cultural diversity, approaches to 40–55; culture, its monolithic conception of 48–9; race, concept of 41–5; tribe, concept of 49–52; *see also* ethnology

archaeological culture: conceptualization of 16–18, 24–5, 108, 137; correlation of with peoples, discussion of 2–3, 15–19, 24–5, 29–31, 106–10; material culture, discussion of the use of to define archaeological cultures 16–18; new archaeology's retention of a normative conceptualization of 26–7, 109; *see also* Childe, culture, culture-history

archaeology: archaeological classification, discussion of 36–9, 130–1; colonialist archaeology, definition of 9; and the construction and legitimation of cultural identity, discussion of 1–2, 8–10, 135–44; culture, its monolithic conception of 49; data, discussion of the implications of its theory-laden nature for the study of ethnicity 138–40; empiricism, its retreat in response to nationalist use of 3, 5, 11–12; imperialist archaeology, definition of 9; and the legitimation of national identity 2–3, 6, 8–10, 12, 135–44;

nationalist archaeology, definition and development of 6, 8; Nazi Germany, discussion of its use of archaeology 2–3; objectivity, discussion of the undermining of 10–11, 138–40, 143; world-orientated archaeology, definition of 9; *see also* archaeological culture, culture-history, nationalist archaeology, new archaeology, post-processualism

assimilation: *see* acculturation

Barth, F.: ethnic boundaries, explanation of the persistence of 73; ethnic group, discussion of the definition of 59–60; ethnicity, subjectivist approach to 59–60; instrumentalism, role in the development of 72–4

Bentley, G.C.: practice theory of ethnicity, critique of 93–5; practice theory of ethnicity, definition and discussion of 90–1, 92–4; *see also* practice theory of ethnicity

Binford, L.R.: artefact and assemblage variation, discussion of his theorization of 110–11; culture-history, critique of its conceptualization of culture 26, 107; ethnicity, use of the concept to explain stylistic variation 111; *see also* new archaeology

Boas, F.: culture, discussion of the role of in the development of the concept of 46–7; unilinear evolution, discussion of his opposition to 47

Bourdieu, P.: agency, conceptualization of 91; *doxa*, concept of 94, 95; *habitus*,